Clash of Worldviews

CLASH OF WORLDVIEWS. Copyright © 2025 by Haneul Jung. All rights reserved. No part of this book may be used or reproduced in any way without written permission of the publisher, except for brief quotations.

Published by System for International Law and Order (SiLO) LLC
Book Design by Sungmin Oh

ISBN 979-11-984119-2-1

CLASH of WORLDVIEWS

HANEUL JUNG

SILO

To my Family

CONTENTS

INTRODUCTION ⋯ 10
ABBREVIATIONS ⋯ 15

CHAPTER 1 **WELCOME TO OUR CHANGING WORLD**
: WHY THE WORLD ORDER IS SHIFTING AND WHY IT MATTERS ⋯ 17

CHAPTER 2 **DECODING GLOBAL POLITICS**
: HOW INTERNATIONAL RELATIONS WORK ⋯ 25

CHAPTER 3 **THE ENDS JUSTIFY THE MEANS? REALPOLITIK'S CLASH WITH LEGITIMACY THROUGH HISTORY** ⋯ 39

CHAPTER 4 **THE AGE OF REASON**
: HOW THE EUROPEAN ENLIGHTENMENT SHAPED MODERN CIVILIZATION ⋯ 49

CHAPTER 5 **KANT'S PERPETUAL PEACE**
: THE FOUNDATION OF THE LIBERAL WORLDVIEW ⋯ 61

CHAPTER 6 **THE EUROPEAN BALANCE OF POWER**
: THE 19TH CENTURY GEOPOLITICS BEHIND THE WORLD WAR I ⋯ 77

CHAPTER 7 **AMERICAN EXCEPTIONALISM AND LIBERAL INTERNATIONALISM** ⋯ 95
1. The Story behind Global Leadership ⋯ 96
2. America's First Major Role in Global Governance ⋯ 106

CHAPTER 8 **WORLD WAR II**
: IDEOLOGICAL CONFLICTS AND THE BIRTH OF THE COLD WAR ⋯ 117

CHAPTER 9 **THE DYNAMICS OF THE COLD WAR** ⋯ 127
1. Strategy, Ideology, and Superpower Rivalry ⋯ 128
2. The Dawn of True Multilateralism ⋯ 143

CHAPTER 10 **PAX AMERICANA**
: UNPACKING THE U.S.-LED LIBERAL INTERNATIONAL ORDER ⋯ 153

CHAPTER 11 **RISE OF REGIONAL ORDER**
: CHINA AND RUSSIA'S REVISIONIST QUEST FOR HEGEMONY ⋯ 175

CHAPTER 12 **THE END OF THE UNIPOLAR MOMENT**
: THE DAWN OF A NEW ERA ⋯ 195

CHAPTER 13 **A WORLD WITHOUT HEGEMON** ⋯ 213
    1. United States: From Hegemon to the Most Powerful ⋯ 216
    2. Russia & China: Rivals and Partners ⋯ 228
    3. Confused Liberal Democracies: Amidst Lost Leadership ⋯ 244
    4. The Global South: A Renewed Geopolitical Middle Ground ⋯ 255

CHAPTER 14 **MULTIPOLARITY VS. MULTILATERALISM**
    : WHY GLOBAL CHALLENGES DEMAND MULTILATERALISM ⋯ 283

CHAPTER 15 **LIBERAL DEMOCRACY'S EXISTENTIAL CRISIS** ⋯ 301
    1. The Expansion and Fragmentation of Liberal Ideologies ⋯ 302
    2. The Perils of Polarization: How Extremism Threatens Liberal Democracy ⋯ 314
    3. Possible Remedy: Rise of the Political Center ⋯ 322
    4. The Future of Liberal Democracy and the Fate of the Multipolar World ⋯ 330

CHAPTER 16 **NAVIGATING THE UNCERTAINTIES**
    : CONCLUDING REFLECTIONS ON A CHANGING WORLD ⋯ 339

    BIBLIOGRAPHY ⋯ 345
    About the Author ⋯ 366

INTRODUCTION

I open this book's preface with a personal story—a pivotal experience that profoundly shaped my views on politics, law, and the elusive nature of truth.

At a certain point in my career, I was tasked with leading a legal dispute of extraordinary political sensitivity. It was a difficult case, full of legal and factual complexities. Ultimately, thanks to the dedication of a remarkable team—and, admittedly, a stroke of good luck—we achieved a favorable final outcome. Midway through the proceedings, however, an unfavorable interim ruling was rendered, igniting a political firestorm. Conspiracy theories began to spread, with some alleging that the unfavorable interim outcome resulted from covert political interference during the legal preparation process. These accusations were wholly baseless. Yet, despite their lack of merit, they cast a long shadow over our team, deeply affecting those who had devoted themselves to the case from the outset.

As the team leader, I felt a personal obligation to address these rumors and defend the integrity of our work. I publicly explained that the outcomes of the dispute—both interim and final—were the product of careful legal reasoning and sustained effort. Those in positions of responsibility, regardless of political affiliation, largely understood and accepted this explanation. But not everyone was persuaded. Some accused me of defending a flawed legal preparation out of loyalty or pride.

Despite my repeated efforts to clarify that my defense was not political but professional, the criticisms persisted. One encounter, in particular, stands out in my memory. After I explained that I was simply presenting the 'facts' to defend my team's work, the individual responded with a remark that has stayed with me ever since:

"Facts? The truth stands above them!"

I realized that his notion of "truth" transcended mere empirical accuracy—it spoke to deeper convictions, values, and ideological frameworks. In that moment, I glimpsed something essential about the nature of political conflict.

But such truth claims are inherently subjective. Likewise, political behavior seldom adheres to pure logic. Intuition, emotion, and entrenched beliefs frequently eclipse factual analysis, and once facts are filtered through ideological prisms, they lose their universal authority.

In principle, logical reasoning should produce objective conclusions. Yet reality proves more complex: logic often serves not as a tool for discovery, but as a post-hoc justification for decisions already shaped by intuition. Legal systems, aware of these pitfalls, are meticulously designed to prioritize objective standards and empirical evidence. But human adjudicators—whether judges, arbitrators, juries or others—remain subject to intuitive influences. Seasoned legal practitioners recognize this dynamic, skillfully steering adjudicators' intuitions to their advantage. Meanwhile, there are adjudicators who make up their minds long before they hear the argument, driven by preconceptions and intuition rather than reasoned analysis.

What, then, shapes human intuition? It emerges from a constellation of factors: accumulated knowledge, cognitive frameworks molded by experience, emotional states, innate biases (from pattern-seeking to confirmation bias), and even subconscious inclinations. Even absent direct self-interest, intuition frequently determines judgment—nowhere more visibly than in political opinions. However, when it comes to political judgment—and indeed in all value-based judgments—there is one overriding influence: the value system of the individual.

People with different value systems can interpret the same set of facts and arrive at radically different 'truths.' Whether by instinct or analysis, it is almost impossible to escape one's own value system completely. These systems—forged through upbringing, personality, and lived experience—ultimately reflect broader worldviews. If the judgments people make are so heavily influenced by their value systems, and if these value systems are themselves grounded in a particular worldview, then it is the worldview that serves as the fundamental framework shaping human thought and behavior.

But what happens when a worldview is not limited to an individual? What if a community, a nation, or even entire segments of the global population share a common worldview? Such shared worldviews exert immense influence over collective decision-making. In this sense, not only individuals or groups, but entire societies, nation-states, and the international system itself become expressions of the dominant values and worldviews they embody. Thus, worldviews are the lens through which people interpret reality and determine how they ought to act within it.

These shared worldviews are usually forged through the cultural and historical experiences of a society. Societies with common cultural foundations tend to perpetuate their worldviews through education, collective memory, and tradition. But the shaping of a worldview is not merely a cultural or historical process—it is also deeply philosophical. Time and again, history has witnessed moments when great thinkers emerged at pivotal junctures to either systematize an existing worldview or articulate a bold new vision. Once formed, such ideas often transcend the realm of theory, permeating all aspects of life and reshaping entire societies.

By influencing the worldviews of an era's people, these ideological forces have in turn shaped the course of history and international affairs. From this perspective, every major transformation in the international order can be understood not only as a shift in the balance of power, but also as a confrontation between worldviews—between the ideas that justify the existing order and those that seek to legitimize a new one.

The title of this book, *Clash of Worldviews: Understanding the 21st Century International Order Through Ideas*, captures its central purpose: to explore the major ideologies and worldviews that have decisively shaped human history at critical junctures. If historical events create the external conditions that influence the behavior of states, then understanding the "thoughts" that guided individuals and nations to act as they did requires an inquiry into the ideas and worldviews that informed their perceptions.

This task feels especially crucial today, as the U.S.-led liberal international order that defined the post–Cold War era has effectively come to an end, giving way to competing visions of world order now emerging across the globe. In this context, understanding the ideological foundations of these rival paradigms is essential to grasping the nature of the new international landscape taking shape before us.

As the title suggests, this book is a follow-up to my previous work, *Understanding 21st-Century International Order in Context: South Korea's Future in an Era of Hegemonic Transition*, published in 2023 (in Korean). That book examined key historical developments that shaped the current international order—touching upon important ideological shifts along the way. This volume, by contrast, inverts the approach: here, ideas take center stage, providing the interpretive lens through which historical transformations are analyzed. Despite significant overlap in subject matter, the two works are structured differently. In that sense, they may be best understood as two sides of the same coin.

The final section of this book confronts a defining challenge of our time: the escalating political polarization threatening to destabilize liberal democracies worldwide. As a self-identified centrist, I have long avoided making overt political statements. Centrists are often criticized from both the left and the right, and the very nature of centrism—grounded in an instinct for balance and a wariness of extremes—can make it difficult to adopt rigid ideological positions. Indeed, some of my colleagues observed that in my previous book, I stopped short of fully articulating my own views. Yet in this unprecedented moment—as democratic institutions face sustained pressure and societal fractures deepen—I have resolved to speak plainly. Not because I naively believe that my personal reflections will have any significant social impact, but because at a time of increasing polarization and the possible erosion of liberal democracy, it seemed irresponsible in its own way to remain silent when I had something to contribute.

To be sure, this book is not without its flaws. It contains errors and limitations, and many readers will no doubt be more knowledgeable, insightful, and discerning than I. Still, even the smallest object—like a pebble kicked up on the side of the road—can inspire a moment of reflection. If this book can serve, even in a small way, as a catalyst for deeper thought and discussion among readers, that alone would be enough for me.

I can only hope that humanity will face its current challenges with wisdom, and in solidarity. And for all that we lack, I pray that the grace of a good and just God will make us whole.

ABBREVIATIONS

"AI"	Artificial Intelligence
"A2/AD"	Anti-Access/Area Denial strategy
"CCP"	Chinese Communist Party
"CSTO"	Collective Security Treaty Organization
"EEZ"	Exclusive Economic Zones
"EU"	European Union
"EV"	Electric Vehicle
"FDI"	Foreign Direct Investment
"FTA"	Free Trade Agreement
"GATT"	General Agreement on Tariffs and Trade
"GDP"	Gross Domestic Product
"IBRD"	International Bank for Reconstruction and Development (World Bank)
"ICC"	International Criminal Court
"ICJ"	International Court of Justice
"ICSID"	International Center for Settlement of Investment Disputes
"ISDS"	Investor-State Dispute Settlements
"IDA"	International Development Association
"IFC"	International Finance Corporation
"IMF"	International Monetary Fund
"IT"	Information Technology
"ITO"	International Trade Organization
"LIO"	Liberal International Order
"MAD"	Mutually Assured Destruction
"MAGA"	Make America Great Again
"MFN"	Most-Favored-Nation principle

"MIGA"	Multilateral Investment Guarantee Agency
"NATO"	North Atlantic Treaty Organization
"NPT"	Treaty on the Non-Proliferation of Nuclear Weapons
"PRC"	People's Republic of China
"PSI"	Proliferation Security Initiative
"Quad"	Quadrilateral Security Dialogue
"SCO"	Shanghai Cooperation Organization
"SOE"	State-Owned Enterprises
"SWIFT"	Society for Worldwide Interbank Financial Telecommunication
"UDHR"	Universal Declaration of Human Rights
"UN"	United Nations
"UNCLOS"	United Nations Convention on the Law of the Sea
"U.S."	United States of America
"USSR"	Union of Soviet Socialist Republics (Soviet Union)
"WMD"	Weapons of Mass Destruction
"WTO"	World Trade Organization

CHAPTER 1

WELCOME TO OUR CHANGING WORLD
: WHY THE WORLD ORDER IS SHIFTING AND WHY IT MATTERS

*Ignoranti quem portum petat,
nullus suus ventus est.*
If a man knows not to which port he sails,
no wind is favorable.

Lucius Annaeus Seneca

Is the world changing? The question almost answers itself. Change has always been a constant throughout human history, but the current transformations are unique. What sets this moment apart is not change itself, but the profound reordering of the global system that appears to be taking shape.

The scale of this transformation rivals the most consequential turning points in modern history. At the very least, it marks the most significant realignment since the geopolitical shock of 1991, when the Soviet Union's collapse redrew the global map. Viewed through a broader historical lens, it may even signal a civilizational shift—one whose ripple effects will touch every society, whether they recognize its onset or not. The signs are everywhere: international institutions groan under obsolete mandates; economic alliances fracture and reconfigure; the once-unstoppable tide of globalization is receding. Even the liberal frameworks that upheld the postwar order increasingly seem unfit to interpret—let alone manage—the world now emerging. This is not gradual evolution. It is rupture. Not a continuation of familiar patterns, but the birth of a new and still-unformed paradigm.

Three tectonic forces—among others—are reshaping the foundations of global order.

The first is the global redistribution of power. Every international system rests on a balance of power. For nearly three decades, the world has operated under a unipolar order, with the United States as its hegemon. That era is now drawing to a close. A growing consensus holds that American preeminence is in decline—and with it, the architecture of the current global system must inevitably be reimagined. While many anticipate a return to great-power rivalry, the contours of the next phase remain profoundly uncertain.

The second is the transformation of the international economic order. Since the Cold War's end, the liberal international order has been anchored in free trade. Its intellectual lineage—from Immanuel Kant through Adam Smith to David Ricardo and most contemporary economists—held that open markets would not only maximize global welfare, but also promote peace through economic interdependence.

But that consensus has unraveled. Beginning around 2016—and unmistakably by 2022—the United States, long the chief architect of global integration, began to retreat from free trade. In a striking reversal, it now openly prioritizes domestic resilience and strategic autonomy. The free-trade era, for all practical purposes, is over. Supply chains are splintering, markets fragmenting, and economic efficiency increasingly subordinated to national interest—not as a tactical deviation, but as a new governing logic.

The third is the erosion of liberal ideals. For decades, values such as human rights, democracy, and environmental stewardship structured global discourse. Even authoritarian regimes, though resistant to liberal norms, often paid rhetorical homage to them or countered them with appeals to cultural relativism. That era, too, is ending. Today, many states do not merely resist liberal norms—they reject them outright. Some claim these ideals are incompatible with their cultural traditions; others dismiss them as deeply flawed or ideologically bankrupt. The

West, for its part, has struggled to mount a coherent response.

This growing normative divergence carries profound implications. Cultural difference has always held the potential to become a source of conflict; now, the deepening fragmentation of values is rendering global consensus increasingly elusive. As shared understandings break down, multilateral institutions falter—and geopolitical tensions mount.

Among these three forces, the redistribution of power concerns material capability. In contrast, economic restructuring and ideological divergence pertain to legitimacy—to the erosion of the normative and institutional consensus that upheld the post-Cold War liberal order.

These forces do not operate in isolation. They are mutually reinforcing. Together, they portend a deceleration—or even reversal—of globalization, heightened fragmentation among states, and a rise in regional tensions and conflict. At the same time, nationalism and traditionalist ideologies are resurging as countercurrents to liberal ideals, both domestically and internationally. We are living through a pivotal era—one marked by uncertainty, flux, and the potential for systemic upheaval. It is little wonder that many now characterize this as the age of 'post-globalization.'

Yet, in order to grasp the structural essence of this moment, a more precise term is warranted: this is a period of hegemonic transition.

As U.S. global hegemony recedes, non-liberal revisionist powers—chiefly China and Russia—are seeking to reassert influence over their historical spheres of dominance. China, in particular, is attempting to reclaim the status of global superpower. The models pursued by these powers are not liberal. They seek to establish hierarchical regional orders grounded in traditional authority, deference, and civilizational identity—reminiscent of pre-modern patterns of dominance.

By contrast, liberal democracy is predicated on sovereign equality and fundamentally rejects hierarchical relations among states. Therefore, liberal hegemony cannot draw legitimacy from dominance or coercion;

such notions are antithetical to its values. Instead, a liberal hegemon must lead through consent—deriving legitimacy from shared norms, institutional participation, and voluntary alignment of values. Only by aligning its global posture with its ideological foundations can a liberal hegemon sustain its legitimacy in the eyes of both allies and adversaries. This is why the United States has long insisted on framing its role not as 'hegemon,' but as global leader. Especially in the aftermath of World War II and the Cold War, the U.S. positioned itself as *primus inter pares*—a "first among equals"—within an international system grounded in liberal principles. The architecture it built formally allowed allies, and even adversaries, to challenge its leadership—so long as such challenges remained within the framework of the system it governed.[1]

That model is now under strain. Increasingly, the United States appears tempted to reassert itself not as a liberal hegemon, but as the most powerful actor in an emerging multipolar world.

This shift is consequential. Power transitions are inherently volatile. History teaches that when a reigning hegemon is challenged by a rising power, the risk of conflict increases dramatically. One possibility is that the declining power reacts forcefully to arrest its relative decline—what Graham Allison call the 'Thucydides Trap.'[2] Another is that the rising power, sensing its advantage is fleeting, acts precipitously to seize the moment—what Hal Brands and Michael Beckley term the 'Peaking Power Trap.'[3]

We are, unfortunately, caught between both traps. The United States, unwilling to relinquish its primacy, increasingly views China as a strategic threat—applying pressure across economic, technological, and military fronts. At the same time, China faces growing domestic headwinds. Many analysts believe Beijing's relative military advantage in the Taiwan Strait may soon peak—raising fears that it might act militarily before that window closes. The trajectory of U.S.-China relations in the coming years will therefore be pivotal to global peace and stability.

At its deepest level, this global inflection point is also a clash between our primal instincts and our aspirational ideals.

On one hand lies the instinct for relative gain—the drive for power, security, and advantage in a competitive world. This mirrors the Hobbesian state of nature: a "war of all against all." Like gravity, it is ever-present—capable of being managed, but never fully escaped. On the other hand lies our aspiration toward peace and cooperation. Time and again, in the wake of catastrophic conflict, states have attempted to construct universal frameworks for peace. This tension—between instinct and ideal—shapes the arc of modern history.

After World War I, the League of Nations collapsed under the weight of its flaws. After World War II, a more resilient international order emerged. And after the Cold War, the United States led efforts to extend that order globally. Today's international system is thus the product of two "hot" world wars and one "cold" one—an architecture forged through trauma, effort, and collective resolve. Even revisionist powers like China and Russia do not seek to destroy this order entirely. While they contest its power distribution and challenge U.S. primacy, they stop short of advocating for systemic anarchy. The same is true of many globalization skeptics and critics of neoliberalism.

The danger lies not in contestation per se, but in its potential unintended consequences. Efforts to reshape the international order may destabilize it—and absent a coherent alternative, the world risks slipping into fragmentation and lawless competition. What is ultimately at stake is not just the fate of U.S. leadership or the liberal order, but the fragile scaffolding of global stability itself.

Endnotes:

1 Nevertheless, the United States has frequently been criticized for asserting its hegemonic authority when it deems its core national interests to be at stake.

2 International political scientist Graham Allison examined 16 historical cases in which a dominant hegemon confronted a rising power, finding that roughly 75% of these encounters resulted in major wars. This dynamic is called the 'Thucydides Trap.' According to Allison, war was avoided in rare instances—such as between the United States and the British Empire—due to key factors: the rising power shared a similar cultural and political sphere with the incumbent, refrained from direct territorial challenges, and largely accepted the prevailing international order, fostering cooperation rather than outright confrontation. Allison's 'Thucydides Trap' theory has been criticized for oversimplifying the causes of conflict. Some scholars argue, for example, that the relationship between Athens and Sparta during the Peloponnesian War does not neatly fit the model of an 'established hegemon' confronting a 'rising power,' as both were already dominant Greek city-states before the Persian Wars. Nonetheless, a broader truth remains: when one state's power rises rapidly, its rivals often perceive this shift as a threat, leading to overreactions and escalating tensions. If the emerging state aspires to hegemonic status while its competitor seeks to maintain dominance, the likelihood of strategic rivalry intensifying becomes even greater.

3 See Hal Brands and Michael Beckley, "China is a Declining Power – and That's the Problem," Foreign Policy (24 September 2021).

CHAPTER 2

DECODING GLOBAL POLITICS
: HOW INTERNATIONAL RELATIONS WORK

No single approach can capture all the complexity
of contemporary world politics.
Therefore, we are better off with a diverse array of
competing ideas rather than a single theoretical orthodoxy.
Competition between theories help reveal their strengths
and weaknesses and spurs subsequent refinements,
while revealing flaws in conventional wisdom.

Stephen Walt

The purpose of this chapter is to provide a concise overview of the key theories of international relations, which will serve as the basis for the analyses that follow. Readers who are already well-versed in the subject, as well as those who wish to proceed directly to the core arguments of the book, may choose to skip this chapter. Nonetheless, all readers are encouraged to at least skim through this chapter.

Domestic Politics vs. International Politics

When most people think of politics, they picture elected officials, legislative chambers, and campaign rallies. Yet these formal institutions represent only the most visible layer of a phenomenon that pervades all human interaction. Politics exists wherever people engage with one another—whether in corporate boardrooms, community organizations, or even within households—because power dynamics, the interplay of influence and control, shape every collective decision.

At its core, politics is about the exercise of power: the strategic processes by which resources are allocated, priorities are set, and competing interests are resolved. This understanding applies equally to domestic governance and international relations, both of which function as arenas of contested authority.

However, there are two fundamental distinctions that set them apart.

1. Enforceability of Rules

Domestic systems function within a rule-bound hierarchy, where governments, courts, and other institutional norms serve as society's 'Leviathan' (to borrow Hobbes' metaphor). This central authority enforces laws, adjudicates disputes, and punishes transgressions, whether through formal legal mechanisms or informal social and political sanctions. Even in flawed or corrupt states where institutions are weakened, the possibility of accountability still exists and continues to shape how actors compete for power and influence.

By contrast, the global arena inherently lacks a sovereign enforcer. International law exists, but it functions through voluntary compliance, mutual consent, and reciprocal incentives—not through centralized coercion. States remain the ultimate arbiters of their own conduct, giving rise to the structural 'anarchy' that realist theorists such as Kenneth Waltz identified as the defining characteristic of international relations. In this environment, power does not operate within rules—it defines them.

2. The Nature of Political Actors

Domestic decision-making revolves around individual agency—voters, legislators, and civil servants navigating codified legal frameworks. These actors operate within a system shaped by competing pressures: electoral mandates, ideological commitments, and institutional checks such as judicial oversight and media (public) scrutiny. Crucially, their choices bear direct personal consequences—career longevity often depends on satisfying constituents and adhering to established norms.

In the international realm, however, states themselves become the central actors, driven by cold calculations of national interest and relative power. Absent a supranational 'Leviathan,' no overarching authority compels compliance; enforcement rests on precarious networks of treaties, reciprocal expectations, and reputational costs. This structural vacuum creates a moral hazard: foreign policy decision-makers—particularly in autocratic regimes—can shield themselves from the human consequences of their choices on war, sanctions, or alliances. The result is a greater tolerance for risk, with strategies that privilege state survival over individual well-being.

3. The Broader Implications

These structural divides—enforceable rules versus anarchic norms, individual accountability versus state abstraction—reveal the enduring paradoxes of international relations. States, like individuals, vie for power and influence, yet they do so in a realm where consequences are diffuse, compliance is voluntary, and authority rests not on codified enforcement but on shared perceptions and mutual expectations. Understanding this dichotomy is not merely academic—it is essential to making sense of everything from trade wars to security dilemmas.

Understanding Hegemony: The Key to World Politics

One of the most important—if not the most important—drivers of state behavior in the international system is the pursuit of hegemony.

The idea that "great powers inevitably seek hegemony" was famously articulated by John Mearsheimer. Yet the core insight predates Mearsheimer and resonates across civilizations. Scholars, commentators, and statesmen have long invoked this principle—whether to analyze it, caution against it, or challenge it.

As discussed above, politics is fundamentally about the exercise of power—the strategies by which actors acquire, exercise, and maintain influence over others. Hegemony, in this context, represents the attainment of such dominance or the capacity to enforce it. It is, in many ways, the logical endpoint of political ambition. For states, the anarchic nature of the international system makes the pursuit of hegemony even more urgent and unrestrained than in domestic settings. Unsurprisingly, this pursuit stands at the core of many realist theories of international relations.

While realists differ in their explanations of why states seek power, they generally converge on the idea that power is a means to ensure national security. At the risk of oversimplification, here are three key realist perspectives on why states pursue power:

Hans Morgenthau, the godfather of classical realism, argued that states, like individuals, are inherently driven by self-interest. Just as individuals seek to advance their personal standing, states act to promote their national interest, which invariably entails the accumulation of power.

Kenneth Waltz, who pioneered 'defensive realism,' viewed survival as the central goal of state behavior. In an anarchic international system, where no overarching authority guarantees safety, states must rely on their own capabilities to secure their existence.

John Mearsheimer, developing the theory of 'offensive realism,' maintained that the inherent uncertainty of international politics compels states to maximize their power. Because no state can ever be certain of another's intentions, the most reliable path to security is to become the most powerful actor—a hegemon.

In my view, all states pursue three core objectives: security, prosperity, and autonomy—typically in that order.

Since the dawn of civilization, the international system has operated under conditions of anarchy, lacking any higher authority to regulate state behavior. There is no overarching sovereign to enforce rules, mitigate crises, or sanction violations. In such a system, the logic of "survival of the fittest" prevails. Absent a 'Leviathan' to impose order, self-help becomes the organizing principle, and power relations define the contours of international interaction.

What, then, motivates state behavior in this environment? The answer lies in national interest—comprising both tangible assets, such as resources and territory, and intangible imperatives, most notably security. Each state seeks to advance its interests within the limits of its capabilities. Without an effective enforcement mechanism to restrain opportunism, there is little reason for a state to forgo actions that might undermine others if doing so strengthens its own position.

For weaker states, the most immediate concern is survival. Once that is secured, the pursuit of prosperity follows. Yet even as states grow wealthier and ascend to great power status, the problem of autonomy remains unresolved. In a competitive system populated by other powerful actors, no state can fully guarantee its freedom of action. To address this vulnerability, great powers seek to carve out spheres of influence—strategic buffers that secure their borders and extend their economic and political reach.

This logic has driven the formation of empires throughout history. When great powers respect each other's spheres of influence, a measure of stability is possible. But when those boundaries are contested, conflict often ensues. Thus, states must remain vigilant, continually defending their position against actual or potential rivals. Whether through diplomacy, economic leverage, or military force, interstate relations are inherently competitive.

This struggle—to enhance one's own position while countering the ambitions of others—has a natural culmination. The ultimate goal is to become so dominant within a region that no competitor can plausibly challenge one's supremacy. Once a state achieves this status and is widely recognized as the regional preeminent power, its core interests become self-sustaining. That condition is known as hegemony.

Not all great powers can attain hegemony, but few—if any—would forgo it if the opportunity arose. Hegemony offers security, prosperity, and the autonomy to shape regional affairs to one's advantage. As long as these remain the foundational goals of states, the pursuit of hegemony will remain a defining feature of international politics.

Hegemonic Stability and Legitimacy

Military strength is the single most important factor in establishing hegemony. However, once a stable hegemonic order is in place, further expansion can become counterproductive, as it may destabilize the very system that underpins the hegemon's dominance. At that point, the hegemon's primary task shifts: from accumulating power to preserving the system that sustains its supremacy.

Historically, many great empires paused their expansion upon reaching regional dominance. These periods of consolidation often coincided with the emergence of stable hegemonic orders.[1] In this sense, a defining characteristic of a hegemon is not unchecked expansion but a vested interest in maintaining stability.

While a hegemon will act decisively to suppress challengers within its sphere of influence, it also plays a stabilizing role—providing peace, prosperity, and protection to compliant states. In an anarchic international system, the actor most capable and willing to supply public goods such as security and order beyond its own borders is typically the hegemon.[2] This is not an act of altruism, but a strategic investment in preserving the conditions of dominance.

It follows that ensuring the security of those within its sphere of influence is essential to sustaining hegemonic legitimacy.[3] When a hegemon fails to maintain order, its legitimacy erodes, undermining its ability to lead without relying on constant coercion. Over time, the burden of suppressing persistent dissent and managing instability drains resources and gradually exhausts the hegemon's capacity to govern. Hegemony, therefore, is not merely a function of power—it is power exercised with legitimacy.

In this context, the exchange of limited autonomy for security and economic benefits has long been viewed as an acceptable trade-off by lesser powers. This logic remains deeply relevant and continues to shape the structure and dynamics of global politics today.

Realism vs. Liberalism

Now that we have established a foundational understanding of the key actors, concepts, and dynamics in international relations, we can turn to the theoretical frameworks scholars and policymakers use to interpret the complexities of the global arena. These theories are not mere academic abstractions—they function as essential lenses through which we analyze world events, interpret the motivations behind state behavior, and craft strategic responses to international challenges.[4]

Broadly speaking, three major schools of thought offer distinct and often competing explanations for how the international system operates.

'Realism' begins with a stark premise: in the absence of a central authority capable of enforcing rules, power—particularly military and economic power—ultimately determines outcomes. States are viewed as rational, self-interested actors whose primary objective is survival. In this view, the international system is defined by anarchy, competition, and a relentless struggle for dominance. Conflict is not an aberration but a natural consequence of the structure of global politics.

In contrast, 'liberalism' rejects the notion that conflict is inevitable and emphasizes the potential for cooperation. It highlights the role of international institutions, economic interdependence, and shared values in mitigating anarchy and fostering peaceful engagement. From the liberal perspective, diplomacy, norms, and collective action are not only possible—they are essential tools for shaping a more stable and just international order.

'Constructivism,' meanwhile, shifts the focus from material capabilities to the power of ideas, identities, and social norms. Constructivists argue that the international system is not fixed or objective but socially constructed through interaction. What states perceive as their 'interests' is itself shaped by evolving beliefs, identities, and historical context. This perspective opens the door to transformation: if ideas change, so too can the very logic of international politics.

Among these, realism remains the dominant paradigm in geopolitical analysis. Its enduring influence stems from its grounding in historical experience and its ability to explain recurring patterns of conflict, competition, and power balancing. While liberalism and constructivism offer important insights—particularly in accounting for cooperation, ideational change, and institutional influence—realism continues to command significant authority for its perceived explanatory power and pragmatic assumptions.

In this sense, realism functions like a gravitational force in the study of international relations—inescapable, ever-present, and often treated as the default framework for understanding state behavior. And yet, just as revolutionary thinkers once challenged Newtonian physics, so too have many scholars (including realists themselves) questioned the central tenet of realism: must humanity accept a world defined by perpetual competition, or can it transcend this logic through cooperation, institution-building, and the reshaping of global norms?

1. The Balance of Power: A Realist Mechanism for Stability

One of the earliest responses to the dilemma of anarchy came in the form of the 'balance of power'—a concept aimed at preserving stability by preventing any single state from dominating the system. As we shall see in the chapters ahead, this idea forms a core pillar of the realist worldview.

Within the realist framework, great powers seek to maintain equilibrium, ensuring that no single state can achieve unchecked dominance within a given region. A stable balance of power acts as a system of checks and balances, deterring aggression by making conquest prohibitively costly. Even regional hegemony—where one state dominates a specific area—can sometimes be viewed as a form of balanced stability, insofar as it prevents wider conflict through a predictable power structure.

Still, realism's portrayal of international politics as a never-ending power struggle can be deeply unsettling. When the balance is disrupted, the likelihood of war increases. Is this truly the best humanity can aspire to? After all, humans are social beings. Within many modern nation-states, people have successfully replaced the law of the jungle with the rule of law, and built cooperative political communities that constrain self-interest through governance and institutions. If gravity can be overcome through science and engineering, perhaps the realist 'gravitational pull' in international relations can also be transcended.

But how? This is where liberalism offers a vital alternative.

2. A Liberalist Vision: A Path Beyond Realism

The intellectual foundation for liberal alternatives to realism was laid by the great German philosopher Immanuel Kant in his 1795 essay *Perpetual Peace*. He begins with a darkly humorous observation: a Dutch inn bore a sign reading "Perpetual Peace," illustrated with a cemetery—implying that true peace is only found in death. Kant rejected this fatalism. In his essay, he outlined a vision for peace that could be realized during life, offering the philosophical groundwork for what would later evolve into liberal international thought.

Liberalism, the chief rival to realism in international relations, builds on Kant's ideas and transforms them into a systematic framework. If realism is the gravitational force that pulls states toward power competition, liberalism proposes countervailing forces that can push back against it.

Four such forces stand out: legitimacy, interdependence, multilateralism, and the spread of liberal democracy.

Legitimacy: The Soft Power of International Politics

Legitimacy is a foundational force in all political systems. Power alone rarely suffices—rulers and states alike must justify their authority. Even from a realist perspective, legitimacy is essential to hegemony. It facilitates not only the acquisition of power but also its durability. A hegemon that lacks legitimacy must rely on coercion, which in turn breeds resistance and instability.

Over time, the sources of legitimacy have evolved. In ancient times, absolute monarchies claimed divine sanction; modern states often derive legitimacy from national sovereignty, self-determination, or democratic representation. In recent decades, liberalism has expanded the legitimacy discourse to include human rights and rule-based governance. Yet, legitimacy remains a contentious and contested arena in international politics, reflecting profound ideological and cultural divides.

Today, the struggle over legitimacy is one of the primary battlegrounds between nationalism and liberalism, shaping global debates on sovereignty, intervention, and governance.

Interdependence: The Economic Case for Peace

One of liberalism's most significant contributions to international relations is the argument that economic interdependence reduces the likelihood of war. Grounded in classical economic theories of absolute and comparative advantage, this principle has underpinned the logic of globalization for decades.

As economic ties deepen, the costs of conflict rise—making war an increasingly irrational choice.[5] For many, the post–Cold War era of globalization seemed to embody this vision—until Russia's invasion of Ukraine in 2022 shattered that assumption.

To be clear, realists also acknowledge that economic interdependence can advance national interests by fostering prosperity. However, they view it as a contingent factor: if a state believes that disrupting trade yields greater strategic gains, interdependence ceases to function as a deterrent. In other words, economic ties may reduce the risk of war—but they cannot eliminate it.

Multilateralism: Institutionalizing Cooperation

The United Nations (UN) defines multilateralism as a commitment to shared norms, collective decision-making, and cooperative problem-solving.[6] It is often described as the international equivalent of democracy. At its core, multilateralism provides structured forums for dialogue, consensus-building, and conflict resolution.

Institutions such as the UN and the World Trade Organization are foundational pillars of the multilateral system. They embed legitimacy, foster cooperation, and deepen economic integration. In doing so, they reduce uncertainty and miscalculation—two key drivers of conflict.

Moreover, multilateralism helps level the playing field by empowering smaller states and limiting the unilateral actions of great powers. In this way, it contributes to a more stable and inclusive international order.

The Spread of Liberal Democracy: A Long-Term Solution?

Kant famously argued that republican governments are less likely to go to war. Many liberal theorists maintain that this idea remains valid:

liberal democracies[7] rarely, if ever, fight one another.

Several mechanisms help explain this phenomenon. First, electoral accountability: democratic leaders must answer to their citizens, making them cautious about engaging in unpopular wars. Second, shared norms and values: liberal democracies tend to uphold principles that discourage aggression. Third, economic ties: democracies often maintain strong trade relations, further reducing the incentives for conflict. Finally, institutional constraints—checks and balances—limit the ability of a single actor to unilaterally launch military campaigns within a liberal democracy.

Though liberal democracies are a relatively recent development in human history, empirical evidence supports the notion that wars between them are exceptionally rare. If this pattern continues, the global spread of liberal democracy may offer one of the most promising paths to lasting peace.

Can the gravity of realism be overcome?

No single liberal mechanism can guarantee perpetual peace. Yet, taken together, they form a powerful alternative to realism's bleak vision of unending conflict. Realism's gravitational pull remains strong. But liberalism offers tools to resist it—mechanisms for cooperation, stability, and mutual prosperity. The future remains uncertain, but the pursuit of a more peaceful international order is not only possible—it is essential.

Still, an uncomfortable question lingers: Are these liberal solutions sufficient—especially amid today's hegemonic transitions and mounting geopolitical rivalries? Can humanity truly move beyond the logic of power politics, or will the gravitational weight of realism once again prevail?

As global power shifts and international uncertainties grow, these questions become ever more pressing. They demand not only deeper reflection but deliberate and coordinated action.

Endnotes:

1 The Roman Empire, successive Chinese dynasties, the British Empire, and, more recently, the United States have all demonstrated this pattern.

2 Thus, leading scholars such as Charles Kindleberger, Robert Gilpin, and Stephen Krasner have developed what is known in international relations as 'hegemonic stability theory.' This theory posits that the international system is more likely to remain stable and peaceful when a dominant state—a hegemon—exists. The hegemon upholds global order by providing essential public goods, including security, economic stability, and a framework for international trade. These contributions benefit most, if not all, states within its sphere of influence, thereby reducing the likelihood of conflict.

3 David Easton defined legitimacy as "a strong inner conviction of the moral validity of the authorities or regime." See David Easton, *A Systems Analysis of Political Life* (John Wiley & Sons, 1965).

4 Perhaps the most compelling articulation of this point comes from Joseph Nye, who once reflected: "When I was working in Washington and helping formulate American foreign policies as an assistant secretary in the State Department and the Pentagon, I found myself borrowing elements from all three types of thinking: realism, liberalism, and constructivism. I found all of them helpful, though in different ways and in different circumstances." See Joseph Nye and David Welch, *Understanding Global Conflict & Cooperation: Intro to Theory & History* (9th Ed.), Pearson Education (2014), p. 16.

5 Modern empirical studies on trade and military conflict seem to reveal mixed outcomes: trade can either deter war or exacerbate it, depending on the conditions and circumstances. See Stephen Brooks, "The Trade Truce? – When Economic Interdependence Does – and Doesn't – Promote Peace," Foreign Affairs (18 June 2024).

6 See United Nations on "The Virtues of Multilateralism and Diplomacy" (https://www.un.org/en/observances/multilateralism-for-peace-day)(last visited on 13 September 2024)

7 Kant's republican ideals are deeply intertwined with the core principles of modern liberal democracy. He emphasized individual liberty, the rule of law, and representative government—values that remain foundational to contemporary liberal democratic systems. Specifically, his preference for representative over direct democracy, along with his insistence on legal equality and civil rights, closely aligns with the normative framework of liberal democracy. For a more detailed discussion of these connections, see Chapter 5.

CHAPTER 3

THE ENDS JUSTIFY THE MEANS? REALPOLITIK'S CLASH WITH LEGITIMACY THROUGH HISTORY

> History is …
> an unending dialogue between
> the present and the past.
>
> E. H. Carr

The U.S.-led liberal international order endured for nearly three decades—but that era has now drawn to a close. We have entered a new period marked by turbulence and uncertainty. There are many ways to interpret this moment of upheaval, but what is particularly striking is how people's perceptions of today's disorder are deeply shaped by their memories—and assumptions—about the preceding liberal order.

Liberal thinkers often regarded the post–Cold War liberal order as a landmark in the moral and institutional advancement of civilization—a deliberate departure from the 'rule of the jungle' that had long governed international relations. For them, it represented a significant step toward a more peaceful, rules-based global system. From this perspective, today's disorder is not only geopolitical but also ideological. It reflects both the failure of the United States to live up to its global responsibilities and the opportunistic ascent of authoritarian states determined to erode liberal norms.

Realists, by contrast, regard the liberal international order as a historical anomaly—a brief interlude during which a single hegemon faced no serious challengers. From their perspective, the United States was simply behaving as any dominant power would—maintaining order within its sphere of influence, primarily to serve its own national interests. Today's growing instability is thus viewed as the predictable consequence of a shifting distribution of power, driven by the relative decline of U.S. primacy.

Both perspectives offer important insights. Yet I propose a different analytical lens—one that bridges the core assumptions of realism and liberalism: the concept of legitimacy.

Legitimacy is where these traditions converge and clash. For liberals, legitimacy stems from shared norms, institutional governance, and public consent. For realists, it is often instrumental—a tool that enhances a hegemon's ability to lead without constant coercion. In both cases, however, legitimacy is what allows order to be sustained over time. As we move deeper into this period of hegemonic transition, the crisis of legitimacy—both within and between states—may offer the most illuminating way to understand the erosion of the international order and the challenges of building a new one.

Legitimacy and Realpolitik

I have previously emphasized the interplay between realpolitik and legitimacy. Legitimacy is fundamental to political power—not merely as a practical tool, but as a force that transcends narrow self-interest. In any political endeavor, actions should ideally be either intrinsically legitimate or broadly perceived as such by the public.

Within the realm of realpolitik, I distinguish between two dimensions of legitimacy: (i) hard legitimacy, which provides the structural basis for political authority, and (ii) soft legitimacy, which shapes public perceptions of morality and justice. While hard legitimacy secures the authority of a state, soft legitimacy strengthens its durability and acceptance.

1. Hard Legitimacy: The Foundation of Power

Hard legitimacy encompasses elements such as legal and institutional authority, a monopoly on the use of force, control over territory and resources, and recognition by other political entities. Yet at its core, hard legitimacy derives from the most essential duty of governance: ensuring survival and prosperity.

Throughout history, societies have expected their governing institutions to deliver security and economic stability. When states fail to meet these basic expectations, their legitimacy is called into question—and often, their very existence is threatened. The Chinese philosopher Mencius (孟子) argued that a ruler who failed to ensure the safety and welfare of the people could rightfully be overthrown. This principle resonates in Western political thought as well, particularly in the social contract theories of Thomas Hobbes, John Locke, and Jean-Jacques Rousseau. These thinkers held that the legitimacy of government rests on its ability to protect the well-being of its citizens. Even today, a state that fails to fulfill this foundational role is often labeled a "failed state."

In this sense, hard legitimacy and realpolitik are inseparable. Maintaining security and prosperity—the core imperatives of realpolitik—form the basis of hard legitimacy.

2. Soft Legitimacy: Shaping Perceptions

Soft legitimacy operates in a different domain. It is grounded in moral, cultural, and ideological judgments about what is considered 'right' or 'just.' It draws strength from public approval, alignment with cultural values, ethical justification for actions, and persuasive ideological narratives.

Whereas hard legitimacy pertains to material structures, soft legitimacy shapes the interpretation of those structures. It influences how people perceive political decisions, imbuing them with (or stripping them of) moral weight and meaning. Soft legitimacy is inherently more malleable—and often more fragile—than its hard counterpart. When moral or ideological justifications clash with the imperatives of realpolitik, history suggests that realpolitik usually prevails.

Nationalist conflicts provide a clear example. Ask nationalists from opposing sides to justify their state's actions, and both will likely assert moral righteousness—despite offering contradictory claims. This highlights the subjective and narrative-driven nature of soft legitimacy: it is contingent on perspective, and its power lies in who controls the story.

History's Lessons

History has demonstrated this dynamic time and again, across civilizations, cultures, and eras.

One of the earliest and most influential historical accounts is *The History of the Peloponnesian War*, written by the Athenian historian Thucydides. It chronicles the conflict between the Peloponnesian League, led by Sparta, and the Delian League, led by Athens. Initially, the two powers had been allies against the Persian Empire in 480 BC. But following their victory, Athens began to expand its influence across the Greek world. Thucydides famously observed that "the growth of Athenian power, and the alarm which this inspired in Sparta, made war inevitable." For Sparta, Athens' rise threatened to upend the regional balance of power—what Thucydides identified as the true cause of the war. This insight laid the intellectual foundation for realist theories in international relations. Power—not justice or morality—was the decisive force in state behavior. This principle is most vividly illustrated in the Melian Dialogue, a pivotal episode in Thucydides' account.

During the war, Athens launched a campaign against Melos, a small and neutral island state in the Aegean Sea. Despite Melos maintaining strict neutrality, Athens demanded its unconditional submission. Thucydides presents a stark account of the ensuing negotiations, exposing the raw logic of power politics. The Melians appealed to their neutral stance, insisting they posed no threat to Athens. But the Athenian envoys responded that allowing Melos to remain independent could encourage defiance among other city-states within Athens' sphere of influence.[1] When the Melians invoked principles of justice, morality, and the dangers of persecuting neutral parties, the Athenians dismissed such ideals as irrelevant. They argued that, in the natural order of things, "the strong do what they can, and the weak suffer what they must." When negotiations broke down, Athens besieged the island, executed the male population, and enslaved the women and children.

Ironically, it was Athens—the cradle of Western philosophy and democracy, home to Socrates and Plato—that committed such acts. Sparta, often caricatured for its militarism, played no part in this episode. The stark dissonance between Athens' internal ideals and its foreign conduct underscores a central truth: in the realm of international politics, power and security often trump virtue and moral aspiration. The philosophical discourse on justice and morality that thrived in the Athenian agora had little bearing on its external affairs.

This realist perspective was not unique to ancient Greece. Similar ideas emerged independently in other civilizations.

In ancient China during the 3rd century BC, *Legalism* (法家) rose as the dominant political philosophy. Legalists advocated for a powerful, centralized state underpinned by strict laws and harsh punishments. They viewed human nature as inherently selfish, and believed that only through rigid legal enforcement could order be maintained. Although later eclipsed by Confucianism in domestic governance, Legalist principles left a lasting imprint on Chinese thinking about interstate relations. Legalists insisted that rulers prioritize power, military strength, and state survival above all else. Morality, in their view, was subordinate to strategic necessity.

This emphasis on pragmatic statecraft endured through Chinese history. A striking example is the *Thirty-Six Stratagems* (三十六計), a classic text of military strategy. One of its maxims advises: "befriend the distant, attack the near." The idea is that proximity breeds threat—so align with far-off powers to contain immediate rivals. If a state becomes too friendly with a neighboring state, that proximity could become a liability and a path to subjugation.

Ancient Indian political thought also embraced realism. The *Arthashastra*, an influential treatise attributed to Kautilya, advisor to Emperor Chandragupta in the 4th century BC, laid out an elaborate theory of statecraft rooted in power politics. Kautilya described a 'circle of states' framework (or the "Mandala Theory") in which immediate neighbors are natural enemies, and more distant powers are potential allies—a striking parallel to the Chinese strategic logic.

Within this framework, Kautilya asserted that the primary duties of a ruler are to secure the state's power, stability, and survival. He unapologetically recommended the use of deception, espionage, and even assassination, if necessary. Like the Legalists and Thucydides, Kautilya viewed ethical concerns as secondary to the demands of power.

Across these ancient civilizations, we see recurring themes: that state behavior is driven primarily by self-interest and survival; that rulers must navigate a world defined by threat and competition; and that moral ideals, however noble, often yield to the imperatives of power. These foundational insights continue to shape realist thought in international relations to this day.

Realism vs. Religion

Even religious movements, which often claim the highest moral authority, have historically bowed to the logic of realpolitik.

Religions have long served as powerful motivators of state behavior. In medieval Europe, the Crusades were launched under the banner of faith, with the goal of reclaiming Jerusalem from Islamic powers. Within Europe, religious schisms fueled prolonged conflict between Catholic and Protestant states. Likewise, Islamic empires undertook centuries-long campaigns to expand the *Dar al-Islam*—the "House of Islam"—driven by a theological imperative to extend Islamic governance beyond its original borders.

Yet, history shows that when religious conviction collided with the imperatives of realpolitik, it was often realism—not faith—that prevailed.

The Thirty Years' War (1618–1648) offers a compelling example. While the war began as a bitter struggle between Catholic and Protestant states within the Holy Roman Empire, it soon evolved into a broader geopolitical contest. Catholic France, under the leadership of Cardinal Richelieu—a senior churchman and statesman—sided with Protestant powers to curb the growing influence of the Catholic Habsburgs. Richelieu's justification was unambiguous: "Man is immortal; his salvation is in the afterlife. But the state has no immortality; its salvation is now or never." This statement captured the essence of realpolitik: the security and interests of the state override all else, including religious allegiance.

A similar dynamic played out in the Islamic world. After the schism between Sunni and Shia Islam, political rivalry emerged alongside theological division. In the 16th century, the Shia Safavid Empire in Persia formed alliances with Catholic European powers (Austria and Spain (Habsburgs), as well as the Papacy) against the Sunni Ottoman Empire—while the Ottomans, despite their role as leaders of the Sunni Muslim world, entered into a strategic partnership with Catholic France. Here again, religious identity did not preclude pragmatic alliances. When strategic interests demanded it, realpolitik reigned supreme.

These cases reinforce a fundamental truth: even when politics is infused with religious or ideological fervor, it is the hard calculus of power that often determines the course of state behavior.

The Dawn of a New Paradigm

For most of recorded history, realism dominated the logic of international affairs. The principles articulated by Thucydides, Richelieu, Kautilya, and the Legalist thinkers of China formed the bedrock of global statecraft. Power, survival, and strategic interest governed international conduct.

But beginning in the 14th century, a gradual transformation began in Europe. Though realist imperatives remained—culminating in colonial conquests and two world wars—an ideological shift had quietly taken root. This shift was seeded during the Renaissance, nourished by the Reformation, and brought to bloom in the Enlightenment.

Ideas of human rights, individual liberty, democracy, and national self-determination began to challenge the long-standing supremacy of power politics. Though slow to shape the actual behavior of states, these ideas laid the intellectual groundwork for what would eventually become known as the 'liberal international order.'

Endnotes:

1. In particular, the Athenian envoys argued that allowing Melos to remain independent within Athens' sphere of influence—the Aegean—could lead other city-states to question Athens' strength and dominance.

CHAPTER 4

THE AGE OF REASON
: HOW THE EUROPEAN ENLIGHTENMENT SHAPED MODERN CIVILIZATION

*Sapere aude! Habe Mut, dich deines eigenen
Verstandes zu bedienen.*
Dare to know! Have courage to use your own reason
—that is the motto of enlightenment.

Immanuel Kant

Europe is home to two of history's most influential ancient civilizations: the Greeks and the Romans. However, with the fall of the Western Roman Empire in 476 AD, Western Europe entered the Early Middle Ages, a period marked by the cultural and political dominance of the Catholic Church.

The Early Middle Ages became known as the 'Dark Ages,' a term popularized by 14th-century European scholars who viewed the era as one of cultural and intellectual decline following Rome's collapse. While modern historians debate the fairness of this characterization, it is undeniable that, during this time, Western Europe lagged behind other civilizations, particularly in Asia, in economic and technological development.[1]

A transformative shift began in Italy in the late 14th century with a movement later called the Renaissance, meaning 'rebirth' in French. This era saw a revival of classical knowledge from ancient Greece and Rome, inspiring renewed interest in art, science, literature, and philosophy. Spreading rapidly across Europe, the Renaissance peaked in the 16th century and continued into the early 17th century, serving as a bridge between the medieval world and the dawn of modernity.

One of the Renaissance's most profound contributions was its shift from a God-centered worldview to one that emphasized human potential and achievement. This intellectual movement, known as humanism, celebrated individual expression and critical thinking, laying the foundation for the modern world. The Renaissance also influenced governance, inspiring more secular approaches to political power. Niccolò Machiavelli, for instance, examined politics pragmatically, breaking from medieval traditions and offering a more realist interpretation of statecraft.

Arrival of the Modern Period

The Renaissance ushered in the modern era, a period generally defined as spanning from the late 15th century to the present. Historians typically divide it into three phases: the early modern (1500–1800), the late modern (1800-1945), and the contemporary era (1945~). Of these, the early modern period overlapped significantly with the Renaissance, bringing sweeping cultural, scientific, and political changes.

This era was an age of exploration and global expansion. European explorers such as Christopher Columbus and the notorious Vasco da Gama embarked on ambitious voyages seeking new trade routes, marking the beginning of European global dominance and, in one way of another, the era of interconnected economies. Equally transformative was the scientific revolution, which revolutionized humanity's understanding of the natural world. Visionaries such as Galileo Galilei and Isaac Newton laid the foundations of modern science, fostering a spirit of inquiry that propelled technological advancements. The early modern period also witnessed a monumental shift in religious and political structures. The Protestant Reformation, led by figures like Martin Luther in the 16th century, challenged the authority of the Catholic Church and reshaped Europe's religious and political landscape. In political philosophy, this period saw the emergence of ideas that would shape modern governance. Thinkers like Thomas Hobbes, John Locke, Voltaire, Montesquieu, and Jean-Jacques Rousseau championed concepts of individual liberty, secularism, and rational government. Their works heavily influenced the Enlightenment and laid the groundwork for modern democratic institutions. By fostering scientific progress, cultural transformation, and political reform, the early modern period set the stage for Europe's global influence. Through colonial expansion, industrialization, and two world wars, European civilization reshaped world history, making this period a pivotal turning point not just for Europe, but for humanity as a whole.

But how exactly did the early modern period ignite such profound changes in Europe—and why did these changes occur uniquely in Europe? Many scholars and commentators have proposed their own explanations for this complex, enduring question. Jared Diamond, in his acclaimed bestseller *Guns, Germs, and Steel,* famously attributes Europe's dominance to its geographical and environmental advantages, as well as a long history of intense intra-continental competition.[2] Others argue that Europe's geographic proximity to the Americas, which opened the door to the vast resources of the 'New World,' was the decisive factor. These explanations are compelling, and I see merit in each of them. However, I also note that the defining aspects of modernity were essentially shaped by the contributions of individual visionaries and intellectual giants. In other words, critical differences were made at the individual level, albeit collectively. Given the remarkable emergence of such influential figures in different fields, almost simultaneously in Europe and only in Europe, I cannot help but wonder: was it mere coincidence? Perhaps not.

As with every historical period, these luminaries were not isolated actors but products of their time, influenced by what might be called the 'spirit of the age,' or zeitgeist.[3] The early modern period, too, was imbued with a unique zeitgeist that indirectly empowered and guided these individuals, enabling their remarkable achievements. Their collective contributions ushered in the modern era, raising an intriguing question: what was it about the European 'spirit of the age' that set its progress apart from the rest of the world? Many commentators point to factors such as Europe's rich cultural heritage, evolving institutional frameworks, innovative commercial ventures, experimental approaches, and pluralistic perspectives. These elements undoubtedly played a role, as Europe experienced transformative advancements across culture, governance, commerce, science, and social diversity during this period. However, this broader picture invites a deeper inquiry: what underlying force drove Europe to become a hub of progress at that time? In my view, the common driving force behind these progressive movements was 'individualism.'

Individualism—in its emphasis on personal autonomy, creative expression, and the pursuit of self-interest—provided the intellectual and cultural foundation that enabled Europeans to challenge traditional authorities and reimagine society. It was this spirit of individual initiative, combined with the unique historical and cultural conditions of Europe, that set the stage for the profound changes of the early modern period.

Enlightenment: The Birth of Modern Ideas

The humanist legacy of the Renaissance shifted social focus away from overarching symbols such as God, rulers, or social hierarchies, centering instead on the individual.

During the early modern period and beyond, the moral worth, autonomy, and societal role of individuals gained unprecedented intellectual attention and recognition. This emphasis on individualism fostered greater personal responsibility, economic freedoms such as property rights, and an expanding spectrum of individual liberties. It was such newfound focus on the individual that spurred daring expeditions, innovative commercial ventures, and groundbreaking scientific advancements. It also catalyzed sweeping societal changes, including institutional and religious reforms across various European states. These developments, occurring in remarkable synchrony, propelled Europe toward unprecedented progress during the early modern period. Ultimately, this growing emphasis on individual liberty culminated in the emergence of classical liberalism in the late 17th century, marking a decisive shift from the Dark Ages to the 'Age of Reason.'

The Enlightenment, the intellectual and cultural movement that defined this era, was grounded in the belief that human reason could be harnessed to understand and improve society. Critical thinking became the defining method of the era's intellectual giants, and many consider René Descartes' 1637 declaration, *"Cogito, ergo sum"* ("I think, therefore I am"), to symbolize the dawn of the Enlightenment.

A key political development of this period was the rise of social contract theory. In 1651, Thomas Hobbes published *Leviathan*, a seminal work that challenged the notion of divinely ordained ruler. Hobbes argued that, in the absence of political authority, society would descend into *bellum omnium contra omnes*—a "war of all against all"—where life would be chaotic and dominated by brute force. To escape this anarchy, individuals collectively agreed to form a government, surrendering certain freedoms in exchange for security and the protection of their lives and property. This foundational idea, known as the social contract, laid the groundwork for modern political thought.

Hobbes' theory was later expanded by thinkers such as John Locke and Jean-Jacques Rousseau, who refined and adapted his ideas to emphasize different aspects of governance and individual rights. Locke, for instance, argued that all individuals possess natural rights to life, liberty, and property. He viewed property rights as an extension of personal freedom,[5] asserting that any government failing to safeguard these rights forfeited its legitimacy. Rousseau, while sharing Hobbes' and Locke's belief in the natural equality of all men, had a distinct vision of the state of nature. He argued that primitive humans, lacking concepts of good and evil, lived in morally neutral conditions, cooperating or opposing one another only as needed. As societies evolved, customs and conventions emerged, leading to disparities in wealth and power. Rousseau contended that these inequalities were perpetuated by social institutions that primarily served the elite rather than reflecting the collective will of all individuals. To rectify this, he advocated for a political system in which laws and institutions were established through the participation of all citizens. A governing body, such as a government, would then be responsible for enforcing the collectively decided laws and ensuring adherence to the general will of the citizens.[6] His vision laid the theoretical foundation for modern liberal democracy.

The 17th and 18th centuries saw an intellectual flourishing, with figures such as Voltaire, Montesquieu, and David Hume championing principles of liberty, human rights, and equality. This period also gave rise to Adam Smith, widely regarded as the father of modern economics. In *The Wealth of Nations*, Smith argued that individual freedom was essential for efficient markets and economic prosperity.[7] His concept of the 'invisible hand' suggested that self-interested actions within a competitive market could inadvertently benefit society as a whole.

The Enlightenment's impact was not merely theoretical—it directly influenced key historical turning points. The French Revolution (1789) was deeply inspired by Rousseau's ideas on popular sovereignty and the general will, while the U.S. Constitution (1787) institutionalized the separation of powers, a concept drawn from Montesquieu's *The Spirit of the Laws* (1748), which emphasized checks and balances to prevent tyranny.[8]

By accelerating historical change and shaping its direction, the Enlightenment awakened humanity's capacity for universal reason, leaving an enduring legacy on modern political and intellectual thought.

The Enlightenment's Global Impact

The ideas and philosophies of the Enlightenment had profound implications not only for Western society but also for international politics. The Enlightenment's focus on safeguarding individual life, liberty, and property helped form a framework for addressing global political challenges.

Hobbes, for example, contributed to the realist school by describing the state of nature as a condition of anarchy. At the same time, his idea that individuals created governance to escape this natural threat also influenced liberal thought. Building on Hobbes, some theorists envisioned a global 'Leviathan' in the form of sovereign states working together to mitigate international anarchy. Conversely, Rousseau offered a more cooperative vision: an international community of sovereign states united in pursuit of the common good.

This period also saw a shift in how international trade was understood. The mercantilist view, which framed trade as a zero-sum competition, began to give way to more liberal ideas. Adam Smith argued that free trade could increase a nation's output and promote mutual economic prosperity.[9] Montesquieu further linked commerce with peace, suggesting that economic exchange fosters stability and harmony among nations.

Around 1800, Europe entered the late modern period, which lasted until 1945. The intellectual advancements of the Enlightenment continued to shape Europe during this time. The Industrial Revolution, which began in the mid-18th century and lasted until the mid-19th century, fueled rapid industrialization and technological innovation. This phase propelled Europe to the height of global dominance, transforming it into the most advanced civilization of the era.

However, increased wealth and technological superiority did not lead to peace; instead, they exacerbated conflicts. Geopolitical rivalries among European powers fueled wars within the continent and spurred imperial expansion. Armed with technological advancements, European nations extended their dominance across the globe, often with little resistance and a disregard for the consequences.

Sadly, the modern period not only fostered intellectual progress, but also marked an era of global colonialism and imperialism. In response, some of Europe's greatest thinkers sought ways to transcend realpolitik and achieve 'perpetual peace' in the international community. Among them was Immanuel Kant, a towering figure whose death in the early 19th century even symbolized the end of the Enlightenment era.

Endnotes:

1   Even the neighboring Byzantine Empire—the Eastern Roman Empire's successor—flourished during this period.

2   Diamond argues that Europe's strategic location, favorable climate, and the availability of domesticable plants and animals provided a significant advantage in agricultural development. This, in turn, paved the way for technological innovation, the formation of states, and the accumulation of surplus resources. He further underscores the importance of Eurasia's east-west axis in enabling the dissemination of crops, animals, and technology. Additionally, he highlights how Europe's fragmented geography fueled intense intra-continental competition among states, fostering innovation while preventing unification under a single, stagnant empire.

3   The concept of the 'spirit of the age' is prominently featured in the philosophical writings of Georg Wilhelm Friedrich Hegel. It refers to the prevailing attitudes, ideals, values, beliefs, and cultural norms that define and shape the way people think, feel, and behave during a specific historical period.

4   This is the first principle of Descartes' 1637 work Discourse on the Methods.

5   While Locke's emphasis on the protection of property is often highlighted alongside life and liberty, it is worth questioning whether private property can truly be regarded as a natural right. One could argue that property is essential to individual freedom—after all, if a person cannot secure the means to live independently, can they truly be considered free? From this perspective, property becomes a fundamental pillar of liberty, justifying its status as a natural right alongside life and freedom. However, the legitimacy of property rights becomes more complex when wealth is accumulated by one person to the extent that it suppresses the freedom of others. Should property that exceeds what is necessary to secure one's own freedom be equally protected under natural law? Locke asserted that individuals have a natural right to property in themselves and that ownership arises from one's labor. Yet, even within his framework, the justification for great wealth becomes questionable when it is not solely the product of an individual's labor but also of the labor of others. Does wealth derived from systems of labor and exploitation retain the same moral legitimacy as property acquired through personal effort? Locke's reasoning is less clear on this point, raising important questions about the intersection of natural rights, economic structures, and social justice.

6   Rousseau did not advocate for unconditional adherence to majority rule or equate it with justice. Unlike Hobbes' Leviathan, in which a sovereign authority governs its subjects, Rousseau envisioned the state as a moral and collective body formed by individuals united under a social contract. This collective entity embodies what he called the 'general will.' Crucially, the general will is distinct from both the 'particular will' and the 'will of all.' The particular will reflects individual self-interest, while the will of all is merely the sum of individual interests, which may not align with the true

common good. By contrast, the general will transcends private interests, representing the collective good of the community. It arises when individuals see themselves not merely as private persons but as integral members of a larger whole. For Rousseau, the general will inherently promotes freedom and equality, but its realization depends on a strong sense of civic identity. If individuals prioritize self-interest over communal belonging, the will of all—an aggregation of competing private interests—prevails, corrupting the general will and undermining social cohesion. A well-functioning society, in Rousseau's view, requires citizens to see themselves as active participants in the sovereign, prioritizing the common good over personal gain. All in all, Rousseau believed in democratic processes as a means to determine the general will, provided that individuals voted with the common good in mind rather than private interests. In his view, this idealized form of democracy emphasizes deliberation and civil responsibility of its people.

7 In *The Wealth of Nations*, Adam Smith explored the principles of wealth creation and management from both moral and economic perspectives. He began with the premise that human nature is complex, encompassing both selfishness and altruism. While altruism sustains communities, he argued, self-interest drives economic activity. Smith observed that self-interest motivates individuals in economic exchanges, but it is guided by bargaining and negotiation within markets. Markets enable specialization, allowing individuals to focus on tasks where they have expertise. This specialization fosters a division of labor that integrates even those without specialized skills into production, increasing efficiency, expanding the workforce, and boosting demand. As a result, the division of labor serves as a catalyst for economic growth and national wealth. Smith famously described the market as an 'invisible hand' that aligns individual self-interest with societal welfare, fostering prosperity unintentionally. He also advocated for a limited governmental role, emphasizing its responsibilities in maintaining law and order, enforcing property rights, and providing public goods—such as infrastructure—that private actors cannot efficiently supply. In international trade, Smith opposed government-imposed restrictions, arguing that market principles should operate freely across national boundaries. He believed that trade fosters an international division of labor, where nations specialize in producing goods in which they have an advantage. Through this mechanism, international trade expands wealth globally and establishes a more interconnected economic system.

8 Montesquieu argued that the fundamental purpose of law is to safeguard individual liberty by limiting the abuse of power. In particular, Montesquieu famously warned that "there can be no liberty if the judiciary is not separated from the legislative and executive." He asserted that the most effective safeguard against tyranny is the separation of powers, which divides governmental authority into distinct branches—executive, legislative, and judicial—each capable of checking and balancing the others. When these branches remain independent yet interdependent, he contended, a stable and moderate system of governance can be maintained. Beyond institutional design, Montesquieu emphasized the role of civic virtue in sustaining a republic. He believed that a republic thrives when its citizens possess a deep sense of patriotism—devotion to their country and its legal order. However, he cautioned that political leaders who

manipulate this virtue for personal or factional gain risk destabilizing the republic and undermining its foundational principles.

9 During Adam Smith's era, the dominant economic doctrine was mercantilism, which viewed international trade as a zero-sum game—where one nation's gain necessarily came at another's expense. This perspective framed economic relations between states as an ongoing struggle between winners and losers. Smith, however, fundamentally challenged this notion. He argued that under a system of free trade, nations could specialize in producing goods for which they have a natural or acquired advantage, thereby maximizing overall global wealth. This groundbreaking idea, known as the theory of 'absolute advantage,' demonstrated that trade could be mutually beneficial rather than a contest of exploitation. Smith's advocacy for free trade laid the intellectual foundation for economic liberalism, shaping modern theories of globalization and interdependence. His vision extended beyond economics—he believed that economic openness could foster international stability by reducing incentives for conflict and promoting cooperation among nations. In this way, his ideas contributed to the broader ideal that a liberal international order, grounded in free trade and economic integration, could serve as a pathway to global peace.

CHAPTER 5

KANT'S PERPETUAL PEACE
: THE FOUNDATION OF THE LIBERAL WORLDVIEW

In relations between nation,
the progress of civilization may be seen as movement from
force to diplomacy, from diplomacy to law.

Louis Henkin

Immanuel Kant, one of the foremost philosophers of the Enlightenment, sought to reconcile the era's ideals with the harsh realities of international relations amid the volatile geopolitical landscape of 18th-century Europe. His essay *Perpetual Peace* embodies this ambition, providing a classical blueprint for securing enduring peace among nations.

Kant argued that peace is not only possible but a moral necessity. This claim is rooted in his ethical philosophy, particularly the categorical imperative, which stresses the obligation to treat individuals as ends in themselves, not merely as means to an end. In the realm of international relations, Kant applied this principle to advocate for actions that respect the dignity and rights of all people. Consequently, the pursuit of peace goes beyond pragmatic strategies such as the balance of power or strategic alliances; it is a moral duty grounded in justice, human dignity, and reason. This ethical approach calls for the creation of an international order that fosters cooperation and upholds individual rights as foundational principles.

While Kant's vision may initially seem idealistic, *Perpetual Peace* moves beyond mere ethical aspiration. Kant carefully examined the relationship between rationality and ethics, concluding that perpetual peace is not a utopian dream but a realistic goal achievable through specific political and social reforms. His ideas have made a foundational contribution to the liberal theory of international relations, establishing a counterpoint to the long-standing realist perspective.

One could, perhaps with a touch of hyperbole, claim that the essence of liberal international theory is encapsulated within this nearly 250-year-old essay. Though subsequent thinkers have expanded and refined Kant's concepts, many of his original propositions in *Perpetual Peace* remain relevant and influential in contemporary discussions on global diplomacy and peace.[1] Therefore, dedicating an entire chapter to this classic work is definitely worthwhile.

Perpetual Peace is organized into six Preliminary Articles,[2] three Definitive Articles, two Supplements, and two Appendices. Among these, the three Definitive Articles are particularly crucial, as they outline the core conditions necessary for the attainment of lasting peace.

The First Definitive Articles: Republicanism

The first Definitive Article stipulates that every state should adopt a republican form of government. Kant revisited a theme extensively explored by Enlightenment philosophers: the transition from a state of nature to one of security and peace.

Like his contemporaries, Kant strongly advocated for republicanism, arguing that the social contract—which is crucial for establishing peace and security among individuals emerging from the state of nature—finds its truest expression in a republican constitution. For Kant, the republican system embodies the principles of liberty, equality, and the rule of law, all of which are essential for cultivating lasting peace.[3]

According to Kant, the essence of a republican constitution rests on three fundamental principles. First, freedom for all members of society: this principle ensures that every individual has the liberty to act according to their will, provided their actions do not infringe upon the freedom of others. Second, dependence on a single common legislation: here, Kant argued that all individuals are subject to the same laws, fostering unity and shared responsibility within the state. Third, legal equality of all citizens: this principle emphasizes that every citizen is equal before the law, ensuring fairness and justice in governance.

Kant contended that these principles render the republican constitution uniquely legitimate, as it emerges directly from the concept of an original social contract, which forms the foundation of all lawful legislation. Moreover, Kant argued that the republican constitution is not only pure in its inception—rooted in the concept of right—but also the only system capable of genuinely fostering perpetual peace within its borders. A key reason for this is the republican mechanism for declaring war. In a republic, the decision to engage in military conflict must be ratified by the citizens who will bear the brunt of war's costs, whether through personal loss or taxation. This participatory requirement makes citizens, who directly suffer from war's consequences, more reluctant to endorse military actions than an autocratic leader who might be detached from these burdens.

Thus, Kant concluded that adopting a republican form of government is essential for achieving perpetual peace. However, he clarified that this is merely the starting point. Building upon the republican foundation, Kant's second Definitive Article expands these principles to an international scale, further developing his blueprint for global peace.

The Second Definitive Articles: A Leage of Peace

In his second Definitive Article, Kant advocated for the creation of a federation of free states as the foundation for perpetual peace. He began by drawing a parallel between nation-states and individuals in a state of nature—existing without a governing authority, where each poses a potential threat to the other. Just as individuals escape this precarious condition by forming a civil society governed by a republican constitution, Kant suggested that independent states should consider forming a federation bound by shared laws and principles. This federation differs from an international system with a hierarchical structure in which a central authority governs subordinate states. Instead, Kant envisioned a voluntary association in which states retain their sovereignty while adhering to a legal framework that mitigates mutual threats.

Kant contrasted "lawless freedom"—the freedom of savages—with "true freedom," which is guided by reason. He argued that reason, as the supreme moral authority, unequivocally condemns war and compels states to pursue peace as a moral duty. Yet, peace cannot be established or maintained without a collective agreement among nations. Therefore, Kant called for a pacific federation, distinct from traditional peace treaties that merely conclude individual conflicts. Instead, this league would work to eliminate war altogether, creating a stable international order based on mutual cooperation and the rule of law.

Kant believed that such a federation was not only ideal but also feasible. He envisioned a powerful and enlightened republic, naturally inclined toward peace, as the nucleus of this federation. Over time, other states would voluntarily join, strengthening the principles of freedom and mutual security in accordance with international law. This gradual expansion would eventually encompass all nations, just as individuals abandon their lawless freedom to live under civil law.

In this context, Kant challenged the so-called natural rights of states, particularly the presumed right to wage war. He warned that conflating international law with the right to war would allow states to justify aggression not through universally valid legal principles, but through unilateral assertions of power. Thus, true international law must be rooted in a shared commitment to peace, rather than in the mere regulation of conflict.[4]

The Third Definitive Articles: Cosmopolitan Right

In his third Definitive Article, Kant introduced the concept of 'cosmopolitan right,' which he limited to the "conditions of universal hospitality." Nevertheless, he stressed that this is a right, not merely an act of philanthropy.

At its core, cosmopolitan right ensures that a stranger arriving in another territory is not met with hostility. For Kant, this principle arises from the idea that the earth belongs collectively to all of humanity.[5]

Kant viewed cosmopolitan right as a crucial step toward an eventual international constitution, akin to a republican constitution, which he termed a 'cosmopolitan constitution.' He believed that as peaceful and lawful relations among states evolved under international law, humanity would gradually move toward realizing this cosmopolitan framework.

The Guarantee of Nature: A Hidden Force for Peace

Kant recognized that his ideas might be dismissed as overly idealistic. To preempt such criticism, he provided further analysis in the First Supplement and the two Appendices, where he sought to counterbalance the dominance of realpolitik by identifying an opposing force within human nature—one that could drive humanity toward perpetual peace.

He argued that the state of nature compels individuals to form groups for mutual protection. The presence of a potential threat prompts individuals to band together, and the threat posed by neighboring groups encourages them to establish a group capable of wielding greater armed power. But how can we be certain that such a group will be 'good?'

Kant acknowledged that human beings are inherently selfish. However, even the most self-interested individuals recognize the necessity of a just legal system that ensures their own security. No rational person would tolerate legal loopholes that others could exploit to destabilize society, thus threatening their own well-being. This desire is distinct from the selfish individual's urge to manipulate the system behind the scenes for his or her personal benefit. This distinction between overt and covert selfishness helps explain why people—despite their self-interest—support laws that promote stability and fairness.[6]

Kant applied this logic to international relations. Just as individuals seek protection under good laws, states will align themselves with legal frameworks that shield them from external threats. Naturally, states would be cautious of laws that could be exploited by other states in ways that jeopardize their own security and stability. Thus, Kant argued, the selfish tendencies of states are counterbalanced by nature's mechanism. Even without moral virtue, their self-interest naturally inclines them toward rules that promote universal stability and security. This, Kant argued, is the "irresistible will of nature," through which justice ultimately prevails.

Kant acknowledged that differences in language and religion could impede the progress of international integration.[7] He argued that such differences could foster mutual hatred and be used as pretexts for war, but he also believed that cultural exchange and the gradual convergence of values would foster mutual understanding over time.

He also identified another natural force that unites nations: common self-interest. Expanding trade, property rights and financial exchange would therefore promote peace, regardless of moral motivations.

Ultimately, Kant maintained that nature itself guarantees perpetual peace, as the fundamental workings of human self-interest drive nations toward cooperation and stability.

Morality and Politics: Bridging the Divide for Peace

In the *Appendices*, Kant explored the tension between morality and politics in the pursuit of lasting peace. He acknowledged that while ethical governance is essential, it often clashes with the pragmatic demands of statecraft. Politicians frequently prioritize expediency over moral law, justifying deception or aggression as necessary for state survival. This creates a disconnect between what is morally right and what is politically expedient, leading political leaders to place national interests ahead of moral obligations to peace, thus making peace seem unattainable.

However, Kant argued that disregarding morality for political gain is ultimately shortsighted. He critiqued the concept of realpolitik, which subordinates ethics to power and self-interest, warning that the belief in peace's impossibility can become a self-fulfilling prophecy. Instead, he advocated for a cosmopolitan order in which nations cooperate based on mutual respect and shared values.

Kant contended that the realist approach is self-defeating, as it erodes trust and the foundations of a just society. In contrast, moral political action fosters sustainable peace by building trust and promoting cooperation. He emphasized that morality and enlightened self-interest are not opposing forces—acting according to moral principles often yields the best long-term outcomes for states. Thus, morality is not a hindrance to politics but the universal foundation of legitimate political action.

Ultimately, Kant called for a paradigm shift in political thought, where morality is not merely a tool for political expediency, but a guiding principle. He argued that only when politics is guided by public right—a just and fair legal framework governing relations between individuals and states—can it become a tool for achieving justice and promoting peace. Morality provides the foundational principles for just action, while politics is the practical application of these principles within society. Therefore, Kant believed that morality and politics are not in conflict, but mutually supportive. By adhering to moral principles in political affairs, states can foster a more just and peaceful international order. The harmony between morality and politics is essential for achieving perpetual peace.

While morality must guide politics, Kant recognized that wisdom and prudence are necessary for effectively implementing moral principles in complex situations. Political reality may require temporary compromises, but practical wisdom should serve morality, not override it.

Kant also stressed that public engagement is crucial in ensuring that politicians uphold moral principles. He argued that reason and critical thinking is essential to align politics with morality. An informed and engaged public is crucial for holding leaders accountable and ensuring that governance remains consistent with the principle of public right. Naturally, only a republican system can foster such an informed and engaged public.

Ultimately, Kant called for a federation of free republics, bound by laws reflecting moral obligations, as the best framework for bridging moral aspirations and political realities. By integrating ethics into political structures, states can work toward a just and lasting peace.

Key Takeaways

Two central ideas run through Kant's theory of perpetual peace: freedom and law. If freedom is the foundation of peace, law is the mechanism that secures it.

Kant saw the spread of republican government as essential for international peace, arguing that freedom must be respected both within states and in the international community. At the same time, he emphasized the 'rule of law'—republics should be governed by laws that reflect the will of the people, rather than the arbitrary rule of despots (i.e., the 'rule *by* law'). This principle extended beyond domestic governance: Kant envisioned an international order based on law, upheld by a federation of states that would protect cosmopolitan rights and replace power politics with legal norms.

Historical Impact of Kant's Perpetual Peace

Kant's vision of lasting peace—grounded in democratic institutions, international cooperation, legal order, and respect for human rights—continues to shape modern discussions on global governance.

First, his vision of a league of peace foreshadowed the creation of the League of Nations after World War I and, more significantly, the United Nations (UN) after World War II. His skepticism toward the sovereign right to wage war—justified or not—is reflected in the UN Charter, which categorically prohibits the use of force in international relations, except in cases of self-defense or UN Security Council authorization.

Kant's republicanism—the idea that liberal democratic states[8] are less likely to wage war—directly influenced modern 'democratic peace theory,' particularly the work of Michael Doyle, which empirically demonstrated that liberal democracies rarely, if ever, fight each other. His advocacy for international law and peaceful dispute resolution laid the groundwork for the development of international legal institutions, including the International Court of Justice, the International Criminal Court, and the dispute settlement body of the World Trade Organization (WTO). Kant's emphasis on universal hospitality and world citizenship also helped shape modern human rights discourse and cosmopolitanism. Moreover, his belief that trade and commerce reduce the risk of war was later expanded by liberal thinkers like Norman Angell, Robert Keohane, and Joseph Nye, who developed the theory of economic interdependence—the idea that increased economic ties among nations lower the likelihood of conflict. This theoretical foundation, alongside the economic principles of absolute and comparative advantage, contributed to the creation of the General Agreement on Tariffs and Trade (GATT) in 1946 and later the WTO in 1995.

Ultimately, modern liberal peace theory is best summarized by the concept of 'Triangulating Peace,' which consists of three core elements: (i) the spread of liberal democracy; (ii) economic interdependence; and (iii) multilateralism. All three pillars are directly rooted in Kant's *Perpetual Peace* (1795), demonstrating his enduring influence on the global order.

The Reality Gap: Colonialism and Power Politics

Unfortunately, the gap between idealism and reality is often stark. The Age of Discovery expanded Europe's horizons, but it quickly turned from exploration to conquest. Not long after Kant published *Perpetual Peace*, European powers embarked on a colonial era, subjugating much of the world even as Enlightenment ideals flourished at home.

Ironically, many European intellectuals—supposedly enlightened by classical liberalism—justified colonial imperialism under the guise of cultural and racial superiority. Popular caricatures from the late 19th and early 20th centuries vividly illustrated how colonial rule was framed as a 'civilizing mission.' This reflects the deep-seated sense of Western cultural dominance that persisted despite liberal ideals. The spread of liberal thought in Europe did not immediately translate into a more peaceful world order.

At the same time, Europe itself remained mired in geopolitical struggles. The French Revolution led to the Napoleonic Wars, followed by the Crimean War, where Britain, France, and the Ottoman Empire fought to curb Russian expansion. Meanwhile, Prussia waged wars against Austria and France, culminating in German unification (1871) and shifting Europe's balance of power. Then, in 1914, World War I erupted.

In this volatile era, liberal ideals remained largely aspirational. The realist concept of international anarchy—the idea that power, not law, governs relations between states—was an undeniable reality. The liberal vision of a peaceful international order seemed idealistic, even naïve. For liberalism to be realized, it required a collective effort among nations, including the effort by that "powerful and enlightened republic." Such an effort did not materialize until after the devastation of the world wars, long after these ideas were first articulated.

Endnotes:

1 This is not to suggest that every aspect of *Perpetual Peace* holds the same relevance today as it did in 1795. While each component of Kant's work carries timeless philosophical value, not all of them retain practical applicability in the modern context. For instance, even the most devoted Kantian would hesitate to argue that the *Preliminary Articles* or the *Second Supplement* remain fully valid when subjected to contemporary scrutiny. In this chapter, my primary focus will be on the three *Definitive Articles*, the *First Supplement*, and the two *Appendices*. The six *Preliminary Articles* are only touched upon briefly in endnote 2 below.

2 In the first part of the essay, Kant outlined six preliminary articles aimed at reducing the likelihood of war, even among states that are not yet true republics. These preliminary articles represent essential political reforms designed to eliminate the structural conditions that make war more likely. To this end, Kant advocated for the prohibition of secret treaties and diplomacy, the annexation of territory by force, standing armies, the accumulation of national debt for foreign ventures, interference in the constitution or policies of other states, and, in general, all acts of hostility that would undermine mutual trust.

3 Kant argued that any form of government other than a republic inevitably leads to despotism. This, he maintained, occurs when the executive and legislative powers are not separated, allowing laws to be both made and executed arbitrarily by the same authority. For Kant, the ideal government must be based on a representative system to ensure accountability and the protection of individual rights. However, he warned strongly against the dangers of direct democracy, in which the power to govern is supposedly vested in the people as a whole. Kant foresaw that such a system would inevitably deteriorate into despotism. He feared that, in the absence of institutional constraints, executive power could suppress individual freedoms under the guise of acting on behalf of the people. This, he warned, would create a self-contradiction within the general will, undermining the very liberties it claimed to uphold. Viewed through a modern lens, Kant's insights closely align with the principles of a republican system grounded in liberal democracy, where the separation of powers and protection of individual rights serve as fundamental safeguards against tyranny.

4 Kant critiqued traditional 'just war' theory, particularly as developed by medieval jurist Hugo Grotius, arguing that such frameworks can be easily manipulated by the powerful to justify acts of aggression. He rejected the notion that military action can ever serve as a legitimate or effective means of resolving disputes. For Kant, war cannot bring an end to the state of war itself; rather, just war thinking perpetuates the state of nature in international relations instead of seeking to eliminate war altogether. In essence, Kant shifted the focus from justifying war to actively pursuing lasting peace. Nevertheless, he considered that the 'just war' theory inherently reveals that states are capable of distinguishing between 'just' and 'unjust' wars; this recognition, according to Kant, reflects a deeper moral capacity in human beings—the ability to discern right from wrong. Kant believed that this same capacity enables humans to

overcome their destructive instincts and to trust in the potential for others to do the same. This moral potential, in turn, fuels the hope for progress toward lasting peace.

5   Building on the principle that all human beings share common ownership of the earth's surface, Kant asserted that cosmopolitan right includes two key entitlements: (i) the right of visitation – Strangers have the right to present themselves in foreign lands without facing hostility; and (ii) the right to temporary shelter – Hosts must provide refuge, particularly when a traveler's life is in danger. However, Kant made a crucial distinction: cosmopolitan right does not extend to permanent settlement (ius incolatus) without a formal agreement.

6   A clear example of this tendency appears in Walt Disney's 2016 film *The Jungle Book*. During a severe drought, all the animals of the jungle observe a natural law that forbids fighting or killing. Even Shere Khan—the ferocious tiger and main antagonist who relentlessly pursues the wolf-raised man-cub Mowgli—acknowledges this "Water Truce." When warned, he begrudgingly complies, remarking, "I am deeply respectful of these laws *that keep us safe.*"

7   In advocating an International Federation, Kant expressed skepticism about the feasibility of a single, unified world government. He argued that as a government expands its reach, its laws would gradually lose their effectiveness, and an overly centralized global authority could ultimately descend into anarchy. Instead, Kant proposed a voluntary federation of free states, designed to preserve state sovereignty while promoting peace and cooperation. Through this framework, states could gradually develop common principles and mutual understanding, fostering the long-term emergence of a more unified international order—not through coercion, but through the natural evolution of shared interests and norms.

8   To be clear, Kant harbored profound concerns about 'direct' democracy. He believed it could easily devolve into a 'tyranny of the majority,' where the will of the majority overrides individual rights and freedoms. In Kant's view, direct democracy risks degenerating into despotism because it reflects the collective private interests of the majority, rather than the general will aimed at the common good. Such a system, he argued, violates the principles of freedom and justice, as it enables citizens to act as rulers without accountability or regard for the broader welfare of society. Instead, Kant advocated for a republican system—one grounded in the separation of powers, checks and balances, and the rule of law. In this framework, individual liberty is protected through representative institutions rather than direct popular rule. His republican ideals closely align with modern liberal democracy, which combines representative democracy with constitutional safeguards and protections for minority rights. When Kant criticized 'democracy,' he was referring to systems like ancient Athens, which lacked liberal restraints and often subordinated individual rights to majoritarian rule—as seen in the execution of Socrates. In contrast, contemporary liberal democracies incorporate institutional mechanisms designed to prevent such abuses, ensuring a balance between popular sovereignty and the protection of fundamental rights. Thus, Kant's republicanism can be seen as a precursor to modern

liberal democracy, emphasizing the need for structured legal frameworks to safeguard individual liberty against the excesses of unmediated popular rule.

CHAPTER 6

THE EUROPEAN BALANCE OF POWER
: THE 19TH CENTURY GEOPOLITICS BEHIND THE WORLD WAR I

> The test is not absolute satisfaction
> but balanced dissatisfaction.
>
> Henry Kissinger

In the modern era, Europe witnessed remarkable progress across various spheres of society. Yet, in the realm of realpolitik, it remained a stage for relentless geopolitical rivalry. Europe's great powers continuously vied for supremacy in nearly every aspect of statecraft, and these prolonged and intensifying conflicts eventually culminated in two devastating world wars.

In *Perpetual Peace*, Kant envisioned an international framework designed to foster peace within the anarchic global order—marking a bold departure from the traditional 'balance of power' system. However, it is crucial to acknowledge that in the absence of such a balance, the international system often defaults to the natural principle of 'survival of the fittest.' This anarchic state is aptly captured by Thomas Hobbes' famous description of a "war of all against all."

Hegemon the Peacekeeper?

The most traditional approach to achieving peace, as history suggests, often involves the establishment of hegemony. When a great power achieves the status of a regional hegemon, it dominates its sphere of influence and seeks to maintain a hegemonic order that serves its interests. Motivated by self-preservation and the promotion of its system, the hegemon often assumes the role of regional peacekeeper. Yet, relying on hegemony as a means of peace presents significant challenges. This raises important questions about whether hegemonic stability can truly deliver enduring peace—or if it merely suppresses conflict temporarily while sowing the seeds of future discord.

In addition, the path to hegemony is usually paved with blood. As explained earlier, all states are fundamentally driven by the pursuit of security and prosperity, which often requires the constant acquisition of greater power and control. This process often involves the subjugation of neighboring states and the creation of empires, which paradoxically exposes them to increased internal instability and external threats. As states extend their reach, the pressures of securing borders, sustaining economic strength, and managing internal cohesion push them to expand even further. The pursuit of greater influence becomes not just a reaction to external threats but also a means of ensuring continued dominance and staving off internal decline. This self-reinforcing cycle continues until the state either exhausts its capacity to expand or, by rare chance, achieves uncontested regional hegemony.

In this context, it is crucial to recognize that hegemony is a rare and fortunate exception to the otherwise brutal dynamics of international relations. History provides only a few examples where true hegemons emerged and managed to sustain peace and stability within their spheres of influence for any significant period. For the most part, power struggles have resulted in protracted, senseless conflicts and countless casualties.

Furthermore, maintaining hegemony is an exceptionally difficult task, making it even more unrealistic to rely on a hegemonic order for lasting peace. History offers clear evidence of this. The so-called Pax Romana, Pax Sinica, Pax Britannica, and even Pax Americana—all eventually came to an end. The fall of hegemonies is often accompanied by intense violence. The collapse of Pax Romana plunged Europe into centuries of chaos, while the end of each phase of Pax Sinica brought bloody turmoil to East Asia. The decline of Pax Britannica led to the outbreak of World War I, despite the relatively peaceful transfer of Britain's legacy to the United States. Even today, as we stand on the brink of Pax Americana's decline, the world watches with uneasy anticipation.

Moreover, hegemony is often synonymous with imperialism. By its very nature, hegemonic rule erodes the autonomy of subordinate nations. This loss of sovereignty is inevitable because every hegemonic system is fundamentally designed to serve the interests of the hegemon.

In sum, peace through hegemony is neither sustainable nor desirable. Fortunately, history offers a proven alternative: a balance of power. When great powers achieve a balance among themselves, the resulting system of checks and balances promotes stability and peace—at least until that balance is disrupted.

The Utility of the Balance of Power System

While Kant's noble vision of permanent peace deserves every commendation, the value of the 'balance of power' system cannot be underestimated. For centuries—until the outbreak of the world wars—it represented the most realistic and progressive framework for maintaining peace in an inherently anarchic international system.

The balance of power system is often preferred to peace through hegemony because it is comparatively easier to achieve—at least in theory. As long as a region consists of multiple powers, a balance can theoretically be established through skillful diplomacy. When great powers possess comparable strength, they can easily form a balanced system. Alternatively, if one power begins to dominate and seeks hegemonic status, other powers can form alliances to counterbalance it. Balance becomes impossible or impractical only when the dominant power is so overwhelmingly strong that even a united opposition cannot effectively challenge it.

However, achieving balance is far easier in theory than in practice. Establishing such a system requires tremendous effort, and maintaining it presents even greater challenges. The fundamental problem lies in the inherent uncertainty of international relations—the inability to predict or trust the actions of other states. This issue, part of the broader security dilemma, is not new; the same "primordial fear" that haunted Sparta during the time of Thucydides still influences state behavior today. Consequently, this conditional peace cannot rely on mutual trust but must instead rest on the continuous recalibration of power dynamics to sustain balance in an ever-evolving international landscape.

Given these challenges, it is no surprise that history has witnessed only a few periods where an effective balance of power system was achieved. Each of these instances required immense strategic commitment, careful diplomacy, and, at times, a significant degree of luck. This underscores a crucial point: the balance of power system is not a natural state of affairs but an artificial construct—an intentionally crafted mechanism for peace.

When the Balance of Power System Works

The European balance of power system traces its origins to the Peace of Westphalia in 1648, which is often regarded as the foundation of the modern state system. The series of treaties that ended the Thirty Years' War and the Eighty Years' War introduced key principles—such as territorial sovereignty and non-interference in the internal affairs of states—that reshaped interstate relations in Europe. These norms curtailed the overarching authority of empires and supranational institutions (e.g., Catholic Church), promoting a more decentralized international order.

While the modern concept of the nation-state would not fully emerge until the 19th century,[1] the Westphalian settlement laid the institutional groundwork for its eventual rise by affirming the autonomy and equality of sovereign states within a balance of power framework.

While the principle of balance of power was not explicitly articulated in the Westphalian treaties, it nonetheless served as a central guiding force in shaping the post-war diplomatic order. The treaties implicitly advanced this principle by fostering a web of alliances and counter-alliances that functioned as a system of checks and balances among European states. By dispersing power across multiple sovereign actors, the Westphalian settlement helped prevent the rise of a single hegemon and laid the foundation for a more decentralized European order. Moreover, the Westphalian system established a durable tradition of alliance-building as a means of counterbalancing stronger powers—a practice that became a hallmark of European diplomacy and a key mechanism for preserving stability and restraining hegemonic ambitions.

The Westphalian model faced its greatest challenge in the late 18th and early 19th centuries. Following the French Revolution, France's army underwent transformative reforms, emerging as the most formidable land force in Europe. Under the command of Napoleon Bonaparte—a military strategist of extraordinary brilliance—revolutionary France systematically dismantled the coalitions assembled under the balance of power framework.

Ironically, the revolutionary republic that had overthrown its monarchy soon evolved into an empire. Napoleonic France extended its dominance across the continent, subjugating or neutralizing major powers such as Prussia, Austria, and various Italian and German states. In response, a series of coalitions—comprised of powers like Britain, Austria, Prussia, and Russia—formed to contain French expansion. Yet, despite their efforts, these alliances repeatedly faltered in the face of Napoleon's military genius. Ultimately, it was a combination of British naval and financial supremacy, along with the unforgiving Russian winter, that brought Napoleon's historic campaigns to an end. The collapse of Napoleonic France marked a turning point for the Westphalian system, demonstrating both the fragility and resilience of the balance of power principle in the face of extraordinary challenges.

Following Napoleon's defeat in 1814, the European powers embarked on an ambitious effort to restore the prewar balance of power and prevent future continental domination. From 1814 to 1815, the Congress of Vienna—a series of high-level diplomatic negotiations—sought to redraw Europe's political map and establish a durable framework for peace. These efforts involved a range of territorial adjustments: France was returned to its prewar borders; buffer states such as the Netherlands and the German Confederation were established; and, most significantly, the Concert of Europe was created. This informal but influential diplomatic mechanism brought together the five great powers—Great Britain, France, Russia, Prussia, and Austria—in a cooperative effort to preserve continental stability through a shared commitment to balance. Remarkably, France—despite its recent aggression—was included in the system to counterbalance the growing strength of Russia.

At the heart of this postwar restoration was Austrian Foreign Minister Klemens von Metternich, famously dubbed the 'Coachman of Europe.' As the chief architect of the Concert of Europe, Metternich's overarching goal was the preservation of the status quo. He championed the restoration of traditional monarchies and the suppression of liberal and nationalist movements, which he saw as existential threats to the established order. Metternich also advocated for collective security, urging the great powers to hold regular diplomatic consultations to manage emerging crises and prevent unilateral action. Serving as a mediator between rival powers—particularly Britain and Russia—he worked to defuse tensions before they could erupt into open conflict. While criticized for his reactionary stance, Metternich's diplomacy helped to maintain a remarkably stable European order for much of the 19th century.

Still, the relative peace of this era cannot be credited to Metternich alone. The balance of power system relied heavily on Great Britain's active role as an offshore balancer. At the height of its global influence, Britain's naval supremacy and skillful diplomacy were instrumental in preserving the continental equilibrium. Together, the Concert of Europe and British engagement fostered an extended period of geopolitical stability that would come to define the post-Napoleonic age.

Yet, as Metternich himself anticipated, the 19th century would be increasingly shaped by the rising force of nationalism. One of the most consequential expressions of this dynamic was Pan-Slavism—an ideology strongly associated with the Russian Empire. Initially emerging as a cultural and intellectual movement that emphasized the shared heritage of Slavic peoples, Pan-Slavism gradually evolved into a political doctrine. In Russia, it became a powerful rhetorical tool for advancing expansionist ambitions, particularly in Eastern Europe and the strategically critical Crimean Peninsula.

These regions, under the control of two non-Slavic empires—the Austrians and the Ottomans—soon became flashpoints for confrontation. While Russia and Austria vied for influence in Eastern Europe, the broader conflict between them was restrained for much of the 19th century by the stabilizing influence of the Concert of Europe. However, such diplomatic architecture did not extend to the more volatile Black Sea and Balkan regions, where Slavic populations and rising nationalist tensions gave Russia fertile ground to pursue its geopolitical aims under the guise of Pan-Slavism. This ideological pretext ultimately escalated Russian confrontations with the Ottoman Empire, culminating in the Crimean War.

In the mid-19th century, Russia intensified its longstanding pursuit of maritime access to the Mediterranean. Control of the Black Sea—and, by extension, the Bosphorus Strait—became a strategic imperative. This narrow waterway, linking the Black Sea to the Mediterranean, flows through Istanbul (formerly Constantinople), the capital of the Ottoman Empire and a city of immense geopolitical significance. For centuries, Russia had been geographically constrained by its lack of warm-water ports. Securing the Bosphorus would not only break the Ottoman grip on the region but also enable Russia to project naval power beyond its traditional confines.

Though the Ottoman Empire had once stood as a formidable power, by the 19th century it was in visible decline. While industrialization transformed the great powers of Europe, the Ottomans lagged behind in both military and technological modernization. Russia, by contrast, had reemerged as a major European power following its pivotal role in defeating Napoleon. This newfound strength emboldened its ambitions in the Black Sea region, alarming other European powers—particularly Great Britain.

The British Empire, which famously spanned a quarter of the world's landmass, regarded Russian expansion as a direct threat.[2] It saw the Mediterranean and the routes to India as vital strategic corridors. Russia's growing presence near the Bosphorus was thus perceived as an encroachment on British geopolitical interests. These two empires—Britain and Russia—were the primary antagonists in what became known as the 'Great Game,' a century-long rivalry centered on control over Central Asia. Russia's gradual southward advance toward the Indian subcontinent, and its quest for warm-water ports, collided with Britain's determination to safeguard its imperial crown jewel: India. The Crimean Peninsula became one of the most intense theaters of this imperial competition.

In an ironic twist of history, Britain and France allied with the Ottoman Empire—once cast as the "enemy of Christian Europe"—to contain Russian expansion. France, motivated by its own aspirations in the Middle East, joined the alliance. These coalitions set the stage for the

Crimean War (1853–1856), one of the defining conflicts of 19th-century geopolitics.

The Crimean War mobilized hundreds of thousands of troops and inflicted heavy casualties, bringing an end to the relatively peaceful era that had followed the Napoleonic Wars. It concluded with the Treaty of Paris (1856), which reaffirmed the territorial integrity of the Ottoman Empire and curtailed Russian naval power in the Black Sea. While the war was a significant setback for Russia, it did little to diminish the broader rivalry between the Russian and British empires. The Great Game would continue to unfold across the Middle East, Central Asia, Tibet, and East Asia, remaining a dominant theme in global geopolitics until the early 20th century.

Despite their global competition, Britain and Russia continued to operate within the continental diplomatic order established after 1815. The Concert of Europe remained intact, with Britain and France often aligned on one side and Austria and Prussia on the other. This structure helped preserve European stability, even as the great powers projected their rivalries onto the colonial periphery.

By the early 20th century, however, tectonic shifts were underway. In 1904–1905, Russia suffered a stunning defeat in the Russo-Japanese War—marking the first time in modern history that an Asian power decisively defeated a European one. The destruction of Russia's Baltic and Pacific fleets forced Britain to recalibrate its strategic priorities. Meanwhile, a newly unified Germany—since 1871—had risen rapidly as a dominant continental power, fundamentally altering Europe's balance. Recognizing this shift, Britain moved to end the Great Game. In 1907, the two powers signed the Anglo-Russian Convention, which demarcated their respective spheres of influence in the Middle East and Central Asia. With this agreement, they turned their attention from the imperial periphery back to Europe, where a new and far more dangerous confrontation loomed on the horizon.

In the 19th century, the Kingdom of Prussia emerged as a formidable continental power. Since the Napoleonic Wars, Prussia had steadily consolidated its position, expanding its influence through key military engagements, including the Schleswig War against Denmark. However, it was the ascent of Otto von Bismarck in the mid-century that truly transformed Prussia's role in European affairs. A master strategist and one of history's most astute geopolitical thinkers, Bismarck—with the full support of King Wilhelm I—pursued the unification of Germany, a project that would profoundly reshape the European balance of power.

Central to German unification was a decisive reckoning with Austria, which had long regarded the German-speaking states as part of its traditional sphere of influence. In 1866, Prussia defeated Austria in the Austro-Prussian War—a swift and decisive campaign that lasted only seven weeks. The victory consolidated Prussian dominance over northern Germany and effectively removed Austria from German political affairs.

Having secured the north, Bismarck turned his attention to the southern German states. France, under Emperor Napoleon III, viewed the prospect of a unified Germany with growing alarm, seeing it as a direct challenge to French hegemony in continental Europe. In a carefully orchestrated diplomatic maneuver, Bismarck provoked France into declaring war in 1870. The Franco-Prussian War united the German states against a common enemy, and once again, Prussian military efficiency proved decisive. France was swiftly defeated, and in 1871, Bismarck proclaimed the establishment of the German Empire in the Hall of Mirrors at the Palace of Versailles. King Wilhelm I of Prussia was crowned Kaiser (Emperor) of a newly unified Germany.

Bismarck is widely regarded as a diplomatic genius—not only for his role in unifying Germany but also for ensuring that its emergence did not destabilize Europe. The post-Napoleonic order, crafted to prevent the rise of any one hegemonic power, had been upended by Germany's rapid ascent—having vanquished both Austria and France. Yet rather than seek continental dominance, Bismarck exercised strategic restraint. He recognized that any attempt to assert German hegemony would likely provoke a countervailing alliance, particularly from Britain and France. Although Germany possessed the industrial and military potential to rival even the British Empire, Bismarck deliberately eschewed such ambitions.

Following Austria's defeat, Bismarck took deliberate steps to mend ties with Vienna. Austria, now reorganized as the Austro-Hungarian Empire, became a crucial ally rather than a lingering adversary. Bismarck also moved to secure relations with Russia, ensuring stability between two of Europe's largest land empires. His diplomacy culminated in a web of interlocking alliances—including the League of the Three Emperors and the Dual Alliance—that anchored Germany in a network of strategic partnerships. At the same time, he avoided antagonizing Britain, which remained vigilant against any shifts that might threaten the continental balance of power. France, Germany's most immediate rival, was left diplomatically isolated.

Bismarck's foreign policy was guided by realism, caution, and a deep understanding of European dynamics. Rather than pursue expansion, he focused on consolidating Germany's position within the existing international order. His commitment to maintaining peace among the great powers helped preserve the post-Napoleonic system well into the late 19th century. Among his many diplomatic accomplishments were the Congress of Berlin in 1878—where he mediated tensions in the Balkans—and the Berlin Conference of 1885, which sought to manage imperial rivalries in Africa.[3] Under Bismarck's stewardship, Germany emerged not only as a powerful state but as a stabilizing force in European diplomacy.

When the Balance of Power System Fails

It is truly remarkable that a state with the potential to dominate the European continent—such as Germany under Bismarck—chose not to pursue hegemonic ambitions. Bismarck's diplomatic genius lay in his ability to masterfully navigate the complex web of European rivalries, preserving the post-Napoleonic peace while securing Germany's place within the continental order. Yet even a statesman of his caliber could not fully suppress the deeper structural impulses of international politics. Just as Napoleon's military brilliance was ultimately checked by the realities of European geopolitics, Bismarck's pragmatic diplomacy could only delay, not eliminate, the latent forces of German nationalism and imperial ambition.

Following the death of Kaiser Wilhelm I, Bismarck found himself increasingly at odds with Wilhelm II over the direction of German foreign policy. Whereas Wilhelm I had endorsed Bismarck's careful balancing act, Wilhelm II rejected such cautious restraint in favor of a more assertive and expansionist approach. In 1890, Bismarck was dismissed from office—a turning point that marked the end of an era. Freed from Bismarck's moderating influence, imperial Germany embarked on a path of geopolitical ambition, clashing with Britain, France, and Russia in precisely the way Bismarck had sought to prevent. The foundations of a fragile peace began to erode, and the stage was set for the great conflagration of 1914.

In the 19th century, Great Britain's strategic priorities were clear: to maintain stability on the European continent in the wake of Napoleon's defeat and to secure the vast global reach of the British Empire. Through a combination of military strength and astute diplomacy, Britain preserved a balance of power that prevented the rise of another continental hegemon. This strategic posture forestalled large-scale conflicts like the Napoleonic Wars and contributed to an extended period of relative peace in Europe.

Benefiting more than any other nation from the Industrial Revolution, Britain became the wealthiest state in Europe, though its power was not rooted in a large standing army. Instead, British dominance was built on economic strength, global trade, and the liberal principles of free commerce championed by thinkers like Adam Smith. This era—commonly referred to as the Pax Britannica—represented the apex of British global influence.

While Britain did not seek to dominate continental land wars, it was unwavering in its commitment to naval supremacy. Control of critical sea lanes and trade routes (including those linking it to its overseas colonies) was crucial to maintaining Britain's position as the linchpin of global commerce. As such, maritime supremacy was central to British security, enabling it to deter continental threats and protect its far-flung empire. Following its decisive victory at the Battle of Trafalgar in 1805, the Royal Navy became the world's preeminent maritime force. By the late 19th century, Britain had codified its naval dominance in the form of the 'two-power standard,' enshrined in the Naval Defence Act of 1889. This doctrine required that Britain's fleet be larger than those of the next two largest naval powers combined.

Germany's rise under Kaiser Wilhelm II directly threatened both pillars of British strategic doctrine. First, Germany's late entry into the imperial competition placed it in direct conflict with the established colonial powers—particularly Britain and France. By the late 19th century, most of the world's strategically significant territories had already been claimed, leaving little room for new imperial entrants. Germany's attempts to secure overseas markets and colonies clashed with British and French interests, prompting an Anglo-French rapprochement and aligning the two powers in opposition to Berlin.

Second, Germany's aggressive naval buildup challenged Britain's dominance at sea. Influenced by the seminal work of American naval theorist Alfred Thayer Mahan—*The Influence of Sea Power upon History* (1890)—Wilhelm II became convinced that great power status required a powerful navy.[4] This belief led to a rapid expansion of the German fleet, sparking a naval arms race with Britain, often referred to as the 'Gunboat Race.' The two nations increasingly viewed each other through the lens of strategic rivalry, undermining the maritime equilibrium that had long underpinned the Pax Britannica.

The immediate catalyst for World War I was the escalating confrontation in the Balkans, where Russia—having allied with Britain and France after Bismarck's dismissal—sought to expand its influence amid the decline of the Austro-Hungarian Empire. The Balkans, long viewed as Vienna's strategic backyard, became the flashpoint for great power conflict.[5] But the deeper tensions had been building for decades. At its core, the war was driven by the structural rivalry between a status quo superpower—Britain—and a rising challenger—Germany. By 1914, this geopolitical contest had reached its breaking point, unleashing a cataclysm of violence and destruction unprecedented in European history.

Endnotes:

1 The claim that the concept of the nation was introduced by the Treaty of Westphalia (by codifying state sovereignty) is difficult to substantiate. The idea of nationhood predates the modern state and developed organically over time, rather than being the product of a specific diplomatic agreement. In Europe, national identity was significantly weakened during the Middle Ages by the overarching authority of Christianity and the decentralizing structure of feudalism. Yet it re-emerged with renewed vitality in the modern era. In much of the non-Western world, including Asia, there are comparatively fewer historical instances of such a profound erosion of national identity—suggesting that the evolution of nationhood followed different trajectories across regions.

2 At its imperial zenith, the British Empire was the largest in history, controlling nearly 25% of the world's landmass. Its vast holdings spanned Europe (e.g., Britain and Malta), the Americas (e.g., Canada and Jamaica), Oceania (e.g., Australia and New Zealand), Southeast Asia (e.g., Malaysia and Brunei), South Asia (e.g., India and Afghanistan), West Asia (e.g., Oman and Cyprus), and Africa (e.g., Egypt and South Africa). This unprecedented global reach inspired the adage, "The sun never sets on the British Empire." Britain's primary geopolitical rival in the 19th century was Russia. While less industrialized than Britain, Russia's vast empire stretched from the Baltic to the Pacific, controlling large swaths of northern Eurasia. In short, Britain dominated the southern halves of most continents, while Russia asserted control over the northern regions. At one point, Russian territory even extended to Alaska, bringing the two powers into direct proximity not only in Europe but also in Central Asia, the Americas, and East Asia.

3 Africa became a battleground for Western powers during the 19th and early 20th centuries. The French colonial empire, stretching across the continent from east to west, and the British Empire, spanning from north to south, were locked in a fierce power struggle. Other European nations, including Germany, Spain, Portugal, Italy, and Belgium, also sought to claim their share of the continent. As tensions escalated and threatened to ignite full-scale war, Bismarck intervened. Having already mediated a power struggle in the Balkans in 1878 to preserve the European balance of power, Bismarck was determined to prevent a similar conflict from destabilizing Europe over distant African territories. From November 1884 to February 1885, intense negotiations were held in Bismarck's office, culminating in the Berlin Conference. At the conference, European powers drew arbitrary borders, dividing Africa into spheres of influence. While the Berlin Conference helped maintain peace in Europe for several more years, it condemned Africa to a legacy of division. These borders, drawn without regard for local geography, cultures, or ethnic groups, still define Africa's nations today. Much like in the Middle East, these artificial borders merged diverse peoples and tribes into single political entities, setting the stage for civil wars and conflicts that would ravage the continent in the following century—resulting in immense loss of life and property.

4 In his seminal 1890 work, *The Influence of Sea Power upon History, 1660-1783*, Alfred

Thayer Mahan argued that control of the seas was fundamental to national power and prosperity. He emphasized the critical importance of a strong navy to safeguard trade routes, project military power, and control strategic waterways. Britain, already the dominant naval power, saw Mahan's theories as a validation of its existing naval strategy, viewing naval supremacy as essential to protecting its vast empire and global trade interests. Germany, an emerging industrial power, also embraced Mahan's ideas. In 1894, Wilhelm II, deeply influenced by Mahan's work, wrote to the author to express that he had not only read but memorized the 557-page book. This newfound understanding of naval power led Germany to challenge British naval dominance, as it sought to build a formidable fleet to secure its growing overseas colonies and trade routes. In response, Britain accelerated the expansion and modernization of its own navy. Both powers, guided by Mahan's emphasis on the doctrine of decisive battle and the importance of superior firepower, embarked on an intense naval arms race, focusing on the construction of large battleships, particularly the revolutionary dreadnoughts. See among others, Holger Herwig, *The Influence of A. T. Mahan upon German Sea Power* (U.S. Naval War College, 1990).

5   The immediate cause of World War I was the assassination of Archduke Franz Ferdinand of Austria-Hungary and his wife on June 28, 1914, by Serbian nationalists in Serbia's Sarajevo. At the time, Serbia was a Russian ally, which further complicated the diplomatic situation. The Austro-Hungarian Empire demanded that Serbia punish those responsible for the assassination of Archduke Franz Ferdinand, disband all anti-Austrian organizations within Serbia, remove anti-Austrian officials, and allow Austria to investigate the assassination on Serbian soil. However, Serbia rejected these demands. In response, Austro-Hungary declared war on Serbia on July 28, 1914. As Serbia's tutelary power, Russia declared general mobilization on August 2, 1914. Germany, an ally of Austro-Hungary, demanded that Russia rescind its mobilization order. When Russia refused, Germany declared war on Russia on the same day. The next day, August 3, 1914, Germany declared war on France, a Russian ally, and invaded Belgium as part of its plan to invade France. In response to Germany's violation of Belgium's neutrality, the United Kingdom declared war on Germany on August 4, 1914. Following the Anglo-Japanese Alliance, Japan declared war on Germany on August 23, 1914. By 1917, the war expanded further, with the Ottoman Empire, Italy, Bulgaria, Portugal, the United States, Greece, Thailand, China, and Brazil all joining the conflict.

CHAPTER 7

AMERICAN EXCEPTIONALISM AND LIBERAL INTERNATIONALISM

Die Weltgeschichte ist der Fortschritt im Bewußtsein der Freiheit – ein Fortschritt, den wir in seiner Notwendigkeit zu erkennen haben.

World history is the progress of the consciousness of freedom —a progress which we have to recognize in its necessity.

Georg Wilhelm Friedrich Hegel

1. The Story behind Global Leadership

Everything comes to an end. The European balance of power system, which had maintained relative peace for nearly a century, finally collapsed at the dawn of the 20th century, giving way to a war of unprecedented scale and devastation: World War I.

The war, which began in 1914 and lasted over four years, ended on November 11, 1918, with Germany's unconditional surrender. While initially a conflict among European powers, it quickly spread across the globe. The vast reach of European colonial empires ensured that battles erupted not only in Europe but also in the Middle East, Africa, and Asia.

World War I claimed approximately 40 million military and civilian casualties, leaving Europe in ruins. The destruction was not just physical but psychological and societal, as the war's impact reverberated worldwide. Its consequences reshaped the course of human history, triggering geopolitical upheavals that included the collapse of four imperial dynasties,[1] the emergence of new nation-states in Europe, the rise of communism following the Russian Revolution and the ascent of the United States to become the world's preeminent power.

The major battles of the war, fought primarily on European soil, pitted the Central Powers—led by Germany and Austria-Hungary—in a brutal war of attrition against the Allied Powers, which included Britain, France, Russia, and later the United States. Although the Russian Revolution of 1917 forced Russia's withdrawal in early 1918, the grinding stalemate continued. By the time the United States entered the war in 1917, Germany was drained of manpower, resources, and morale. American intervention decisively tipped the scales. After four years of devastating warfare, the German army was no match for the military might of the United States, which began deploying nearly ten thousand troops a day. In November 1918, both the Austro-Hungarian Empire and Germany surrendered to the Allies, marking the end of World War I.

By the end of the Civil War in 1865, the United States had already established itself as an industrial and military powerhouse. Its entry into World War I signaled a turning point, cementing its position as the world's most powerful nation.

The war not only redrew the political map but also signaled the dawn of a new global order. Europe was no longer the center of power; the torch had passed to the 'New World.' Yet this shift raised a crucial question: With all its might, did the United States have the will—or even the desire—to shape the course of history?

Arrival of a Powerful and Enlightened Republic

In *Perpetual Peace*, Immanuel Kant argued that the spread of republican governments was the first condition for lasting peace. He further envisioned a voluntary federation of free republican states as the second. However, Kant introduced a pragmatic caveat: for such a federation to take shape, "a powerful and enlightened republic" must take the lead. This republic, acting as the nucleus, would attract other states to join its peaceful order. It would need to balance strength with principle—combining the realism of power with the moral example championed by liberalism. When Kant theorized about such a republic, he was illustrating the practical feasibility of his ideas. Yet, more than a century later, history has produced a nation that appears to fit his criteria: the United States of America.

Nations rise to greatness through various factors. Sometimes, a single leader alters history. Other times, technological advancements—such as the Industrial Revolution—reshape global power dynamics. But history teaches that geography is the most enduring foundation of great power status. A nation occupying a strategically advantageous position within its region often becomes dominant. If it lacks a serious geographic rival, it can rise to regional hegemony. While the fortunes of nations fluctuate, geography remains constant. Many of today's great powers owe their status to geographic advantages that have persisted for centuries. As long as their territorial integrity holds, these nations retain their geopolitical significance—or the potential to reclaim it. As the British journalist Tim Marshall aptly noted in the title of his bestseller, nations are in fact "prisoners of geography."

Unlike transient powers whose rise and fall were dictated by historical contingency—such as the Latin Empire in the 13th century or the Dutch Republic in the 17th century—some nations possess geopolitical advantages that have allowed them to remain relevant across centuries. A unified China, for instance, will always possess the potential to dominate East Asia. India is well-positioned to consolidate influence over the Indian Ocean. Russia, with its vast expanse, will always have the potential to shape a unique geopolitical order across Eurasia. Geography dictates these possibilities.

But what about the United States? No nation in history has enjoyed a stronger geographic advantage than the United States. Not only is it positioned to dominate the Americas, but with the Treaty of Guadalupe Hidalgo in 1848, it became the first and only nation with the potential to achieve true global hegemony. That treaty, which ended the Mexican-American War, secured U.S. borders in a way that cemented its geopolitical supremacy.

Stretching from the Atlantic to the Pacific, the United States spans a landmass nearly as large as Europe. Unlike other great powers, its access to the world's two largest oceans is unrestricted. This advantage is unparalleled and sharply contrasts with the constraints faced by China and Russia. China's maritime access, for example, is geographically restricted. The Korean Peninsula, Japanese archipelago, Taiwan, and Southeast Asia form a chain that impedes its ability to project naval power freely. Meanwhile, its landlocked borders with South Asia and the Middle East further limit its strategic reach. Russia, too, faces severe geographic constraints. Its Arctic coastline is frozen for much of the year. Its western access to the Atlantic is vulnerable to Scandinavian and British naval blockades. To the east, its Pacific ports are hindered by icy waters and Japan's maritime presence. These limitations have historically shaped Russia's and China's geopolitical behavior, often pushing them toward territorial aggression as a means of compensating for their geographic disadvantages. The United States faces none of these challenges. Its oceanic access is completely open, allowing it to trade freely, project power globally, and expand its influence without geographic hindrance.

Beyond maritime supremacy, the United States enjoys an extraordinary wealth of natural resources. Throughout the 19th and 20th centuries, it was the only nation in the world fully self-sufficient in essential resources. Today, advancements in shale gas and oil extraction have made the United States the world's leading exporter of energy. Environmental concerns aside, this development underscores its exceptional energy security. Even rare earth elements, once seen as a U.S. vulnerability, are now a potential strength. Recent discoveries suggest the United States may possess some of the world's largest reserves of these critical materials. This resource abundance extends to agriculture as well. The U.S. possesses the most fertile farmland in the world, ensuring food security and economic strength. Moreover, America's internal geography has facilitated an unparalleled infrastructure network. The Mississippi River Basin—the largest inland waterway system in the world—acts as a natural transportation network, reducing costs and enhancing economic integration.

If any nation were capable of thriving in complete isolation, it would be the United States. Historically, its dependence on foreign trade has been minimal. During World War I, international trade accounted for only a small fraction of its GDP. Even today, while deeply integrated into the global economy, the United States remains uniquely positioned to sustain itself independently. Yet, even these extraordinary advantages do not fully capture the extent of America's geopolitical dominance.

As the shadow of American dominance eventually fades, China and Russia will inevitably be forced to contend with each other. History reminds us that China's greatest geopolitical rival during the Cold War was not the United States, but the Soviet Union. Their long border and overlapping spheres of influence make lasting cooperation difficult. At the same time, China faces an emerging challenger in the south: India, a country with the demographic and economic potential to rival its power. To the east, Japan—a formidable naval power—remains a strategic counterbalance. Meanwhile, in the west, European nations remain wary of Russian expansionism, especially in the wake of its invasion of Ukraine.

In contrast, the United States remains unburdened by such rival constraints. Unlike China and Russia, which must constantly navigate powerful neighbors and shifting alliances, the United States faces no serious regional rivals. To the north, Canada is a longstanding ally with a shared cultural and political foundation. Despite its vast size, its small population ensures it poses no strategic challenge to the U.S. To the south, Mexico, while a neighboring power, has never represented a true geopolitical threat. The same is true for the rest of Latin America.

Across the globe, the U.S. alone enjoys the security of a vast, resource-rich homeland with no existential threats on its borders. The United States towers over the world with a level of security that no other great power has ever enjoyed.

Classic Crossroads: Isolationism vs. Interventionsism

From the perspective of realism, the United States' unparalleled geographic and geopolitical advantage affords it two reasonable paths. The first is to project its unmatched power beyond its continental borders, establishing itself as the global hegemon—something no empire in history has ever achieved. The second is to consolidate its regional hegemony, prioritizing security and stability within its immediate sphere of influence while avoiding the risks of overextension.

Historically, the second option has been the more common choice. While some empires—such as Alexander the Great's Macedonian Empire—sought expansion beyond regional dominance, most major powers ultimately prioritized consolidation once they secured their immediate surroundings. The Roman Empire, after reaching its territorial zenith, focused on stabilizing its borders rather than continuous conquest. Likewise, unified Chinese dynasties usually turned inward to maintain governance and security. These examples underscore a fundamental principle of power: expansion carries increasing costs and diminishing returns, making long-term consolidation the more rational strategy.

Moreover, the United States is not an empire in the traditional sense but a democratic republic in which public sentiment shapes policy. This democratic structure makes the pursuit of global hegemony even less likely, as American leaders must justify overseas engagements not just in terms of strategic interests but also in a way that resonates with the public. As history has shown, Americans have often been reluctant to support foreign interventions unless provoked by direct threats.

For much of its early history, the United States maintained a deliberate distance from global conflicts, focusing instead on securing its dominance over the Americas.[2] This policy, articulated in the Monroe Doctrine, was not merely ideological but a rational choice for a nation that was both self-sufficient and geographically insulated from foreign threats. Even as global tensions rose in the early 20th century, the U.S. avoided entanglements in overseas conflicts until direct provocations—such as unrestricted submarine warfare in World War I and the attack on Pearl Harbor in World War II—forced its hand.

During these wars, the United States faced the potential emergence of rival hegemons in Europe and Asia—Germany in both world wars and Japan in the second world war. Realist calculations dictated that these powers had to be contained, yet convincing the American public to engage in global affairs required appeals beyond pure strategy. Consequently, U.S. leaders frequently presented their interventions as idealistic struggles for democracy and a new world order, rather than mere defensive geopolitical maneuvers.

After each war, the United States championed a departure from the traditional balance-of-power system, instead advocating for a new order based on cooperation and multilateral institutions. It positioned itself as the "powerful and enlightened republic" that Immanuel Kant had envisioned—a nucleus around which a federation of free states could coalesce to preserve global peace. This vision led to the creation of the League of Nations after World War I and the United Nations (UN) after World War II.

However, both domestically and internationally, these efforts often proved overly ambitious. The U.S. itself never joined the League of Nations, undermining its effectiveness, and it later rejected membership in the International Trade Organization. Without sustained American leadership, these institutions were ultimately unsuccessful.

This pattern reveals a recurring tension in U.S. foreign policy: while it has frequently sought to shape a liberal international order (in fact, it was the first nation in history to seriously attempt the establishment of a liberal order—repeatedly, despite setbacks), domestic politics and competing strategic priorities have often constrained its commitments.

American Exceptionalism: The Call of History?

Nevertheless, Americans and their leaders have long viewed themselves as distinct from European powers and peoples. They saw the United States as unique, special, and, in many ways, exceptional. This belief was articulated by Thomas Jefferson, who envisioned America as "a standing monument and example" for the international community.

This sense of exceptionalism, commonly referred to as 'American exceptionalism,' has deep historical roots. The term was first popularized by the French historian Alexis de Tocqueville in the 1830s, based on his observations during his 1831 visit to the United States. In modern political discourse, the concept gained renewed prominence during Barack Obama's 2008 presidential campaign, when his views on American exceptionalism were challenged by John McCain, cementing the term as a defining feature of American political identity.

This enduring belief in exceptionalism has often driven the United States to pursue international goals that might seem idealistic. Much of this sentiment stems from America's vast geographic advantages. A nation endowed with exceptionally immense resources and territorial wealth may naturally come to see itself as exceptional. However, American exceptionalism runs deeper than material prosperity; it is embedded in the nation's history, culture, and identity.

Every nation has its own foundational myths that shape its collective identity. As Yuval Harari noted in *Sapiens*, these narratives serve to bind societies together. The United States, though founded relatively late in history, developed a national identity centered not on ancient myth but on liberal ideals.

One of the earliest and most enduring symbols of this identity is the story of the Pilgrims—English settlers who crossed the Atlantic seeking religious freedom. The Mayflower and Plymouth Colony became powerful national symbols representing the pursuit of freedom and a fresh start. Unlike the divine selection narratives that underpin many older civilizations, America's self-conception revolves around the ideals of 'freedom' and 'the American Dream.'

A century and a half later, these ideals became the foundation for a new republic. The American Revolution was not merely a war for independence but a radical experiment in governance. Unlike virtually every other state of the era, which established monarchies, the United States embraced Enlightenment principles, creating a system rooted in liberal democracy, individual liberty, and the rule of law. The U.S. Constitution enshrined the separation of powers and codified fundamental rights—an unprecedented achievement in political history. The so-called American values—freedom, individualism, republicanism, democracy, meritocracy, and laissez-faire economics—became integral to the nation's identity.[3] The republic faced profound challenges, most notably the moral contradiction of slavery. Yet, with the ratification of the Thirteenth Amendment in 1865, which abolished slavery, the United States moved closer to fulfilling its founding ideals.

By the time the United States entered World War I, American exceptionalism had become deeply ingrained in its national consciousness, shaping its approach to global affairs. President Woodrow Wilson, in particular, championed an ambitious vision for U.S. engagement, arguing that America had a moral duty to promote democracy and reshape the international order. This idealism guided the creation of the post-World War I liberal institutions, including the League of Nations and the Permanent Court of International Justice.

American exceptionalism played an even more decisive role in shaping the post-World War II order. The United States spearheaded the creation of multilateral institutions such as the UN and the Bretton Woods system. These institutions, grounded in American ideals of democracy, free markets, and international cooperation, became the backbone of the liberal international order.

2. America's First Major Role in Global Governance

On April 6, 1917, the United States entered World War I, driven by a combination of immediate provocations and broader strategic concerns.[4] Among the most pressing factors was Germany's policy of unrestricted submarine warfare, which had already resulted in the sinking of the RMS Lusitania in 1915. The final catalyst came in early 1917 with the interception of the Zimmermann Telegram, in which Germany attempted to persuade Mexico to join a potential war against the United States, promising to help it reclaim territories lost in the Mexican-American War.

Beyond these immediate triggers, a deeper strategic calculation influenced the United States' decision to intervene. There was growing recognition in Washington that a hegemonic power dominating the European continent could ultimately threaten American security. While the Atlantic Ocean served as a natural buffer, it was the British Royal Navy that effectively ensured a separation between the Old and New Worlds. The ongoing war, however, jeopardized British naval supremacy, raising concerns in the United States that any significant shift in the balance of power across the Atlantic could have long-term security implications.

Thus, the United States resolved to enter the war. However, President

Woodrow Wilson sought to frame American involvement in a way that transcended traditional power politics. Rejecting the European system of balance of power as both morally deficient and strategically flawed, Wilson envisioned the conflict as an opportunity to reshape global order. He saw the war as a means to establish a new international system grounded in American principles—what he considered the nation's new *Manifest Destiny*: the promotion of democracy, self-determination, and the rule of law on a global scale.[5]

First Liberal Reform of the Global Order

To realize this vision, Wilson assembled a group of 150 scholars, historians, and policymakers known as 'The Inquiry.' Their mandate was not only to analyze the causes of the war but also to help Wilson formulate a framework for a lasting peace. Drawing from nearly 2,000 reports and 1,200 maps, their findings coalesced into fourteen key proposals, which Wilson unveiled in his address to Congress on January 8, 1918—an address that would become famous as the *Fourteen Points*.[6]

Deeply influenced by liberal internationalist thought, the Fourteen Points echoed the ideals of Immanuel Kant's *Perpetual Peace*.[7] At its core, Wilson's vision rested on several fundamental principles. Foremost was the principle of national self-determination—the notion that all peoples, regardless of size or power, had the right to govern themselves. This idea, radical for its time, challenged the imperialist and colonial structures that had long defined global politics.

Yet self-determination alone was not enough to guarantee lasting peace. Wilson championed open diplomacy, freedom of the seas, general disarmament, and the removal of economic barriers—all of which he saw as essential conditions for a just and stable international order.[8] Wilson's vision also emphasized legal mechanisms over military force in resolving international disputes. In essence, he sought to replace the traditional paradigm of national security—rooted in power and strategic interests—with a new model in which peace itself would be the fundamental principle of international relations.

In practical terms, Wilson believed that security could only be preserved through 'collective security'—a system in which an attack on one nation would be considered an attack on all, necessitating a unified response. Recognizing the need for an institutional mechanism to uphold this principle, Wilson's Fourteenth Point called for the establishment of a "general association of nations" that would provide "mutual guarantees of political independence and territorial integrity to great and small nations alike." This proposal laid the groundwork for what would later become the League of Nations.

Like Kant, Wilson sought to establish a democratic republican system on an international scale. This ambition was informed by a sense of American exceptionalism that left little doubt that the envisioned global system would reflect that of the United States. Wilson viewed the American model of governance as the most advanced, progressive, and virtuous. From his youth, he believed that America's federal institutions should serve as the foundation for an eventual "parliament of man."[9] The new 'Manifest Destiny' of the United States, as Wilson saw it, was to create an international order in the post-war world that reflected its exceptional political system.

The Fourteen Points marked a stark departure from the European balance-of-power system, which treated nations and territories as negotiable assets in pursuit of equilibrium. At the same time, Wilson's proposals reinforced the Westphalian concept of national sovereignty, ostensibly supporting the self-determination of smaller nations even when it conflicted with the interests of great powers. For the first time in history, multilateralism was seriously considered as a foundational principle of international order.

Wilson's ambitious proposals, however, faced significant resistance.

The Allied powers, still reeling from years of devastating war, were more interested in punishing Germany and securing their own strategic interests than in pursuing Wilson's idealistic blueprint for peace. Nevertheless, they recognized that a decisive victory required continued U.S. support. Moreover, the sheer scale of the war's destruction forced world leaders to acknowledge that the existing international system had failed catastrophically—creating, however reluctantly, an opening for Wilson's revolutionary ideas to be debated and, to some extent, implemented.

In 1919, the Treaty of Versailles was signed, officially ending World War I and establishing the terms of peace between Germany and the Allied Powers. Chapter I of the treaty created the League of Nations, marking the first formal attempt to institutionalize a global system for maintaining peace. Two years later, in 1922, the Permanent Court of International Justice was established to uphold the rule of law in international affairs.

Legacy of Wilsonism

The broad liberal experiment that followed World War I is often remembered as a failure, largely because it did not prevent the outbreak of World War II just two decades later. However, the creation of the League of Nations was historically significant as the first concerted effort to move beyond a purely realist framework in international relations.[10]

For the first time, an international body sought to resolve disputes through legal and diplomatic means rather than military force. The League promoted principles of disarmament and arms control, while also pioneering efforts in human rights—championing causes such as child protection, women's suffrage, labor rights, the abolition of human trafficking, the protection of ethnic minorities, refugee resettlement, and the prevention of war crimes. Many of these initiatives laid the foundation for the UN, which would later assume many of the League's functions. Despite these ambitious efforts, however, the fundamental power dynamics among the European great powers remained unaffected.

For centuries, France's primary strategic goal had been to prevent the unification of Central Europe, fearing that a strong German state would pose an existential threat. Even after Germany's defeat in World War I, it still far outmatched France in industrial capacity and population. Thus, France sought to permanently weaken Germany, advocating for its territorial dismemberment in a manner reminiscent of Cardinal Richelieu's strategy centuries earlier. At the very least, France hoped to establish a buffer state by creating an independent Rhenish Republic. However, these efforts ran counter to Wilson's ideals of national self-determination and ultimately failed. Nevertheless, France succeeded in securing punitive provisions in the Treaty of Versailles, ensuring that Germany remained economically and militarily constrained.

Great Britain, meanwhile, pursued a different geopolitical strategy. Historically, Britain had maintained a balance of power in Europe by preventing any one state from achieving continental dominance. After the Napoleonic Wars, Britain had deliberately refrained from dismantling France, preserving it as a counterweight to Russia and Austria. Following World War I, Britain applied the same logic to Germany. It opposed France's attempts to partition Germany, preferring instead to preserve Germany as a counterbalance to both France and the Soviet Union. Britain's chief priority was to neutralize the threat posed by Germany's High Seas Fleet, which had challenged British naval supremacy before the war.

In the end, the Treaty of Versailles imposed penalties on Germany that historians have often described as "too severe to foster reconciliation, yet not harsh enough to prevent Germany from rising as a great power once again." Germany was stripped of its colonies, forced to cede thirteen territories, and subjected to severe military restrictions. However, its core territories and population remained intact.

The United States, on the other hand, withdrew into a period of isolationism. Despite Wilson's leadership in creating the League of Nations and the Permanent Court of International Justice, his vision of liberal internationalism failed to gain domestic support. Many Americans believed that, with Germany defeated, the country could return to its traditional policy of non-interventionism. The idea of a supranational organization dictating the U.S. foreign policy was met with deep skepticism. Wilson personally campaigned across the United States to rally support for the League, but his efforts were cut short when he suffered a debilitating stroke. Without his leadership, the Senate ultimately rejected the Covenant of the League of Nations.[11] As a result, the United States—the world's most powerful economic and military power—remained outside the League, severely undermining its credibility and effectiveness.

The Gravitational Pull of Realism Returns

The Treaty of Versailles ultimately satisfied no one. It failed to reintegrate Germany into the European order, excluded the United States from the postwar international system, and left France feeling insecure about its long-term security. Furthermore, Wilson's principle of national self-determination, while revolutionary, created unforeseen complications. The dissolution of the German, Austro-Hungarian, and Ottoman Empires led to the formation of new states with deeply fragmented ethnic and political identities. While the rhetoric of self-determination inspired anti-colonial movements worldwide, it often generated instability rather than harmony, as newly independent states struggled to reconcile their diverse populations under singular national identities.

The League of Nations also faced structural weaknesses. At its peak, it had only 58 member states—a stark contrast to the UN today, which has over 190. More critically, League resolutions required unanimous approval, making decision-making slow and often ineffective. Moreover, the League was widely perceived as a tool of British and French interests, further eroding its legitimacy. Britain and France were left to lead the postwar order, but they lacked the economic and military capacity to sustain it alone. From a realist perspective, therefore, the League's greatest weakness was the absence of the United States. Without American participation, there was no enforcement mechanism for the League's principles, creating a power vacuum that contributed to global instability. This imbalance would prove fatal in the years leading up to World War II.

Nevertheless, the League of Nations enjoyed considerable success in mediating international disputes in the 1920s. Several key conflicts were peacefully resolved under its auspices, including the 1921 dispute between Sweden and Finland over the Åland Islands, the 1922 territorial conflict between Germany and Poland over Silesia, and the 1926 dispute between Iraq and Turkey over Mosul. Even in the 1923 crisis between Italy and Greece over an Albanian region, where Benito Mussolini initially resorted to force, the League managed to mediate a resolution before full-scale war erupted. These successes were largely driven by the widespread anti-war sentiment that followed the devastation of World War I.

The anti-war sentiment remained strong through the late 1920s, culminating in the Kellogg-Briand Pact (1928), or the 'Pact of Paris,' which sought to renounce war as a means of resolving international disputes. Initially conceived as a bilateral agreement between the United States and France, the pact quickly expanded into a multilateral treaty, with over sixty nations signing on. Although it lacked enforcement mechanisms, the pact laid the groundwork for later international peace efforts, influencing the development of norms that culminated in the Charter of the United Nations.[12]

However, by the 1930s, the League of Nations' authority came under increasing strain as major powers, now stronger or equal to Britain and France, began to defy its rules in pursuit of their national interests. The

League's failure to respond effectively to Japan's 1931 invasion of Manchuria exposed its fundamental weakness. When Japan withdrew from the League rather than comply with demands to return the region to China, it became clear that the League lacked the means to enforce its decisions.

From that point on, the League's failures multiplied. It was ineffective in preventing the Chaco War between Bolivia and Paraguay (1932), Italy's invasion of Ethiopia (1935), the Spanish Civil War (1936), the Second Sino-Japanese War (1937), the German and Soviet invasions of Poland (1939), and the Soviet invasion of Finland (1939). The League expelled the Soviet Union on December 14, 1939 for its attack on Finland, but by then, World War II was already underway, with Britain and France having declared war on Germany in September.

To dismiss the League of Nations as a complete failure, however, would be overly simplistic. The outbreak of World War II was the result of complex geopolitical forces, and it is uncertain whether a more robust international institution—such as the modern UN—could have prevented the war.[13] E. H. Carr once observed that "no political utopia will achieve even the most limited success unless it grows out of political reality." While this view may seem overly harsh, the failures of the League of Nations serve as a lasting lesson for the 21st century: liberal internationalism cannot succeed without the support of real power. Ultimately, efforts to transcend a realist worldview remain bound by the very forces that realism seeks to explain.

Endnotes:

1 These are the Habsburgs of the Austro-Hungarian Empire, the Hohenzollerns of the German Empire, the Sultanate of the Ottoman Empire, and the Romanovs of the Russian Empire.

2 It should be noted that the United States has not always adhered to liberal principles in practice. Within the Americas and in key strategic regions, it has pursued realpolitik with determination. The 19th-century doctrine of 'manifest destiny' saw the United States expand its territory with a speed and decisiveness that rivaled many historical empires. The scale and swiftness of its territorial growth were, indeed, remarkable in world history.

3 In recent decades, many of these values, such as meritocracy and laissez-faire economics, have come under more progressive criticism due to a greater understanding of structural inequalities and impact of globalization on national economies. However, in the era when blood-based (birthright) monarchy and aristocracy were the prevailing (if not the only) norm, these concepts were truly revolutionary.

4 See American Entry into World War I, 1917, U.S. Department of State Archive.

5 When John O'Sullivan first coined the term "manifest destiny" in 1845, he was primarily referring to the United States' expansionist destiny to stretch across the North American continent. However, by the time of Woodrow Wilson, the concept of 'manifest destiny' had evolved into something broader. It came to signify not only territorial expansion but also the United States' role in setting an example for the world, serving as a "shining city upon a hill" by imbuing and spreading its unique moral virtue.

6 In November 1917, two months before President Wilson's announcement of the Fourteen Points, Vladimir Lenin issued the so-called *Decree on Peace*. In this decree, Lenin called on all nations involved in the Great War to immediately cease hostilities and initiate negotiations for a "just and democratic peace." He defined such peace as one free from the forced annexation of weaker nations or peoples, condemning the continuation of war for territorial conquest by great powers as a crime against humanity. Furthermore, to prevent future conflicts, Lenin proposed the abolition of secret diplomacy and full transparency in treaty negotiations. However, shortly after issuing this proposal, the Soviet Republic began peace talks with Germany, raising suspicions that the Decree on Peace was a mere pretext to justify an agreement with the German Empire. During these negotiations, the issue of Ukraine's independence reignited tensions between the Soviet government and Germany, ultimately leading to a Soviet defeat and the humiliating Treaty of Brest-Litovsk. Under this treaty, the Soviets were forced to cede vast territories—including present-day Finland, Poland, Estonia, Latvia, and Lithuania—to Germany and recognize Ukraine's independence, which ironically set the stage for these nations' eventual independence following Germany's defeat. Given these circumstances, Lenin's *Decree on Peace* remained relatively

obscure, yet it still reflected his ideological convictions. Notably, the decree closely aligns with Immanuel Kant's theory of perpetual peace, especially in its call for the prohibition of territorial annexation and the abolition of secret diplomacy, provisions Kant considered essential to eliminating the state of hostility among nations. However, the most influential and pioneering liberal declaration in this context was undoubtedly President Wilson's Fourteen Points, which more explicitly drew on Kant's vision of perpetual peace than Lenin's decree.

7   However, Wilson never officially acknowledged the influence of the great 'German' philosopher.

8   The Fourteen Points also addressed specific geopolitical issues of the time, such as the impartial settlement of colonial claims, the restoration of Belgium, and the withdrawal of foreign forces from Russian territory.

9   See Henry Kissinger, *Diplomacy*, Simon & Schuster (1994) p. 223.

10 Even before the establishment of the League of Nations, the idea of an international organization aimed at achieving global peace had been proposed. However, it had never been fully realized with a permanent secretariat.

11 In March 1920, the U.S. Senate attempted to ratify the Covenant of the League of Nations, but the vote failed due to a lack of quorum.

12 In particular, the Kellogg-Briand Pact introduced the concept of "crime against peace," which, through a growing consensus and widespread acceptance within the international community, later became a legal basis in international law for the prosecution of leaders responsible for initiating wars of aggression. See generally, Oona Hathaway & Scott Shapiro, *The Internationalist: How a Radical Plan to Outlaw War Remade the World*, Simon & Schuster (2017).

13 The UN, with its Security Council at the core, has a more effective collective security system than the League, whose decision-making was slow and constrained by its rigid respect for state sovereignty. However, even the UN has clear limitations. During the Cold War, ideological divisions between the United States and the Soviet Union frequently paralyzed its ability to act. Today, as the United States steps back from its role as the 'global policeman,' the UN Security Council often remains deadlocked.

CHAPTER 8

WORLD WAR II
: IDEOLOGICAL CONFLICTS AND THE BIRTH OF THE COLD WAR

Only the dead have seen the end of war.

George Santayana

World War I arose from the collapse of the delicate balance of power among European states. In contrast, World War II was even more devastating due to the fusion of ideology and nationalism with geopolitical ambitions.

Nazi Germany, Imperial Japan, and Fascist Italy shared key traits: nationalism, totalitarianism, militarism, and expansionism. Despite differences in political, social, and cultural contexts, their trajectories were strikingly similar—populist leaders rose to power by appealing to nationalist sentiments, consolidated control through totalitarian measures, embraced militarism to sustain their regimes, and ultimately pursued aggressive wars of expansion.

The causes of World War II were complex and multifaceted, offering various frameworks for analysis. The harsh terms of the Treaty of Versailles played a crucial role in setting the stage for renewed conflict,[1] while the Great Depression of the 1930s exacerbated international tensions and fueled the rise of extremist ideologies.[2] Another perspective views the major conflicts that precipitated the war in Europe and Asia as manifestations of neo-imperial expansionism.

War for Sphere of Influence

Unlike 18th- and 19th-century European colonialism, the interwar expansions of Germany, Japan, and the Soviet Union were framed as essential for national survival and self-sufficiency. Nazi Germany justified its territorial ambitions under the ideological banner of *Lebensraum*—'living space'—arguing that the German people needed additional land and resources to secure their future. After repudiating the Treaty of Versailles in 1935, Germany launched an expansionist campaign: re-militarizing the Rhineland in 1936, intervening in the Spanish Civil War, annexing Austria in 1938, and seizing the Sudetenland under the guise of protecting ethnic Germans. The invasion of Poland in 1939, executed in partnership with the Soviet Union under the Molotov-Ribbentrop Pact, marked the start of war in Europe. Yet, as the scope of Lebensraum shows, Nazi ambitions extended far beyond Poland—to Scandinavia in the north and deep into Soviet territory in the east. True to its objectives, Germany pursued these campaigns in the early years of the war.

Imperial Japan promoted the *Greater East Asia Co-Prosperity Sphere* (GEACPS), a vision of regional unity under Japanese leadership, ostensibly to liberate Asian nations from Western colonialism. In practice, however, Japan imposed its own imperial rule, exploiting local resources and labor to sustain its war effort. Like Lebensraum, the GEACPS blended imperialism and nationalism—imperialistic in its territorial ambitions, nationalistic in its justification of Japanese racial and cultural superiority.

Fascist Italy's expansionism was the most straightforward of the three Axis powers. Italy had joined the victorious Entente in World War I but felt betrayed when the Treaty of Versailles failed to deliver its expected territorial gains. This perceived humiliation fueled nationalist resentment and a desire for strong leadership, paving the way for Benito

Mussolini's rise to power under the promise of restoring the glory of the Roman Empire. Italy's expansionist ambitions materialized in its 1935 invasion of Ethiopia, which ruptured relations with Britain and France and pushed Italy closer to Nazi Germany. Italy subsequently supported Franco's forces in the Spanish Civil War, recognized Germany's annexation of Austria, and played a role in the 1938 crisis over Czechoslovakia. After Germany's swift conquest of France in 1940, Italy formally joined the war, declaring war on British and French territories in Africa and the Mediterranean.

The Soviet Union, under Joseph Stalin, was another major expansionist force during the interwar period. After eliminating political rivals and consolidating power by 1938, Stalin turned his attention outward. The Molotov-Ribbentrop Pact temporarily neutralized the German threat, allowing the Soviet Union to pursue its own expansionist agenda. Following the joint invasion of Poland in 1939, it attacked Finland, occupied the Baltic states in 1940, and expanded its territorial reach across Eastern Europe.

Soviet expansionism was driven not only by geopolitical ambitions but also by ideological and security concerns. Historically, Russian expansion had been motivated by the need to create buffer zones against external threats. The aggressive expansion of Nazi Germany to the west and Japan to the east left the Soviet Union in a vulnerable position, reinforcing its longstanding strategy of securing its periphery through territorial acquisitions. At the same time, the Soviet Union sought to advance its ideological mission: the global spread of communism. According to Marxist-Leninist doctrine, socialism could not survive in isolation—it required a worldwide proletarian revolution to dismantle capitalism. This belief partly affected Soviet foreign policy, linking expansionism to the broader struggle against Western capitalism.

The progression of World War II differed significantly from that of World War I in several key ways. Unlike in World War I, where France held its frontline against Germany until the war's conclusion, Germany swiftly conquered France in World War II and launched direct military operations against Britain. In the East, Japan, the most powerful nation in Asia, aligned itself with the Axis powers. At the outset, the Axis appeared stronger than ever, yet each member ultimately made a series of critical mistakes that led to their downfall.

Germany's inability to conquer Great Britain was not necessarily an error but a significant strategic setback. The German military exerted every possible effort to subjugate Britain, but, like many great conquerors before him, Hitler lacked the naval capabilities to overcome the British Royal Navy and cross the narrow Dover Strait. Meanwhile, Italy's disorganized military campaigns, launched with little coordination across Europe and Africa, became a liability for Germany. The Nazi regime was forced to divert significant military resources to the Balkans and North Africa to assist its struggling ally.

After failing to secure air superiority over Britain, Germany embarked on Operation Barbarossa in June 1941, launching a full-scale invasion of the Soviet Union. This strategic miscalculation stretched German forces thin, ultimately dooming Hitler's war effort. Like Napoleon before him, Hitler underestimated the Soviet Union's ability to absorb devastating losses and regroup. The brutal battles on the Eastern Front, combined with the unforgiving Russian winter, eroded Germany's military advantage and shifted the momentum of the war.

The most decisive strategic mistake, however, was made by Japan.

Since 1937, Japan had been engaged in a protracted war with China, which lasted nearly eight years and culminated in September 1945. Despite Japan's superior military technology and tactics, it failed to achieve a swift victory, and the prolonged conflict drained its resources. As World War II escalated, Japan turned its focus to securing the resource-rich colonies of British, French, and Dutch territories in Southeast Asia. In response, the United States imposed a crippling oil embargo in 1941, cutting off more than 80 percent of Japan's oil imports.

The United States demanded that Japan withdraw from China, abandon the Axis alliance, and dismantle its puppet state in Manchuria—terms that would have undone nearly all of Japan's territorial and military gains. Faced with this ultimatum, Japan, like many authoritarian regimes pushed to the brink, chose escalation over concession. Seeking to neutralize the U.S. Pacific Fleet before launching its campaign in Southeast Asia, Japan executed a surprise attack on Pearl Harbor on December 7, 1941. The following day, the United States declared war on Japan.

The entry of the United States into World War II fundamentally altered the course of the conflict. As in World War I, American industrial might proved decisive.[3] The United States' vast production capacity ensured the Allies maintained logistical superiority, outpacing Axis war production on an unprecedented scale. Major American cities, with industrial output rivaling or surpassing Germany's entire wartime manufacturing capacity, became the backbone of the Allied war effort.

For nearly four more years, Germany and Japan—both fully committed to total war—fought with relentless intensity. The Allies, in turn, mobilized unprecedented levels of strategic and tactical ingenuity. Yet, as Winston Churchill had predicted early in the war, the moment the U.S. entered the conflict, the Axis powers' chances of victory were effectively extinguished.

In June 1944, the Allies launched the Normandy invasion, delivering a decisive blow to Nazi Germany. Less than a year later, in May 1945, Berlin fell, marking the end of the war in Europe. In the Pacific, after a grueling island-hopping campaign, the United States dropped atomic bombs on Hiroshima and Nagasaki on August 6 and 9, 1945. On the same day as the Nagasaki bombing, the Soviet Union declared war on Japan and invaded Manchuria. On August 15, Japan announced its surrender via a radio broadcast, and on September 2, 1945, it formally signed the surrender documents aboard the USS Missouri.

With Japan's formal surrender, World War II—the deadliest conflict in human history—came to an end.

Enter the Bipolar World

After World War I, the Allies faced two major challenges. The first was a practical concern: preventing Germany, which had suffered little direct damage to its homeland, from regaining national power and threatening France once again. The second was an ideological challenge: designing and implementing the liberal world order championed by U.S. President Woodrow Wilson. In contrast, the post-World War II landscape was markedly different. The Axis powers had been decisively defeated and no longer posed an immediate threat. However, a new challenge emerged—the growing influence of the Soviet Union.

By the early 1940s, as the Allies gained the upper hand in World War II, the United States and the Great Britain had already begun viewing the Soviet Union as a potential postwar adversary. As the world's first communist state, the Soviet Union was ideologically incompatible with capitalism. As early as 1927, Soviet leader Joseph Stalin had predicted in a discussion with American labor representatives that communism and capitalism were destined for an existential struggle. While the shared threat of Nazi Germany had forged a temporary wartime alliance, the defeat of the Axis powers would inevitably reignite ideological confrontation.

Ironically, Nazi Propaganda Minister Joseph Goebbels was among the first to predict Soviet expansionism after the war. On February 18, 1945—seven months before Japan's surrender and just two months before Adolf Hitler's suicide—Goebbels justified Germany's total war by warning of an impending communist advance. He claimed that a German defeat would result in Soviet control over much of Eastern and

Southeastern Europe, where an 'iron curtain' would descend, accompanied by ethnic purges. Despite his role as a propagandist, Goebbels' prediction proved eerily accurate. Just over a year later, in March 1946, Winston Churchill echoed this warning in his famous Iron Curtain speech, highlighting the Soviet Union's growing dominance over Eastern Europe.

In the immediate aftermath of World War II, however, the United States viewed the Soviet Union and communism as latent rather than imminent threats. Unlike the war-ravaged Soviet Union, which suffered from devastated infrastructure and millions of casualties, the United States emerged from the conflict unscathed, possessing unmatched industrial capacity and sole ownership of the atomic bomb. Isolationist sentiment resurfaced in American politics, with calls for a return to non-interventionism.

Yet, not all Americans supported isolationism. Prominent political scientist Nicholas Spykman warned that disengagement from global affairs would leave the U.S. vulnerable to the rise of continental hegemons in Europe and Asia. He argued that American intervention was essential to maintaining the balance of power. Similarly, economist Charles Kindleberger, a key architect of the Marshall Plan, criticized America's retreat into isolationism after World War I, suggesting that its failure to assume global leadership had contributed to the outbreak of World War II.[4]

Western Europe, in contrast, lacked the capacity to contain Soviet expansion. Germany was partitioned among the victorious powers, while the Great Britain and France struggled to recover from the war. Meanwhile, the Soviet Union established communist regimes in Romania, Bulgaria, Yugoslavia, Albania, Hungary, and Czechoslovakia, transforming them into a buffer zone against Western Europe. These Eastern European nations were either directly absorbed into the Soviet sphere or reduced to satellite states. Under the banner of "Workers of the world, unite!" communism expanded relentlessly.

In 1949, the Soviet Union successfully developed its own atomic bomb, becoming the world's second nuclear power. That same year, Mao Zedong's Communist forces triumphed in the Chinese Civil War, forcing Chiang Kai-shek's Nationalists to retreat to Taiwan. With the fall of mainland China, communism solidified itself as a global ideological rival to capitalism. The world was now divided into two opposing blocs: the so-called 'free world,' led by the United States, and the 'communist bloc,' dominated by the Soviet Union.

Endnotes:

1. The treaty's punitive measures, including territorial losses, military restrictions, and reparations, fueled German nationalism and revanchism. The reparations and economic clauses also contributed to Germany's economic crisis, creating conditions ripe for extremist ideologies.

2. The Great Depression compelled the countries to adopt protectionist policies, intensifying economic rivalries. This weakened international cooperation, which further undermined the basis for collective security. In addition, high unemployment and economic hardship made populations more susceptible to radical political movements.

3. The United States' industrial capacity during World War II was unmatched, far surpassing that of Germany, Japan, the Great Britain, and the Soviet Union—the key belligerents up to that point. The U.S. rapidly mobilized its vast resources to become the "arsenal of democracy," as President Franklin D. Roosevelt had declared. At the start of the Pacific War, the Japanese Navy fielded 10 aircraft carriers. By the war's end, however, the United States had produced an astounding 151 carriers, including both 30,000-ton fleet carriers and 10,000-ton escort carriers. While smaller than Japan's fleet carriers, escort carriers played a critical role in naval operations. A prime example is the Casablanca-class escort carrier, with a displacement of approximately 10,000 tons. Between July 1943 and July 1944, the U.S. commissioned one of these carriers every week, earning them the nickname 'jeep carriers' or 'weekly carriers.' The scale of American shipbuilding extended far beyond aircraft carriers. By the war's conclusion, the U.S. had launched roughly 2,000 transport ships to ferry troops and supplies across both the Atlantic and Pacific. The 10,000-ton Liberty ships, produced at a rate of nearly one per day, ensured that Allied supply lines remained uninterrupted despite Germany's relentless U-boat campaign. In fact, American ship production consistently outpaced the losses caused by submarine attacks. While the bulk of U.S. war production was directed toward defeating Nazi Germany, the resources allocated to the Pacific theater alone created an insurmountable disparity between the United States and Japan. Through the Lend-Lease Act, the U.S. also provided the United Kingdom, the Soviet Union, and other Allied nations with an extraordinary volume of military supplies—tens of thousands of aircraft, tanks, and naval vessels, along with vast quantities of ammunition, food, and clothing. Some reports suggest that after America's entry into the war, the sheer abundance of supplies bordered on surplus, overwhelming the logistical capacities of its allies. To put this in perspective, by 1944, the United States was responsible for producing half of all weapons used in the war. By 1945, it accounted for half of the world's total industrial output.

4. Decades later, Joseph Nye would term this theory the 'Kindleberger Trap.'

CHAPTER 9

THE DYNAMICS OF THE COLD WAR

The Cold War is not a war
in the traditional sense,
but a war of words, ideas, and ideologies.

Unknown (widely attributed to John F. Kennedy)

1. Strategy, Ideology, and Superpower Rivalry

The post-World War II era was unprecedented in several ways. Most notably, the center of the international order decisively shifted away from Europe. Global power now revolved around two superpowers: the United States, representing the 'New World,' and the Soviet Union, dominating 'Eurasia.' Their combined strength so far exceeded that of other nations that traditional great powers were relegated to secondary roles. Each superpower exercised hegemonic control over its respective sphere of influence, establishing, for the first time in history, a bipolar world order.

Another defining feature of this period was the emergence of a 'balance of terror' driven by nuclear weapons. Both the United States and the Soviet Union amassed arsenals capable of annihilating not only each other but all of humanity multiple times over. This condition—where any nuclear conflict would lead to mutual destruction—became known as Mutually Assured Destruction (MAD). Paradoxically, MAD served as a stabilizing force, deterring direct military confrontation between the superpowers.

The unprecedented destructive power of nuclear weapons, coupled with the logic of MAD, diminished the strategic utility of conventional warfare and suppressed the likelihood of full-scale conflict between the United States and the Soviet Union. This marked the beginning of the Cold War era—a prolonged geopolitical struggle fought not through direct military engagement but through economic, ideological, and proxy conflicts.

Grand Strategists

Unable to achieve outright victory through force, both superpowers turned to grand strategy, each seeking to outmaneuver the other through diplomacy, ideological competition, and covert operations. As always, these strategies were shaped by, and in turn influenced, the dominant intellectual currents of the time.

With his seminal work *The Influence of Sea Power upon History*, published in 1890, Alfred Thayer Mahan shaped the geopolitical thinking of the early 20th-century, leading Great Britain, Imperial Germany, and the United States to pursue naval dominance. However, British geographer Halford J. Mackinder soon introduced a competing perspective. In his 1904 paper *The Geographical Pivot of History* and his 1919 book *Democratic Ideals and Reality*, Mackinder proposed the 'Heartland Theory.'

Mackinder argued that the key to global dominance lay not at sea but in the Heartland—a vast, resource-rich region at the core of Eurasia. He believed that as land transportation advanced, the Heartland's strategic value would eclipse maritime power. A state that controlled this region, he asserted, would possess the economic and military strength necessary to dominate the world. Echoing this idea, he famously stated: "Who rules East Europe commands the Heartland. Who rules the Heartland commands the World Island [Eurasia and Africa]. Who rules the World Island commands the world."

Since the 'Heartland' largely overlapped with Russian territory, the Soviet Union naturally embraced Mackinder's theory during the Cold

War, seeking to consolidate its hold over Eastern Europe and expand its influence into Central Asia.

In response, American strategist Nicholas Spykman presented a counterpoint in *The Geography of Peace* (1944), introducing the 'Rimland Theory.' Spykman agreed that Eurasia was the key to world power but argued that the coastal regions—the Rimland—were more strategically significant than the Heartland. Unlike the sparsely populated and landlocked Heartland, the Rimland boasted fertile land, dense populations, and vital sea trade routes. In addition, the Rimland, encircling the Heartland, served as a buffer between land and sea powers. Spykman succinctly summarized his theory: "Who controls the Rimland rules Eurasia; who rules Eurasia controls the destinies of the world."

The United States effectively adopted Spykman's theory as the foundation of its Cold War strategy. Through the policy of containment, Washington sought to prevent Soviet expansion into the Rimland by establishing alliances with key states in Western Europe, East Asia, Southeast Asia, and the Middle East. This strategy was reinforced through economic and military aid, ensuring that Soviet influence remained constrained.

Meanwhile, the Soviet Union attempted to break through U.S. containment by extending its reach into the Rimland. It solidified control over Eastern Europe through the Warsaw Pact, supported communist insurgencies in Vietnam, Cuba, and Africa, and backed Arab nationalist movements in the Middle East. These geopolitical struggles fueled a series of proxy wars, insurgencies, and civil conflicts worldwide. Though the Cold War was nominally "cold," it saw frequent violent clashes through indirect means.

One of the most consequential victories for the United States was its success in driving a wedge between the Soviet Union and China—the two largest communist powers.

In 1969, China and the Soviet Union engaged in military clashes over disputed territories along the Amur, Ussuri, and Heilongjiang Rivers—regions that the Russian Empire had seized from the late Qing Dynasty. When the Soviet Union escalated tensions by threatening China with nuclear strikes, Mao Zedong faced a crisis. Though China had developed nuclear weapons, it lacked the advanced delivery systems necessary to strike Soviet targets effectively. With limited options, China appeared vulnerable—until the United States intervened. Recognizing the risk of nuclear war, the Nixon administration extended de facto nuclear deterrence over China, warning Moscow that a nuclear attack on China would provoke an American response. This unprecedented move bought Beijing time to negotiate a settlement with Moscow, averting war.

The unexpected U.S. intervention paved the way for a thaw in U.S.-China relations. From Beijing's perspective, confronting the Soviet Union—the dominant force in the communist bloc—made rapprochement with Washington a strategic necessity. For millennia, Chinese statecraft had followed the principle of aligning with a distant power to counterbalance a neighboring threat—a concept enshrined in the *Thirty-Six Stratagems*. Meanwhile, Washington saw an opportunity to use China as a counterweight against the Soviet Union.

In 1971, U.S. National Security Advisor Henry Kissinger made a secret visit to China, initiating high-level dialogue. That same year, U.S. diplomatic maneuvering helped secure United Nations General Assembly Resolution 2758, which recognized the People's Republic of China (PRC) as the legitimate representative of China, replacing the Republic of China (Taiwan). In 1972, President Richard Nixon's visit to China marked a historic shift, and by 1979, the U.S. and China had formally established diplomatic ties.

By capitalizing on the Sino-Soviet split, the United States further isolated the Soviet Union, weakening its global position and accelerating the Cold War's eventual outcome.

Battle of Ideology

While geopolitical maneuvering played out at all levels, the Cold War was, at its core, a contest between two competing political and economic systems: liberal democracy and capitalism, represented by the United States, and communism, championed by the Soviet Union. Virtually every part of the Rimland became an ideological battleground where these two rival visions of modernity clashed. In this sense, the Cold War was not merely a geopolitical rivalry but also an ideological war—one between communism and liberal democracy, or more broadly, communism and capitalism.

At the heart of this ideological conflict lay two competing interpretations of modernity, both rooted in Enlightenment thought. Ironically, capitalism—one of liberalism's defining products—played a crucial role in the emergence of communism.

Modern Europe—shaped by rationalism, scientific advancement, commerce, and the market economy—became a fertile ground for intellectual discourse that fueled the development of political philosophy. Central to European thought during this period was the relationship between power and the citizen, and between the individual and society. Liberalism, which emerged in this intellectual climate, challenged hereditary privilege and championed individual liberty. A key tenet of liberalism was that society should impose minimal restrictions on individuals, allowing them to realize their full potential while taking personal responsibility for their actions.

As with most historical developments, the rise of liberalism had an economic basis. At the time of the emergence of liberal thought, Europe was undergoing rapid commercial and industrial expansion. This economic transformation gave rise to the capitalist class, a new social class distinct from the traditional ruling elites of kings and aristocrats. As the era of unregulated economic competition unfolded, the capitalists emerged as the dominant class in society. The assumption that unbridled self-interest would drive relentless innovation and prevent economic stagnation proved false, as powerful capitalists consolidated control over production and markets. Under the monopolization and corporate dominance that stifled competition, the self-regulating market envisioned by early liberals did not function as expected.

As society transitioned from aristocratic rule to capitalist dominance, resentment grew among the working class, which had become the primary oppressed group. Under feudalism, where rigid class distinctions were taken for granted, social inequalities were often accepted as part of the natural order. However, in a world that professed to be governed by principles of fairness and justice under the social contract, structural injustices provoked deeper frustration and unrest. In response, a new ideology emerged—one that sought not merely to challenge capitalism but to overthrow it entirely through revolution. This ideology, communism, envisioned a radically new society in which economic power would be collectivized and class distinctions abolished.

The ideological foundation of communism was laid by Karl Marx and Friedrich Engels, two of the 19th century's most influential political thinkers.[1] Communism framed history as a battlefield of class struggle, asserting that after the bourgeoisie overthrew the feudal aristocracy, the primary conflict became the struggle between the capitalist class and the working class. Marx and Engels advocated for a proletarian revolution to overthrow and eliminate the capitalist class. Their ideas resonated deeply with workers oppressed by the industrial-era bourgeoisie and with progressive intellectuals in 19th-century Western societies. Marx and Engels' ideological legacy was later carried forward by political figures such as Vladimir Lenin and Joseph Stalin.

Like most classical political doctrines, communism evolved into various factions. However, virtually all communist movements, regardless of their differences, shared a fundamental belief: society was divided into two dominant classes—capitalists and workers—and the existing social structure, which allowed the exploitation of the latter by the former, had to be overthrown through revolution. To achieve communism's ultimate goal, the state had to control all means of production, ensuring that the fruits of labor were fairly distributed among all people. Since modern class divisions arose not from aristocratic bloodlines, as in feudal times, but from wealth and capital accumulation, communists argued that state-controlled production would eliminate class distinctions and usher in an era of absolute equality—a supposed utopia.

Under this vision, the Soviet Union and its satellite communist states ruled over nearly one-third of the global population for almost half a century. In these regimes, the state dictated wages and prices, allocating resources through centralized planning. However, the proletarian paradise envisioned by Marx, Engels, and Lenin never materialized. Instead, communist societies became notorious for their totalitarian rule and brutal oppression, often surpassing even the most authoritarian monarchies in history. Far from creating a "worker's paradise," communist regimes built a paradise for the Communist Party elite, stripping workers of even the most basic labor rights they would have enjoyed under a capitalist system. While external factors—such as geopolitical competition with the United States—contributed to communism's downfall, its ultimate failure stemmed from the inherent flaws and contradictions within communist ideology itself.

For communism's ideals to be realized, a revolution must first dismantle the existing class structure. This requires not only the overthrow of the ruling class but also the elimination of so-called "counter-revolutionaries"—those who oppose or resist the revolution. To justify such purges, communism relies on the Machiavellian principle that "the ends justify the means." However, this principle is easily abused by those in power, leading to widespread repression and violence. Indeed, communism necessitates a despotic transitional phase to enforce revolutionary change. Because the system cannot tolerate social diversity—anything that threatens ideological uniformity—an authoritarian regime becomes essential for maintaining order.[2] If purges are justified as a means of establishing the system, they are equally justified as a means of preserving it. Ultimately, it is the ruling dictator who determines the criteria for elimination, making the system inherently unstable and prone to tyranny. Despite its goal of abolishing class distinctions, communism inevitably creates a new class hierarchy: the privileged Communist Party elites and the powerless masses. As the saying goes, "absolute power corrupts absolutely." By its very structure, communism succumbs to totalitarianism, leaving no room for individual liberty or human rights in the face of its grand ideological vision.

In a society that prioritizes ideological conformity over individual expression, personal freedoms are necessarily and severely constrained. Even beyond the well-documented human rights abuses of communist regimes, the absence of private property rights renders resistance nearly impossible. While communism does not explicitly reject private property, it fails to protect property rights in meaningful way. Deprived of economic independence, individuals lack the means to challenge the system. It is no coincidence that liberal thinkers have long regarded the protection of private property as a fundamental prerequisite for individual liberty—a truth that, in hindsight, is both strikingly simple and profoundly significant.[3] In a society where even basic property rights are neither guaranteed nor protected, defying the regime requires extraordinary courage, a risk that few can afford to take.

Thus, the commonly oversimplified belief that capitalism is the sole true antithesis of communism, and that communism and liberal democracy are not inherently incompatible, is misleading. Throughout history, many authoritarian regimes have claimed to be democratic, but no state can be genuinely democratic without guaranteeing individual liberties. Communist states, too, have often adopted the rhetoric of democracy—

many have even incorporated the word 'democratic' into their official names. Yet, in practice, a communist regime that grants its citizens real political freedom and electoral rights is a contradiction in terms. There has never been a single historical instance of a communist government that provided genuine democratic participation, and structurally, such a system is unlikely to ever exist.

It must be noted that capitalism exhibited its own flaws. The economic philosophy of liberal democracy, rooted in liberal thought, initially embraced the principle of a laissez-faire economy—one in which individual economic actors were granted full freedom in the market, with minimal government intervention.[4] This system fostered a free-market economy based on private ownership, free trade, profit-seeking through competition, and the natural fluctuations of supply and demand. While the degree of implementation varied, a free-market economy almost inevitably led to capitalism.[5]

However, as governments refrained from intervening in the market, those who secured dominant positions began to distort both the economy and the market itself. Capitalists exploited workers, and national wealth became increasingly concentrated in the hands of a privileged few, leading to severe economic disparities. The majority of the population—workers—found themselves serving a small capitalist elite. During the height of laissez-faire capitalism in 19th-century Britain, industrialists indulged in extravagant luxuries—some even lighting cigars with high-denomination banknotes—while workers toiled in grueling conditions. Some factory laborers, too exhausted to stand, would rest by leaning against ropes strung along the walls, like laundry hanging out to dry. Given such stark inequalities, it is unsurprising that Marx and Engels predicted capitalism would collapse under the weight of its own contradictions. What communists failed to foresee, however, was capitalism's capacity for innovation and adaptation.

Specifically, Marx and Engels argued that capitalism was inherently exploitative and destined to produce ever-widening economic inequality.[6] While their critique was largely accurate in the context of early industrial capitalism,[7] subsequent reforms—particularly in response to the Great Depression and the rise of communism—enabled capitalism to adapt and evolve. Governments implemented policies to redistribute wealth and mitigate economic disparities, allowing capitalism to avoid the so-called 'capitalist trap' that Marx had predicted.[8] This process of adaptation culminated in the emergence of neoliberalism,[9] which blended elements of early capitalism with select aspects of post-crisis reforms, while often emphasizing a return to market-driven approaches. In this sense, capitalism has continually evolved by addressing both its internal contradictions (such as economic crises) and external challenges (such as ideological competition with communism).[10] Over time, capitalism evolved into regulated capitalism, a system that preserved the market economy while incorporating government intervention to correct its excesses. While the core principle of liberal economic thought remains that government involvement should be limited, the extreme laissez-faire approach—where the state played virtually no role—has long since disappeared.

From a social contract perspective, the communist regimes of the Cold War era, including the Soviet Union, can be understood as having assumed dictatorial power from the people in exchange for two implicit promises. First, they pledged to create a proletarian paradise. Second, they promised to provide a higher standard of living than workers experienced under capitalism. While the first promise was an unattainable ideal, their failure to deliver on the second proved particularly consequential.

In reality, the standard of living in the Soviet Union and other communist states lagged far behind that of citizens in the United States and Western liberal democracies. People under communist rule were deprived not only of political freedoms but also of economic autonomy. They lacked freedom of expression, conscience, and the press, as well as fundamental rights such as freedom of movement, residence, and even basic labor protections like the right to association. To suppress discontent and prevent any sense of relative deprivation, communist regimes rigorously isolated their populations from the outside world.

Yet, the system's inherent contradictions and structural flaws inevitably accumulated. As economic problems became increasingly unmanageable and even essential goods grew scarce, the people recognized the regime's breach of the social contract. In the end, communism's collapse was driven decisively by its economic failure.

Capitalism Wins the Regime Race

In the early stages of the Cold War, the Soviet Union's planned economy at times achieved growth rates that rivaled, or even exceeded, those of the United States. Like modern-day Russia, the Soviet economy relied heavily on natural resources. Its vast territory provided the raw materials needed for industrial production, while goods that were difficult to produce domestically—such as certain food supplies—were secured through trade with other communist bloc nations. Well into the 1970s, the Soviet economy sustained growth, in part due to its role as a major oil producer, benefiting from Middle Eastern oil shocks. Additionally, the Soviet Union maintained scientific and technological capabilities that, for a time, rivaled those of the United States, thanks to centralized research and a highly skilled workforce.

However, the inherent flaws of the centrally planned economy became increasingly evident. Communist economic management concentrated decision-making in the hands of central planners, requiring them to process vast amounts of information to design policies. Yet, the system's authoritarian nature made transparency impossible. Economic targets were not set based on realistic forecasts but as propaganda tools, and once established, they could not be adjusted—even when clearly erroneous. As a result, officials manipulated data to meet preordained objectives, creating widespread inefficiencies. Since failure to meet quotas was unacceptable, false reporting became rampant, leaving even internal economic assessments unreliable. In such a system, corruption and bureaucratic dysfunction were inevitable.

The ban on private competition exacerbated inefficiencies. Communist economies falsely assumed that productivity was determined solely by labor input. Unlike capitalist economies, where management skills influence productivity, communist doctrine dismissed the role of management, leading to systemic inefficiencies.[11] It also ignored market-driven price mechanisms.[12] Naturally, communist economies lacked the adaptability of market-based systems. As inefficiencies accumulated, economic stagnation—and eventual collapse—became inevitable.

Moreover, the Soviet Union, fixated on its rivalry with the United States, disproportionately funneled resources into heavy industry and military production, seeing them as measures of national strength. Meanwhile, essential consumer goods—such as toothpaste, shampoo, sugar, and clothing—remained in chronic short supply, fueling black markets and an informal 'secondary economy' that grew uncontrollably.

Another critical limitation of the Soviet model was its failure to foster paradigm-shifting technological innovation. While they invested heavily in military-related technologies, consumer-oriented advancements were largely neglected. This imbalance was not immediately catastrophic, as heavy industry and military capabilities dominated global innovation for much of the 20th century. However, when information technology (IT) emerged as the driving force of economic growth in the 1970s, the limitations of the Soviet research model became starkly apparent. The rise of personal computing in the West further widened the gap. Unlike the centralized, state-controlled research of the Soviet Union, Western economies fostered decentralized innovation, allowing for rapid technological advancements. In many ways, the moment the Soviets lagged behind in IT marked the decisive turning point in the Cold War's economic competition.

In contrast, the so-called 'free world,' led by the United States, actively embraced market-based capitalism and free trade. Liberal economic policies facilitated economic integration within the Western bloc. The foundation of this global economic order was laid in 1944 at the Bretton Woods Conference, which established the International Monetary Fund (IMF) to oversee exchange rates and financial stability, and the World Bank to finance postwar reconstruction and later, global development.[13] In 1947, the signing of the General Agreement on Tariffs and Trade (GATT) further advanced economic liberalization by lowering tariffs and eliminating trade barriers, fostering unprecedented integration among free-world economies. Together, the IMF, World Bank, and GATT played a pivotal role in dismantling trade barriers, facilitating capital flows, and promoting economic liberalization within the Western bloc.

By institutionalizing market liberalization, capitalism became deeply entrenched in the free world. Unlike communism, capitalism thrived on competition, which ensured efficiency and spurred innovation. The profit motive strongly encouraged individuals and companies to develop cutting-edge technologies and improve productivity. As a result, the capitalist economies of the free world vastly outperformed their communist counterparts.

End of the Cold War

By the time Mikhail Gorbachev became the last General Secretary of the Communist Party of the Soviet Union in 1985, the Soviet Union could no longer sustain its competition with the West. Decades of systemic inefficiencies, economic stagnation, and technological lag had eroded its ability to keep pace with the capitalist world. Around this time, the United States abandoned its long-standing policy of containment in favor of 'Rollback,' actively seeking to bring about systemic change in the Soviet bloc.

In an effort to reform and revitalize the Soviet system, Gorbachev introduced two landmark policies: Perestroika (перестройка, 'restructuring'), aimed at gradual market liberalization, and Glasnost (гласность, 'openness'), which sought to ease censorship, promote transparency, and allow greater freedom of expression. He also sought to end Cold War hostilities, negotiating with the United States and relinquishing Soviet dominance over Eastern Europe. This marked a stark departure from the Brezhnev Doctrine, which had justified Soviet military interventions to maintain control over communist states since 1968. Gorbachev also met with China's Deng Xiaoping in 1989 to mend the Sino-Soviet split and later that year, in a summit with U.S. President George H.W. Bush, formally declared the Cold War over.

Despite his reforms, Gorbachev never intended to dissolve the Soviet Union. Instead, he proposed restructuring it into a looser federation that would grant greater autonomy to its republics while preserving the Union itself. However, on August 19, 1991, hardline communists staged a coup in an attempt to halt reforms and restore the old system. Though the coup collapsed within three days, it irreparably shattered any remaining hopes of maintaining the Soviet Union. The failed takeover emboldened Soviet republics to accelerate their push for independence, sealing the fate of the Union.

Glasnost, by lifting restrictions on the press and public discourse, inadvertently exposed the deep flaws of the Soviet system, fueling mass dissatisfaction. Meanwhile, Perestroika failed to deliver economic stability quickly enough to offset the upheaval caused by political liberalization. Suppressed grievances erupted into full-scale democratic movements, particularly in Eastern Europe, where communist regimes had long relied on Soviet military force to crush uprisings. This time, however, the Soviet Union—under Gorbachev—chose not to intervene.

Between 1989 and 1991, communist regimes in Poland, Hungary, East Germany, Bulgaria, Czechoslovakia, Romania, Albania, and Yugoslavia collapsed in rapid succession. The most symbolic moment came with the fall of the Berlin Wall in 1989, signaling the disintegration of the communist bloc in Europe. As Eastern Europe's regimes crumbled, communist governments across Asia and Africa also began to unravel. The Soviet Union itself fractured as its republics declared independence—beginning with Lithuania on March 11, 1990. One by one, others followed, culminating in the official dissolution of the Union of Soviet Socialist Republics (USSR) on December 26, 1991.

With the Soviet collapse, the Cold War ended in total victory for the United States, marking the definitive triumph of capitalism over communism.

2. The Dawn of True Multilateralism

During the Cold War, the world was structured around a bipolar system, with the United States and the Soviet Union leading opposing blocs. This international order was thus rooted in traditional spheres of influence. At the same time, it differed fundamentally from past hegemonic systems. It was during this period that multilateralism—a form of international democracy[14]—began to take real shape, with the United Nations (UN) at its center.

The United Nations and Its Collective Security Mechanism

In August 1941, amid World War II, British Prime Minister Winston Churchill and U.S. President Franklin D. Roosevelt issued the *Atlantic Charter*, outlining eight key principles for the postwar world. Heavily influenced by Woodrow Wilson's Fourteen Points, the charter emphasized self-determination, economic cooperation, freedom of the seas, and collective security, among others. Within months, key nations—including the Soviet Union—endorsed it, and in January 1942, the *Declaration by United Nations* formally adopted its vision as the foundation of the postwar order.

In his 1945 State of the Union address, Roosevelt famously declared that the United States must work toward "establishing an international order which will be capable of maintaining peace and realizing through the years of more prefect justice between Nations." Even before World War II ended, the UN was officially established in 1945.

Like its predecessor, the League of Nations, the UN was founded on liberal principles: ensuring global peace through collective security, promoting intergovernmental cooperation, and advancing human rights. However, unlike the League, it was far more structured, inclusive, and politically pragmatic. Most critically, the UN differed in one fundamental way: it prioritized political realities over rigid legal frameworks in security decision-making.

The League of Nations suffered from structural ambiguity in the relationship between its Assembly and its Council. While League regulations granted all member states the legal authority to impose economic sanctions on aggressor states, and while the Assembly often assumed responsibilities related to collective security, these mechanisms proved ineffective. Legal authority, unsupported by real power, became meaningless when great powers chose to ignore it. The League's credibility collapsed as Germany, Japan, and the Soviet Union openly defied its resolutions and treaty obligations without facing meaningful consequences. By contrast, the UN, while also structured around a General Assembly and a Security Council, granted the latter clear superiority in matters of collective security.

To fully grasp the functions of the UN and its Security Council, one must first understand the significance of the UN Charter. The Charter fundamentally reshaped the international legal framework governing security and the use of force, concentrating these powers almost entirely in the hands of the Security Council.

Under traditional international law, sovereign states held the authority to use military force, bound only by legal constraints on initiating war (*jus ad bellum*) and conducting military operations (*jus in bello*). However, the adoption of the UN Charter—particularly Article 24—marked a turning point. Member states collectively transferred their primary responsibility for maintaining international peace and security to the Security Council, effectively consenting to let it act on their behalf. While this provision aimed to outlaw aggressive war following two world wars, it also meant that sovereign states largely ceded their authority over the use of force to the Council. Today, UN member states may resort to military force only in response to an armed attack, retaining a temporary inherent right of self-defense under Article 51 of the UN Charter until the Security Council takes collective security measures. Furthermore, under Article 103, obligations arising from Security Council resolutions take precedence over all other international treaty commitments.

The Security Council comprises five permanent members and ten rotating non-permanent members. For a resolution to be adopted, it must receive affirmative votes from at least nine of the fifteen members. However, each of the five permanent members—the United States, the Soviet Union (now Russia), China, the United Kingdom, and France—holds veto power, enabling any one of them to block a substantive resolution. As a result, no Security Council action can proceed if even one permanent member opposes it.

With the exception of the defeated Axis powers, the postwar world's major great powers were granted permanent seats on the Security Council. In practical terms, when the five permanent members reach a consensus, they wield enough hard power to have a decisive influence on global affairs, while all UN member states are legally bound to comply with Security Council resolutions. At the same time, the veto power ensures that no permanent member can be compelled into an action it fundamentally opposes. This structural safeguard also makes it highly unlikely that a permanent member would withdraw from the UN, as Germany, Japan, and the Soviet Union did from the League of Nations in the years leading up to World War II.[15]

This pragmatic approach ensured that major powers retained a decisive role in global governance, preventing the UN from becoming obsolete even amid the intense ideological and geopolitical polarization of the Cold War. In many ways, the longevity and relative effectiveness of the UN can be attributed to the structure of the Security Council, which gave immediate legal authority (and thus legitimacy) to political decisions made within a de facto "great-power league."

However, when a major issue directly involves the core interests of a permanent member, the Security Council often proves ineffective. During the Cold War, persistent U.S.-Soviet tensions limited the Council's role in conflict resolution. The sole exception was the Korean War in 1950—the only real instance during this period when the UN's collective security mechanism was fully enforced in a major war between the Communist and Western blocs.

On June 25, 1950, the Security Council adopted Resolution 82, condemning North Korea's invasion of South Korea and demanding an immediate ceasefire. When North Korea ignored the resolution, the Council passed Resolution 83 on June 27, authorizing military action, followed by Resolution 84 on July 7, which established the composition of UN forces. The Soviet Union, having boycotted Security Council meetings since January 1950 in protest of the UN's recognition of the Republic of China (Taiwan) over the People's Republic of China, was absent[16] and thus unable to exercise its veto.[17] While Yugoslavia, a Communist non-permanent member, was the sole dissenting vote on Resolutions 83 and 84, the support of all attending permanent members ensured their passage. As a result, UN forces, led by the United States, intervened, preventing the fall of South Korea.

After the Korean War, ideological tensions between the Communist and Western blocs escalated, further paralyzing the UN's collective security function in major armed conflicts. Despite the Security Council's inaction in major military conflicts during the geopolitical turmoil of the Cold War, the UN remained a central institution of global governance. The political flexibility embedded in the UN Charter allowed the UN to avoid the fate of the League of Nations.

International cooperation often holds intrinsic value even when it does not yield immediate results. As circumstances and positions shift over time, so too do opportunities for diplomacy. Even at the height of the Cold War, the United States and the Soviet Union managed to agree on deploying UN peacekeeping forces in at least 13 conflict zones, including the Suez Crisis, the Congo Crisis, and conflicts between Lebanon and Israel.

In November 1990, the Security Council authorized another major military intervention. With Resolution 678, it authorized the use of force against Iraq in response to its invasion of Kuwait, marking its first significant military action since 1950 and signaling the eve of the Cold War's end.

UN General Assembly: True Multilateralism in Play

By preserving the framework for multilateral engagement during the Cold War, the UN enabled the international community to build cooperative efforts across various fields, reinforcing global stability in the long term. Much of this international collaboration took place through the UN General Assembly, particularly in advancing human rights and international law.

Despite deep and worldwide ideological divisions, the General Assembly achieved significant progress. In 1948, during its third session, it adopted the Universal Declaration of Human Rights[18] and the Convention on the Prevention and Punishment of the Crime of Genocide. In 1966, during its twenty-first session, it passed the International Covenant on Civil and Political Rights and the International Covenant on Economic,

Social and Cultural Rights. These landmark agreements underscored the UN's ability to drive human rights initiatives even in the midst of Cold War rivalries.

The UN also played a pivotal role in codifying customary international law, primarily through its International Law Commission and General Assembly resolutions. A key example is the United Nations Convention on the Law of the Sea (UNCLOS)—often called the 'constitution of the sea'—which was finalized in 1982 after decades of negotiations. The General Assembly also tackled critical security issues that the divided Security Council could not resolve. The Treaty on the Non-Proliferation of Nuclear Weapons (NPT), a cornerstone of global nuclear non-proliferation efforts, was adopted in 1968. Many other foundational treaties shaping the modern international order also emerged from General Assembly initiatives, solidifying the UN's authority and multilateral influence.

Perhaps the UN's most significant contribution during this period was the formal integration of human rights and the rule of law into international relations. The adoption of international law as a universally recognized normative framework was a transformative development. While the UN did not fundamentally alter the power-driven nature of global politics, it marked the advent of true multilateralism for the first time in history.

Endnotes:

1   In *The Communist Manifesto* (1848), they issued a call to action for the working class, and in *Das Kapital* (1867), they laid out the theoretical framework of communism.

2   Communism emphasized economic equality over political equality, igniting a long-standing debate about whether economic freedom or political freedom should take precedence. E. H. Carr argued that all economic theory assumes the existence of a particular political order, highlighting the inextricable link between economics and politics. In contrast, Friedrich Engels maintained that when political and economic structures clash, political power ultimately aligns with economic forces, asserting that economic development determines the direction of political evolution. (For further exploration, see Robert Gilpin, *U.S. Power and the Multinational Corporation* [Basic Books, 1975], pp. 20-44.) However, in societies where political freedom is firmly established, economic policies can often be altered or reversed through democratic processes. In contrast, political systems that are deeply embedded in a specific economic framework tend to be unable to reform their economic structures without undergoing profound, often revolutionary, changes.

3   John Locke argued that property rights are natural rights, essential to individual freedom. Jean-Jacques Rousseau, while critical of private property for fostering social inequality, also did not advocate for the rigid egalitarianism of communism. Instead, he saw the protection of individual property as a key function of a political system governed by the 'general will' under the social contract. Most decisively, the U.S. Constitution—widely regarded as a culmination of modern liberal thought—explicitly safeguards private property. The Fifth Amendment states, "No person shall be ... deprived of life, liberty, or property, without due process of law; nor shall private property be taken for public use, without just compensation." This enshrines private ownership not only as a fundamental right but also as a cornerstone of a free society.

4   This means that the government entrusts all economic activities to what Adam Smith referred to as the 'invisible hand,' allowing individual economic agents to act in their own self-interest. In essence, it is a system where government intervention is minimal, and market principles govern all economic activities. However, in such an environment, monopolies, collusion, and predatory or unfair trade practices began to dominate the market.

5   Consequently, communism, which rejects market freedom and relies on a command economy controlled by the state, stands in direct opposition not only to capitalism but also to the liberal democracy that underpins it.

6   Marx and Engels argued that capitalist competition would inevitably lead to overproduction, causing supply to outstrip consumer demand and resulting in mass unemployment. They also contended that the exploitation of labor would suppress wages, further reducing purchasing power. As a result, unsold goods would accumulate, triggering economic crises that would ultimately lead to capitalism's collapse. Howev-

er, history has shown that capitalism has repeatedly adapted to and mitigated many of the contradictions Marx predicted. Nonetheless, their core critique—that unchecked exploitation of labor can destabilize the system—remains a valuable insight.

7 In the early days of capitalism, many believed that market forces would naturally correct any economic imbalances. However, unrestricted competition often led to monopolization, fostering a ruthless, 'survival-of-the-fittest' environment that harmed both workers and aspiring entrepreneurs. Established capitalists employed anti-competitive tactics to stifle innovation and erect barriers to entry. In response, later-stage capitalism introduced institutional safeguards, such as competition laws, to curb monopolistic abuses and preserve market dynamism.

8 One of the most significant responses to capitalist crises was the New Deal, introduced in the United States during the Great Depression. Influenced by the economic theories of John Maynard Keynes, the New Deal marked a turning point in capitalism. Keynes argued that laissez-faire capitalism was inherently unstable and that government intervention was necessary to stabilize the economy. His approach emphasized using monetary policy (e.g., adjusting interest rates) and fiscal policy (e.g., infrastructure investment) to regulate aggregate demand and mitigate economic downturns. However, excessive government intervention carried risks. Overregulation could create economic rigidity, making it difficult for markets to adapt to shifting conditions. For instance, overly stringent labor protections might prevent businesses from adjusting costs during downturns, potentially leading to widespread bankruptcies and prolonged recessions.

9 Like early capitalism, neoliberalism upholds the principle of free competition. However, it also recognizes that excessive competition or monopolistic distortions can destabilize the economy. In such cases, state intervention is necessary to maintain economic stability, prevent collapse, and ensure a basic level of welfare and wealth redistribution.

10 One cannot deny that communism, through dialectical opposition, played a significant role in shaping modern capitalism. From a Hegelian dialectical perspective, liberalism can be seen as the thesis (affirmation) and communism as the antithesis (negation). Modern capitalist economies—having integrated social welfare policies, labor protections, and government intervention—could be seen as an evolving synthesis. However, given the challenges and crises brought on by neoliberalism, one can never assume that today's capitalist system represents the final or ideal stage of economic evolution. What is certain, though, is that communism has profoundly influenced the trajectory of modern capitalism, compelling it to reform and adapt in ways that might not have otherwise occurred.

11 Marx argued that the value of a commodity is determined by the labor required to produce it, suggesting that economic value is solely created by workers, while capitalists simply exploit this labor. However, within this framework, communist economic theory overlooked the crucial role of management. While this oversight is significant,

communism's emphasis on the rights and dignity of workers provided valuable insight into the working class's conditions. In contrast, mainstream economics is built upon the principles of specialization and trade—fundamental concepts such as supply and demand. These principles stem from the broader idea of the division of labor, which Adam Smith famously articulated: "The labor necessary to produce any one complete manufacture is almost always divided among a great number of hands." In a self-sufficient, solitary existence, one would not require specialization. However, in any organized society, the division of labor and specialization are essential for increasing productivity. For instance, instead of one worker assembling an entire automobile, assigning workers to specific stages of the assembly process fosters specialization in each task. This method, famously employed by Henry Ford with the assembly line, maximizes efficiency. When applied to society at large, specialization drives economic growth by increasing overall productivity. Greater productivity results in the production and consumption of more goods, reinforcing the dual pillars of economic activity: production and consumption. Additionally, specialization creates more job opportunities, improving workers' purchasing power and boosting trade. The more specialized workers become, the more reliant they are on others for goods and services they cannot produce themselves, spurring broader economic activity. However, this efficiency introduces a critical concern: individuals become mere cogs in a larger system. In this structure, workers become increasingly dependent on capitalists or political elites who control the system. Without a self-correcting mechanism, those in power are prone to exploiting this dependence, an issue that communist thought sought to address.

12 The flaws of communist economic systems extended beyond their neglect of supply and demand. One of the most critical indicators of an economy's health is the "price." Friedrich Hayek, a prominent economic thinker, argued that price is the most essential piece of information for understanding economic conditions. In a market economy, prices act as signals that reflect the needs of both producers and consumers, allowing each to anticipate the other's expectations and adjust accordingly. Economic actors rely on these signals to make informed decisions and plan their activities effectively. However, when price signals are distorted or absent, significant inefficiencies emerge. Producers, unable to accurately gauge consumer demand, misallocate resources, disrupting the balance of production. While price distortions can occur in a market economy due to poor monetary policies, communist systems faced an even more significant challenge: in a command economy, prices do not serve as informational tools at all. Without market-driven prices, communist economies lacked the crucial diagnostic mechanism needed to assess economic performance effectively.

13 Specifically, the conference established the International Bank for Reconstruction and Development (IBRD), which later became part of the World Bank Group, along with institutions such as the International Development Association (IDA), the International Finance Corporation (IFC), the Multilateral Investment Guarantee Agency (MIGA), and the International Center for Settlement of Investment Disputes (ICSID).

14 Multilateralism allows members of the international community to pursue common

goals through constructive cooperation within an internationally governed system. Of the systems that have existed in the international community, multilateralism is perhaps the closest to democracy. Through multilateralism, smaller or developing countries can amplify their voices in the international arena. For multilateralism to work effectively, there must be non-discrimination and reciprocity among participating countries.

15 One notable and possible exception would be the United States, if its isolationist instincts took over. In fact, Republican Senators Mike Lee, Marsha Blackburn, and Rick Scott have introduced a bill, the *Disengaging Entirely from the United Nations Debacle Act*, to fully withdraw the U.S. from the UN in February 2025.

16 From the UN's inception, the Chiang Kai-shek government (now Taiwan) held a permanent seat on the Security Council as the recognized representative of China, one of the victorious powers of World War II. Even after its defeat in the Chinese Civil War and retreat to Taiwan, it continued to occupy China's permanent seat for a significant period.

17 At the time, the Soviet Union maintained that Article 27(3) of the UN Charter—which states that "Decisions of the Security Council on all other matters shall be made by an affirmative vote of seven members, including the concurring votes of the permanent members"—required the explicit consent of all permanent members for any resolution to pass. However, following the adoption of Security Council resolutions on the Korean War, a practice emerged treating abstention or non-participation as not equivalent to a veto. This led to a legal debate over the interpretation of "the concurring votes of the permanent members." The Soviet Union argued that it required the explicit agreement of all five permanent members, while the United States and others contended that, unless the Charter specified "all" permanent members, a resolution could be adopted as long as it secured the affirmative votes of multiple permanent members and at least seven members in total. Over time, the latter interpretation prevailed, establishing that Article 27(3) did not impose automatic paralysis in the absence of a permanent member's vote but instead granted them an active veto right.

18 The Universal Declaration of Human Rights (UDHR), though not legally binding, is of immense significance as it proclaimed fundamental human rights to which all individuals—regardless of race, gender, religion, or nationality—are universally entitled. More importantly, it laid the foundation for the development of international human rights law and the establishment of national human rights standards. This milestone in human history has shaped the global commitment to human dignity and equality.

CHAPTER 10

PAX AMERICANA
: UNPACKING THE U.S.-LED LIBERAL INTERNATIONAL ORDER

> Thus, in the beginning,
> all the World was America.
>
> John Locke

With the dissolution of the Soviet Union, the bipolar international order that had defined the Cold War for nearly half a century came to an end. In its place emerged a unipolar era, marked by the United States' rise as the world's sole superpower. Over the next three decades, the U.S. would be recognized as the only true global hegemon in human history. To understand both the past thirty-odd years and the current era of geopolitical transition, it is essential to first clarify what is meant by American global hegemony.

Nature of U.S. Global Hegemony

There is no disputing that the United States is not only the world's most powerful nation, but also the most dominant state in recorded history. Yet, unrivaled power alone does not necessarily constitute hegemony. While a hegemon must indeed be preeminent, sheer superiority does not automatically confer hegemonic status.

For offensive realists, a hegemon is defined as a state capable of simultaneously overwhelming all potential regional competitors. Absent such dominance, rival states will inevitably form balancing coalitions to counter the would-be hegemon. From this perspective, hegemony is primarily a function of hard power—military capabilities, and the economic and demographic resources that can be converted into military strength. By these standards, the emergence of a true global hegemon has historically been deemed virtually impossible. The international system has witnessed the rise of regional hegemons—states that have secured dominance within a specific geographic sphere. But regional hegemony is a far cry from global hegemony. A global hegemon, in realist terms, would require the capacity to overpower all challengers across the globe, not just within a single region. Even the strongest states have faced structural constraints on their ability to project power globally. Geographic distance, logistical burdens, and geopolitical complexity all present formidable obstacles. Cultural, societal, and ethnic differences further complicate global domination. These enduring limitations make the prospect of exercising unchallenged power over the entire international system exceedingly difficult—if not impossible.

Even at its zenith—whether in the immediate aftermath of World War II, when it dwarfed all competitors in nearly every measure of national power, or in the 1990s, when it stood alone as a consolidated unipolar superpower—the United States never achieved the capacity to unilaterally dominate every global rival at once. It could not, for example, compel China or Russia to submit on all issues, nor did it wield uncontested authority within their immediate spheres of influence.

Nonetheless, the United States held a unique form of power no previous state had possessed: systemic global control. If a hegemon cannot enforce its will everywhere through force, might it still qualify as such if it establishes, regulates, and enforces the rules of the international system—rules that other states, in practice, must follow? If so, then the United States did indeed hold global hegemonic status, at least until quite recently.

During the bipolar Cold War era, the U.S. constructed and presided over a liberal international order within its own bloc, in direct opposition to the Soviet Union's communist sphere. With the collapse of the Soviet Union and its ideological framework, the U.S. entered a unipolar moment in which it exercised an unparalleled degree of global influence. Through its dominance, it not only maintained but actively shaped the post-Cold War order, institutionalizing a system that reflected and reinforced its power.

This is why many liberal international relations theorists characterize American global hegemony not merely in terms of coercive dominance, but as a form of 'hegemonic leadership' or a 'hegemonic order'—an architecture of global governance shaped by a single preeminent power.

The Globalization of the Liberal International Order

With the establishment of a unified international system under effective American hegemony, a period of unprecedented global stability emerged. During this era, the United States and its people embraced an idealistic vision with greater intensity than ever before. For many historians and international relations scholars, America's triumph in the Cold War was not merely a geopolitical victory—it was a moment of historical revelation. It seemed as though history itself had conferred upon the United States a new form of 'manifest destiny.'

It was in this context that Francis Fukuyama famously proclaimed the "end of history," arguing that liberal democracy had achieved a final and decisive victory over rival political systems. His thesis resonated deeply with America's post-Cold War self-image as a global leader uniquely positioned to universalize its values. As the world's unchallenged hegemon, the United States sought to expand the institutional and ideological framework that had unified the Western bloc during the Cold War. Politically, it championed liberal democracy with renewed zeal; economically, it promoted the universal adoption of free-market capitalism.

Thus began an era of expansive liberal internationalism.

At the time, the United States did not shrink from the burdens of hegemonic responsibility. American popular culture reflected a deep-seated belief—rooted in the tradition of American exceptionalism—that the U.S. had a unique moral role as the world's protector. Hollywood films consistently portrayed Americans as defenders of global freedom, confronting tyrants, terrorists, and even existential threats like alien invasions and natural catastrophes. "With great power comes great responsibility"—this iconic line from Sam Raimi's 2002 film *Spider-Man* perfectly encapsulates the ethos of this moment. Indeed, the United States assumed the role of global policeman, using diplomacy, sanctions, and, when deemed necessary, military force to shape world affairs.

Before the end of the Cold War, U.S. foreign policy was guided largely by a realist worldview. In many cases, liberal democratic values functioned more as rhetorical instruments to counter communism than as sincere objectives. After the Cold War, however, U.S. strategy shifted markedly toward idealism. This shift was especially visible in one of the most radical forms of foreign intervention: regime change.

In the late 19th and early 20th centuries, the United States—like other great powers—sought to secure exclusive dominance over key regions, particularly in Latin America and the Pacific. It acquired territories such as Hawaii, Guam, and the Philippines, and installed pro-American regimes in countries like Cuba, Nicaragua, and Honduras. During this period, regime change was driven almost entirely by national interest. This pattern largely persisted during the Cold War. U.S. interventions—covert and overt—were aimed at preventing the spread of communism and curbing Soviet influence. These efforts spanned multiple continents: in the Americas (Guatemala, the Dominican Republic, Brazil, Chile, Grenada, Panama), in the Middle East and Africa (Iran, the Congo), and in Asia (South Vietnam). What distinguished this era was not the objective—strategic dominance—but the method: the United States favored installing compliant governments over direct colonization. In Iran, for instance, the U.S. orchestrated the overthrow of a democratically elected government to restore the Shah—an act that, while justified in Cold War terms, clearly contradicted liberal democratic principles.

After the Cold War, however, the objectives of U.S. interventions changed significantly. In Afghanistan (2001), Iraq (2003), and Libya (2011), the U.S. pursued military campaigns explicitly aimed at establishing democratic regimes. While differing in cause and execution, these operations shared a common goal: replacing authoritarian rule with democratic governance. This new strategy—often termed "democratic nation-building"—demanded immense resources and drew U.S. attention away from other strategic priorities. As such, it would be inaccurate to describe post-Cold War U.S. foreign policy as strictly realist or narrowly strategic—even for critics who regard it as merely an extension of liberal *hegemonic* ambition.[1]

The U.S.-led liberal international order that took shape after the Cold War was not sustained by American power alone. Rather than acting unilaterally, the United States proactively led efforts to build multilateral coalitions to address global challenges. The timing was right. The end of the Cold War marked a dramatic transformation in the functioning of the UN Security Council, which became a more effective vehicle for collective security. In 2014 alone, for instance, the Council passed 60 of 63 resolutions unanimously—an outcome that would have been unthinkable during the Cold War's frequent deadlocks. Multilateralism played a key role in reinforcing and legitimizing the liberal order. A wide array of international organizations—including the UN and its specialized agencies—were created or strengthened to facilitate cooperation in areas ranging from peacekeeping to public health. These developments frequently enjoyed robust U.S. support, reflecting Washington's commitment to an institutionalized world order.

To be sure, the United States did not always defer to multilateralism.

It declined to join certain multilateral institutions, such as the UN Convention on the Law of the Sea (UNCLOS) and the International Criminal Court, when they appeared to threaten core U.S. interests. Nevertheless, American leadership remained the dominant force behind the global structures that underpinned the post-Cold War liberal order.

The United States not only constructed and promoted multilateral regimes, but also retained disproportionate influence within them. Its dominance was not merely a matter of military or economic power, but a structural reality woven into the very fabric of the international system. In this way, U.S. hegemony became both institutionalized and deeply embedded in the architecture of post-Cold War global governance.

Emergence of Neoliberalism

At this juncture, it is helpful to step back and recall that the post–Cold War international system—commonly referred to as the liberal international order (LIO)—is fundamentally grounded in the principles of liberalism. As previously discussed, liberalism is a broad and evolving ideological tradition that has shaped political, economic, and philosophical thought for centuries. By the time of the Cold War's end, the classical liberalism that had flourished in the era of Immanuel Kant was already several hundred years old. While key elements of classical liberalism persisted as the ideological foundation of the LIO, its conceptual framework had undergone significant transformation over time, reflecting shifts in societal values and institutional structures.

The liberalism that underpinned the post–Cold War order thus differed from its 18th-century antecedents. It had evolved throughout the 20th century, culminating in its most dominant and influential modern incarnation: neoliberalism.

Like classical liberalism, neoliberalism is an ideological framework that permeates virtually every sphere of society. However, unlike its predecessor, neoliberalism is not primarily rooted in a moral vision of individual liberty. Rather, it is shaped by a market-oriented economic philosophy that prioritizes competition, efficiency, and the autonomy of individuals as economic actors. While it retains core liberal principles—such as private property rights, limited government, and individual agency—it reframes these ideals within the context of 'global capitalism.' Seen from another angle, classical liberalism primarily emphasized the protection of individual rights and the limitation of state power within the confines of the nation-state. Neoliberalism, by contrast, reinterprets these principles to promote deregulation, privatization, and free trade on a global scale. In doing so, it also integrates national economies into an interdependent international system where domestic policy is increasingly subject to the imperatives of global markets. This shift places a premium on open markets and the reduction of trade barriers, even when such policies may undermine traditional notions of national sovereignty or erode domestic social protections.

In 1989, just a few years before the dissolution of the Soviet Union, American economist John Williamson articulated the key components of this emerging paradigm in what would come to be known as the Washington Consensus.[2] Comprising ten core principles—including fiscal discipline, trade liberalization, deregulation, and privatization—the framework was quickly adopted by the International Monetary Fund (IMF), the World Bank, and the U.S. Treasury Department. It provided the blueprint for economic reform in developing countries, particularly those facing financial crises, with adherence to its doctrines often made a precondition for access to international financial assistance. The Washington Consensus became the dominant policy framework for global economic governance in the post–Cold War era, solidifying the ascendancy of globalized market capitalism.

One of the most consequential developments of this period was the institutional advancement of international trade. In 1995, the World Trade Organization (WTO) succeeded the GATT, dramatically accelerating global efforts to eliminate tariff and non-tariff barriers across a wide range of sectors. This institutional leap forward in trade liberalization played a key role in deepening economic globalization and solidifying the structural foundations of the liberal international economic order.

The globalization of neoliberalism under the LIO was institutionalized through both public and private mechanisms. On the public side, international economic organizations such as the IMF, the World Bank, and the WTO played a central role in promoting and enforcing neoliberal economic norms. On the private side, multinational corporations and global financial institutions reinforced these norms by embedding market-driven practices into the fabric of the global economy. Together, these actors created a system in which neoliberal policy prescriptions became the dominant paradigm for economic governance.

The Pax Americana Arrives

The post–Cold War era was marked by unprecedented levels of global peace and prosperity. Despite ongoing critical assessments, objective indicators consistently demonstrate that the U.S.-led liberal international order facilitated a historically exceptional period of geopolitical stability and economic expansion.

Throughout most of history, the international system operated under conditions of multipolarity. Even the most successful balance-of-power arrangements—such as the 19th-century Concert of Europe—were unable to prevent recurrent major wars. Similarly, while the bipolar structure of the Cold War created a relatively stable strategic equilibrium, it nonetheless witnessed numerous proxy conflicts and regional wars. By contrast, the post–Cold War 'unipolar moment' brought about a remarkably peaceful period in world affairs. From 1991 onward, the frequency of armed conflicts declined sharply. Until the outbreak of war in Ukraine in 2022, large-scale interstate wars had virtually disappeared, with the notable exception of U.S.-led interventions under the banner of the 'War on Terror.' Even when these interventions in Afghanistan and Iraq are taken into account, the overall incidence and intensity of warfare remained historically low. This period of hegemonic stability, maintained under the auspices of the U.S.-led liberal international order, is often referred to as Pax Americana.

At the height of Pax Americana, global security concerns shifted away from interstate wars toward civil conflicts and transnational terrorism. Although civil wars had surged during the Cold War, their frequency and lethality declined in the post–Cold War era. By the 2000s, the peak intensity of civil wars—reached in the early 1990s—had fallen by more than two-thirds. This reduction was largely attributable to proactive U.S. engagement, international humanitarian interventions, and the growing role of United Nations peacekeeping operations, all of which contributed to the de-escalation of intrastate violence. According to World Bank data on state involvement in wars and civil conflicts from 1900 to 2008, global security levels during Pax Americana were comparable to those in the immediate aftermaths of World War I and World War II—periods when the entire world was too ravaged to sustain further large-scale warfare.[3]

In addition to enhanced security, the three decades of unipolarity ushered in an era of unmatched economic prosperity. The liberalization of trade, capital flows, services, and even human mobility catalyzed unprecedented levels of global economic integration. Concurrently, rapid technological advancement and the accelerated diffusion of ideas spurred gains in productivity. According to data from the IMF and the World Bank, the global economy tripled in size during this period, and more than 1.3 billion people rose out of poverty.

Historical data on inflation-adjusted global GDP underscores the singular nature of this economic expansion. For the first 1,700 years of recorded history, global output remained largely stagnant. While the Industrial Revolution initiated a period of sustained growth, its pace was modest by comparison. A more significant economic acceleration began around World War I, driven by early globalization, technological innovation, and European colonial expansion. The post–World War II period, particularly under the Bretton Woods system, saw further growth. Yet even this paled in comparison to the exponential surge in global GDP during the post–Cold War era.[4] Notably, this growth was broadly distributed: nearly every country experienced absolute economic gains, with developing economies growing at a significantly faster rate than their developed counterparts. The resulting shift in the global economic landscape is evident in the rising share of developing countries in world GDP over the transition from the 20th to the 21st century.

The peace and prosperity of the post–Cold War order fostered an unparalleled wave of global interconnectedness—encompassing not only the movement of goods, services, capital, and technology, but also the flow of people, cultures, governance models, and ideas. This deepening cross-border integration, commonly referred to as globalization, became the defining feature of the era, fundamentally reshaping the international system across multiple dimensions.

The Shadow of Pax Americana

Even the most well-intentioned ideologies can yield unintended consequences when translated into real-world policies. During the Cold War, securing the moral high ground over the opposing bloc was often sufficient. But once a dominant global order was established, the core challenges shifted—from ideological competition to questions of governance and legitimacy. The liberal international order, which emerged as the prevailing global framework in the post–Cold War period, did not escape criticism despite its considerable achievements.

Broadly speaking, critiques of the liberal international order fall into two primary categories. The first targets liberal internationalism, which often overlapped with what many perceived as American unilateralism—particularly in the promotion of American-style democracy in regions with distinct historical and cultural contexts. Critics argue that U.S. foreign policy frequently instrumentalized liberal norms as a cover for hegemonic expansion. Military interventions and regime-change efforts, often justified in the name of democracy and human rights, were seen as violations of national sovereignty.[5, 6] This perception reinforced the critique that the liberal international order functioned less as a rules-based system and more as a vehicle for U.S. imperialism.[7] In the post–Cold War era, this dynamic solidified a lasting ideological divide: on one side, liberal internationalism, which advocates limiting state sovereignty in favor of shared values and universal principles; on the other, sovereign internationalism, which prioritizes national self-determination and non-interference in domestic affairs.[8]

A second major line of criticism focuses on neoliberalism, a term that has increasingly acquired negative connotations, particularly in light of globalization's uneven consequences. While globalization undeniably fostered economic integration and technological diffusion, its adverse effects have been deeply felt. Some countries that implemented Washington Consensus reforms managed to stabilize and restructure their economies. But in others, the rapid and unprepared liberalization of markets led to economic disruption. Domestic industries, abruptly exposed to global competition, collapsed; at the same time, market-driven reforms that privileged corporate interests over labor protections produced widespread unemployment and social dislocation.

Critics argue that the neoliberal framework established by the Washington Consensus—and later reinforced by the WTO-led multilateral trading regime—entrenched structural inequalities between developed and developing economies. Although aggregate data show that developing countries grew faster than developed ones in the post–Cold War period, making it difficult to claim that globalization exacerbated absolute wealth disparities, the structural dynamics of global capitalism were far more complex. Under globalization, the push for comparative advantage[9] often locked developing countries into low-value-added roles in the global supply chain. Nations with abundant natural resources became exporters of raw materials; those with inexpensive labor were relegated to manufacturing goods for multinational corporations. Opportunities for technological upgrading or industrial diversification remained limited. While exceptional cases such as South Korea and Taiwan successfully climbed the value chain, most developing economies found themselves trapped in a subordinate position—unable to escape the structural constraints of a global economy dominated by developed countries and multinational corporations.

Importantly, the disruptive effects of globalization were not confined to the Global South. In developed economies, the pursuit of free trade—though beneficial to overall economic output—accelerated the decline of uncompetitive domestic industries. The enduring tension between Adam Smith's free trade liberalism and John Maynard Keynes' emphasis on full employment remains unresolved. As globalization deepened, multinational corporations increasingly offshored production to low-cost labor markets. This generated new employment opportunities in the Global South, but also triggered mass job losses and deindustrialization in the Global North. The decline of both light and heavy manufacturing in advanced economies led to the erosion of working-class living standards. Moreover, as multinational corporations gained the flexibility to relocate operations abroad, they undercut the bargaining power of domestic labor forces and unions—exacerbating wage stagnation, job insecurity, and the deterioration of working conditions.

Despite warnings from economists, labor activists, and critical policymakers about the social and economic costs of neoliberal globalization, the momentum of integration continued largely unimpeded for nearly three decades. For much of this period, globalization was seen as inevitable—a giant wheel set in motion that could not be reversed. It was only when Pax Americana began to fray, and the liberal international order entered a period of crisis, that serious resistance to the prevailing economic orthodoxy began to take shape.

The Twilight of Pax Americana

Although often described as "the most benevolent hegemon in history," the United States has faced considerable resistance across the globe. The exercise of hegemonic power inevitably provokes nationalist backlash, and the broader a hegemon's reach, the more widespread the opposition. As the first truly global hegemon in history, the United States encountered opposition on an unprecedented scale.

A defining moment for Pax Americana and the liberal international order came on September 11, 2001, when the extremist group Al-Qaeda orchestrated a coordinated terrorist attack on U.S. soil. Four commercial airliners were hijacked—two struck the World Trade Center in New York, one crashed into the Pentagon, and the fourth, diverted by passengers, crashed in Pennsylvania. Nearly 3,000 lives were lost in a single morning. It was the first direct attack on a major American city since 1812 and marked the first significant external challenge to U.S. dominance in the post–Cold War era.

In response, the United States launched a sweeping military campaign. Afghanistan, whose Taliban regime had harbored Al-Qaeda, became the initial target. The U.S. invasion began in October 2001, and Kabul fell within weeks. In March 2003, the Bush administration turned its focus to Iraq, toppling Saddam Hussein's regime within 20 days. While both operations appeared initially successful, the U.S. soon became entangled in protracted conflicts that would define the 'War on Terror.' Combating decentralized insurgencies and transnational terrorist networks proved far more difficult than defeating conventional forces—a challenge reminiscent of the Vietnam War, but with a far longer timeline. Efforts to establish stable, pro-American democratic regimes ultimately failed, culminating in the chaotic withdrawal from Afghanistan in 2021 and the Taliban's swift return to power.

Over two decades, the War on Terror drained U.S. military, economic, and diplomatic capital, diverting attention from the rise of rival powers. While Washington was mired in endless wars, China emerged as a global superpower, and Russia began reasserting its influence on the international stage.[10]

Beyond strategic miscalculations, U.S. actions also eroded the ideological legitimacy of the liberal international order. The intervention in Afghanistan was widely supported and backed by UN Security Council Resolutions 1368 and 1373. In contrast, the 2003 Iraq invasion, justified by unverified claims that Saddam Hussein possessed weapons of mass destruction (WMD), lacked definitive evidence and proceeded without UN authorization.[11] Had WMD been discovered, the intervention might have retained certain international legitimacy. In their absence, however, the war came to symbolize the double standards of the liberal order, reinforcing the view that it served as a cover for U.S. imperial ambitions and deepening global anti-American sentiment.

The ideological consequences were profound. The Bush administration framed the post-9/11 world in stark moral terms, pledging to eradicate tyranny and promoting what it called the "Freedom Agenda." Iraq, Iran, and North Korea were labeled the "Axis of Evil," and U.S. foreign policy took a distinctly unilateral and interventionist turn. Military-led nation-building in Iraq and Afghanistan presumed that liberal democracy and free-market capitalism could be exported through force.[12] The name of the U.S. operation—"Enduring Freedom"—reflected this ideological thrust. Yet these efforts backfired, casting doubt on the authenticity of U.S. motives and reinforcing the critique that liberal internationalism had become a euphemism for coercive hegemony.

While the 'War on Terror' strained U.S. power, the 2008 global financial crisis revealed deep vulnerabilities in the neoliberal economic model. The roots of the crisis lay in the deregulatory ethos of the 1990s, particularly the repeal of core provisions of the Glass-Steagall Act through the Gramm-Leach-Bliley Act in 1999.[13] This shift blurred the lines between commercial and investment banking, unleashing a wave of unchecked and risky financial practices. Housing finance policies aimed at broadening homeownership led to an overheated real estate market,[14] fueled by subprime mortgages and complex financial instruments such as mortgage-backed securities (MBS) and collateralized debt obligations (CDOs).[15] When housing prices collapsed, a cascade of defaults triggered a global financial meltdown. Major institutions, including Lehman Brothers and AIG, either failed or required massive government intervention.

The crisis rippled through the global economy. European banks, heavily exposed to U.S. mortgage assets, suffered catastrophic losses. The U.S. auto industry teetered on the brink of collapse. More fundamentally, the crisis laid bare the fragility of a global financial system increasingly detached from productive economic activity, exposing the dangers of excessive financialization and lax regulation.

To stabilize the economy, President Barack Obama pursued an internationalist approach. In past economic crises—such as the collapse of the Bretton Woods system or the 1973 oil shocks—the U.S. had relied on the G7 for coordination. But the scale of the 2008 crisis required broader cooperation. The G20, previously a ministerial forum, was elevated to a summit of world leaders, incorporating emerging powers like China, India, and Brazil. Through coordinated fiscal stimulus, monetary easing, and anti-protectionist pledges, the G20 helped arrest the crisis and facilitated a relatively swift recovery compared to the Great Depression.

The geopolitical implications were far-reaching. First, the crisis marked a turning point in globalization. After decades of rapid expansion, global trade as a share of world GDP fell from 51% in 2008 to 42% by 2020—a phenomenon dubbed 'slowbalization.' Second, the crisis exposed the limits of U.S. economic dominance. Washington's reliance on multilateral solutions signaled that even the world's preeminent power had finite resources. Third and most significantly, the crisis accelerated China's global rise. Unlike the debt-ridden West, China maintained robust growth, launched a massive domestic stimulus, and actively invested abroad, projecting financial strength and geopolitical confidence.

Together, the twin crises of the 'War on Terror' and the 2008 global financial meltdown fundamentally reshaped the liberal international order. Militarily, the failures in Iraq and Afghanistan discredited interventionism. Economically, the crisis shattered the neoliberal consensus that had underpinned globalization. These twin shocks exposed the fragility of American primacy and opened the door for emerging powers to contest the rules and values of the existing world order.

Endnotes:

1 From a realist perspective, U.S. foreign policy in the post-Cold War era often appeared to be driven more by ideological commitments—particularly the promotion of liberal democracy—than by clear national interest or strategic calculations. Realists argue that rather than engaging in costly and often unsuccessful attempts to reshape foreign political systems, the United States should have focused on maintaining its power and security through more traditional means, such as balancing against rising states. Many realist scholars contend that the emphasis on "nation-building" distracted the United States from more pressing geopolitical developments, particularly the resurgence of China and Russia, and ultimately weakened its ability to adapt to shifting global power dynamics. In their view, the post-Cold War shift toward a more idealistic, liberal-oriented foreign policy undermined the United States' long-term strategic position.

2 The Washington Consensus refers to a set of ten economic policy prescriptions. These include maintaining fiscal discipline by reducing deficits and managing public debt, redirecting public spending toward high-impact areas like healthcare, education, and infrastructure, and reforming taxation to widen the tax base while keeping tax rates moderate. The framework prioritizes market-oriented liberalization, advocating for deregulated interest rates, liberalized trade, and flexible exchange rates to boost efficiency and global integration. It also promotes foreign direct investment (FDI) through strong investor protections, privatization of state enterprises to enhance competitiveness, and broad market deregulation to encourage entrepreneurship and competition. Finally, it underscores the critical role of secure property rights as a foundation for economic stability. Intended to create an open, market-driven environment conducive to growth and investment, the Washington Consensus has sparked intense debate over its practical outcomes, with critics arguing it often prioritized market ideology over local context, sometimes exacerbating inequality and economic volatility.

3 See among others, International Bank for Reconstruction and Development (The World Bank): "The 2011 World Development Report."

4 In summary, when viewing world GDP growth over a 2,000-year period, the trend for the first 1,700 years remained nearly flat, with gradual growth from the Industrial Revolution to World War I, followed by a sharp upward curve until the end of World War II. In the last 70 years, global GDP showed a literal "vertical rise." Even within this vertical rise, the trends before and after the 1990s are sharply distinguishable. Many factors contributed to this (though minor variables have likely been naturally controlled over the vast passage of 2,000 years), but the most direct cause was likely "technological advancement." However, it is undeniable that the promotion of globalization led to the overall growth of the "pie" of wealth. See among others, "World GDP over the last two millennia," World GDP – Our World in Data based on World Bank & Maddison (2017).

5 See generally, Jon Western & Joshua Goldstein, "Humanitarian Intervention Comes of Age, Lessons From Somalia to Libya," Foreign Affairs, FRNA, 48, Volume 90 (2011).

6 The 2005 World Summit marked a significant turning point in international law with the adoption of the 'Responsibility to Protect' (R2P) principle by the UN General Assembly. This doctrine establishes that governments have a primary responsibility to protect their populations from genocide, war crimes, ethnic cleansing, and crimes against humanity. It further asserts that if a state fails to fulfill this responsibility, the international community has the right to intervene, if necessary through the UN Security Council. This principle represents a significant shift from the traditional international law principle of non-intervention in internal affairs, particularly internal conflicts such as civil wars. The emergence of R2P creates an obligation for the international community to act in the face of humanitarian crises. See Resolution adopted by the General Assembly on 16 September 2005 (2005 World Summit Outcome), A/RES/60/1 (24 October 2005), paras 138-139. The Libyan civil war of 2011 serves as a prominent example of the application of the R2P doctrine. When the Gaddafi regime used its air force against civilians in Benghazi and other cities during its conflict with rebel forces, the United States, citing R2P, proposed UN Security Council Resolution 1973 on March 19, 2011, establishing a no-fly zone over Libya. It was still the unipolar moment, so neither Russia nor China opposed the resolution (they chose to abstain), and Resolution 1973 was adopted. When the Libyan air force violated the resolution by continuing its attacks, the international community, led by the United States, intervened militarily in the Libyan civil war and enforced the no-fly zone. The Gaddafi regime, having lost control of its air power, was eventually defeated and overthrown by rebel forces. UN Security Council Resolution 1973 has been the subject of much debate. Critics argue that the Libyan civil war was an internal matter within the sovereign jurisdiction of Libya, and therefore external military intervention was unwarranted. They contend that the Libyan people should have been allowed to resolve the conflict themselves. These critics also claim that the R2P principle violates the principle of respect for sovereignty, a cornerstone of international law since the Treaty of Westphalia.

7 In his March 14, 2025, interview, India's Foreign Minister Subrahmanyam Jaishankar aptly remarked that "the virtues of the old order (liberal international order) are somewhat exaggerated," particularly when viewed from the perspective of those on the receiving end of the global decision-making process. See *Indian foreign minister S Jaishankar: "The Virtues of the old order are exaggerated,"* Financial Times (March 14, 2025).

8 According to sovereign internationalism, even human rights can be relative and vary according to cultural and social backgrounds. Therefore, humanitarian intervention, such as the protection of civilians, cannot be a justification that overrides the principle of respect for sovereignty. Thus, many proponents of sovereign internationalism see even values such as human rights, liberal democracy, and the inclusiveness espoused by liberalism not as universal values of humanity, but rather as part of a long-term strategy to expand liberal internationalism. They argue that the protection of human rights or the spread of liberal democracy are used as pretexts to interfere in

the internal affairs of other countries. Those who share this view often hope for the collapse of the US unipolar system, which they see as nothing more than neo-imperialism, and the re-emergence of a multipolar system. On the other hand, liberals point out that the arguments of sovereign internationalists are almost always used to legitimize authoritarian regimes. See Robert Art & Robert Jervis (eds.), *International Politics: Enduring Concepts and Contemporary Issues* (12th ed)(Pearson, 2015), pp. 371-372. Meanwhile, former UN Secretary-General Kofi Annan emphasized that sovereignty includes not only "power" but also "responsibility," arguing that sovereignty cannot prevent humanitarian intervention authorized under the UN Charter to protect human lives. See Kofi Annan, "Reflections on Intervention," The Question of Intervention: Statements by the Secretary-General (United Nations, 1999).

9   Adam Smith's theory of absolute advantage emphasizes the benefits of specialization, arguing that when each nation concentrates on producing goods where it has a competitive edge, global productivity and efficiency are maximized. Building upon this idea, David Ricardo developed the theory of comparative advantage, which refines Smith's concept by showing that, between two trading partners, even if one country outperforms the other in all sectors, the disadvantaged country can still optimize overall productivity (of both countries) by specializing in the areas where it is relatively most efficient.

10 The United States failed to effectively counter China's Belt and Road Initiative in Asia and the Middle East, as well as China's growing influence in Latin America. In addition, the United States' response to Russia's invasions of Georgia in 2008 and Ukraine in 2014 was ineffective. The ineffective U.S. response during this period likely contributed to the outbreak of the Ukrainian war in 2022.

11 The United States also attempted to justify the invasion on the basis of existing UN Security Council resolutions 678 and 687, which authorized the use of force against Iraq after its 1990 invasion of Kuwait, and resolution 1441, which warned Iraq of consequences if it did not comply with WMD inspections. However, Resolution 1441 emphasized continued monitoring by the Security Council, and without additional resolutions, it was widely argued that it did not provide a direct legal basis for military action. The United States also argued that the subsequent UN Security Council Resolution 1483, passed after the invasion, legitimized its actions by authorizing humanitarian aid and reconstruction efforts in Iraq. The international community objected, with then-UN Secretary-General Kofi Annan declaring the invasion "illegal under international law."

12 This approach was also justified as part of the broader 'war on terror,' on the assumption that terrorists were less likely to emerge in democratic states.

13 Since the Great Depression of the early 20th century, U.S. economic policy could be described as "embedded liberalism." The U.S. advocated for market-oriented free trade while avoiding the laissez-faire policies that led to the Great Depression. The market had to be properly regulated. In 1933, the U.S. enacted the Glass-Steagall Act,

which separated commercial banks—which made loans based on deposits and equity—from investment banks, which handled high-risk transactions such as securities investments. However, after winning the Cold War and under the banner of Pax Americana, U.S. economic policy was increasingly influenced by neoliberalism. The new IT revolution demanded that regulation not stifle innovation and growth. Free markets, it was believed, were the most effective means of promoting both economic and technological development. As a result, the Clinton administration began to dismantle the economic policies of the past, which had been influenced by the lessons of the Great Depression. In 1999, in an effort to stay ahead in the global financial competition, the U.S. repealed the Glass-Steagall Act, removing the barrier between commercial and investment banking. After the 2008 financial crisis, the U.S. enacted the Dodd-Frank Act, which, among other things, restricted commercial banks from investing in bonds, stocks, and derivatives with their own equity or borrowed funds. The so-called 'Volcker Rule,' contained in Section 619 of this Act, was implemented in 2015.

14 As affordable housing loans flooded the market, investor funds poured in, driving U.S. housing prices to unsustainable levels. Borrowers, across various income levels, took on excessive debt, assuming that home prices would continue to rise. Predatory lending practices, including NINJA loans (no income, no job, no assets) and risky adjustable-rate mortgages (ARMs), further fueled the housing bubble. Eventually, when mortgage repayments became unsustainable, widespread defaults triggered the collapse.

15 A major difference from the financial markets of the 1930s (during the Great Depression) was the presence of derivatives. In the second half of the 20th century, financial techniques that increased liquidity by securitizing assets and liabilities and using credit derivatives to manage financial risk were considered cutting-edge finance. In the early 2000s, the instability created by derivatives grew, especially as the U.S. pursued a policy of ultra-low interest rates to escape the recession that followed the bursting of the dot-com bubble. Despite warnings from figures such as Warren Buffett, who called derivatives "financial weapons of mass destruction," Wall Street's overconfidence in financial innovation had far outstripped regulatory oversight.

CHAPTER 11

RISE OF REGIONAL ORDER
: CHINA AND RUSSIA'S REVISIONIST QUEST FOR HEGEMONY

> Every civilization sees itself as the center of
> the world and writes its history as
> the central drama of human history.
>
> Samuel P. Huntington

In Korea, there is an old proverb: "Two tigers cannot live on the same mountain." The same principle applies to international politics—two hegemons cannot coexist in the same region. A global hegemon, by definition, seeks to project its power across the entire world, leaving little room for competing regional powers. Thus, the emergence of a regional hegemon necessarily signals the erosion of global supremacy.

As previously discussed, the U.S.-led liberal international order, though imperfect, has delivered significant global benefits. Nevertheless, for a rising great power with the potential to dominate its region, a return to multipolarity may better serve its long-term interests. In a multipolar world, such powers can carve out their own spheres of influence, free from external constraints. Today, the states most poised to assume regional hegemonic roles are China and Russia. Historically geopolitical rivals, they have nevertheless forged a strategic partnership in opposition to U.S. primacy throughout the post–Cold War era.

As early as 1997, Chinese President Jiang Zemin and Russian President Boris Yeltsin met in Moscow and pledged to promote a multipolar world order. Yet, at the height of American unipolarity, their combined influence was insufficient to challenge the status quo. Russia remained circumscribed by NATO's eastward expansion, while China was constrained by U.S. alliances and military presence in the Western Pacific. Under the weight of American hegemony, neither state possessed the strategic autonomy to assert itself as an independent empire. Despite growing in strength, both refrained from direct confrontation with the United States for decades.

But China and Russia are continental powers with deep traditions of regional dominance. Their participation in the U.S.-led order was always a matter of tactical adaptation, not ideological conversion. As American power has waned—militarily, economically, and ideologically—both have moved decisively to reassert their influence and reshape the international system in their favor.

Grand Return of the Middle Kingdom

A Chinese proverb states, "The teacup must be placed lower than the teapot to receive tea." This metaphor aptly captures China's strategic posture in the post-Cold War era. Following the collapse of the Soviet Union and the broader communist bloc, China accepted the liberal international order, recognizing the necessity of working within a unipolar system—what Chinese analysts termed "one superpower, multiple great powers" (一超多强). At the time, the stakes were existential. In 1993, China's per capita GDP stood at a mere $377, the legacy of decades of economic stagnation behind the Bamboo Curtain. Integration into the U.S.-led free trade system became a national imperative. Since at least 1986, China had actively sought membership in the GATT, the precursor to the WTO.[1]

China's accession to the WTO in 2001 marked a decisive turning point. Then-U.S. President Bill Clinton championed China's entry, expressing hope that economic freedom—the foundation of democracy—would eventually take root in Chinese society. From that moment,

China's economic ascent was meteoric. By 2010, it had overtaken Japan to become the world's second-largest economy, with per capita GDP exceeding $4,500—twelve times its 1993 level. By 2020, that figure surpassed $10,000, and by 2022, China's total GDP reached $18 trillion—nearly 70% of the U.S. total of approximately $25 trillion. Given that in the 1990s China's economy was only 6–13% the size of America's, this transformation was extraordinary. The "sleeping giant," marginalized since the late Qing Dynasty, had returned as a peer competitor to the most powerful empire in history. Its vast population, expansive territory, and abundant natural resources created a potent synergy with economic modernization. Growth in material wealth fueled military expansion and bolstered China's comprehensive national power, enabling a confident reassertion of its global ambitions. It was the grand return of the Middle Kingdom.

By the early 2010s, this growing power was reshaping China's foreign policy, rendering it more assertive in both regional and global arenas. This shift was driven by three major developments. First, the 2008 global financial crisis exposed the structural weaknesses of the U.S. economy, boosting Beijing's confidence in the resilience and superiority of its state-led model. Second, in 2010, China surpassed Japan as the world's second-largest economy, leading analysts to predict that it was only a matter of time before it overtook the United States. Third—and most consequential—was a shift in the military balance. Around 2010, China deployed the DF-21 anti-ship ballistic missile, a weapon specifically designed to threaten U.S. aircraft carriers. This milestone in China's Anti-Access/Area Denial (A2/AD) strategy marked a turning point. Combining naval, air, and missile systems, the A2/AD doctrine aims to restrict U.S. military access to China's near seas.[2] For Washington, it signaled a profound strategic complication: projecting power in the Western Pacific would now entail greater risk and uncertainty.

China's growing military capabilities emboldened its behavior in regional disputes. In the East China Sea, tensions flared with Japan over the Senkaku Islands, particularly after Tokyo detained a Chinese fishing boat in 2010. Beijing retaliated by suspending rare earth exports to Japan and curbing tourism—signaling a readiness to leverage economic tools in geopolitical disputes. In the South China Sea, Beijing's expansive Nine-Dash Line claims largely overlapped with the exclusive economic zones (EEZs) of multiple Southeast Asian nations, provoking widespread alarm. In 2013, the Philippines brought the issue to international arbitration. In 2016, the Permanent Court of Arbitration ruled that China's maritime claims lacked legal basis under the UN Convention on the Law of the Sea. China dismissed the ruling outright and accelerated its militarization of artificial islands.

The Taiwan Strait represents an even more volatile and complex theater. Unlike disputes over uninhabited islands, Taiwan involves questions of identity, governance, and sovereignty. For Beijing, reunification remains a core national objective, deeply tied to the legitimacy of the Chinese Communist Party. Yet, Taiwan's increasingly robust sense of distinct identity and its growing resistance to integration with the mainland have fueled rising tensions.

The crisis reached a new level of intensity in 2022, when U.S. House Speaker Nancy Pelosi visited Taiwan despite strong Chinese objections. Her visit, interpreted in Beijing as a violation of the 'One-China principle,' prompted an unprecedented show of force: large-scale Chinese military exercises effectively encircled the island. Taiwan, for its part, has seen a surge in anti-China sentiment, shaped by the perceived erosion of Hong Kong's autonomy under Beijing's control. These dynamics have pushed cross-Strait relations to their most dangerous point in decades.

Empire Strikes Back

Meanwhile, Russia charted its own course toward reestablishing regional dominance in Eastern Europe. At the turn of the century, Moscow initially projected a cooperative stance toward the U.S.-led international order. Still reeling from the collapse of the Soviet Union, it remained economically weakened and geopolitically constrained, navigating a world defined by liberal hegemony. Yet, as Russia began its slow recovery, it grew increasingly alarmed by the continued eastward expansion of the North Atlantic Treaty Organization (NATO).

In 1999, three former Warsaw Pact states—the Czech Republic (formerly part of Czechoslovakia), Poland, and Hungary—formally joined NATO. This was followed by a more expansive wave in 2004, which brought in Bulgaria, Romania, Slovakia (the other successor to Czechoslovakia), and the three Baltic states—Lithuania, Latvia, and Estonia. The latter were not merely former Soviet satellites; they had been constituent republics of the Soviet Union and shared direct borders with Russia. From Moscow's perspective, this was not merely a strategic setback, but a profound erosion of its traditional sphere of influence and the collapse of its post-Soviet buffer zone.[3]

Tensions escalated sharply following NATO's 2008 Bucharest Summit, at which the alliance declared its intention to one day admit Georgia and Ukraine. For the Kremlin, this represented a red line—an existential threat to Russia's ability to maintain influence over its near abroad. That same year, Russia launched a military intervention in Georgia, citing the protection of Russian citizens in the separatist regions of South Ossetia and Abkhazia. The brief but decisive conflict demonstrated Moscow's willingness to use force to prevent further NATO encroachment. The Western response—limited to diplomatic condemnation and modest sanctions—failed to impose meaningful costs, likely reinforcing Russia's perception that it could act with relative impunity within its perceived sphere of influence.

In 2014, Russia escalated its campaign to reassert regional dominance with the annexation of Crimea and the orchestration of armed separatism in eastern Ukraine. The move was driven by a combination of strategic calculus and identity politics: Moscow sought to derail Ukraine's pro-Western trajectory while capitalizing on pro-Russian sentiment in Crimea and the Donbas. Although the West responded with economic sanctions and political isolation, the absence of a robust military deterrent signaled a lack of resolve—at least in Moscow's eyes. The unresolved conflicts in both Georgia and Ukraine reinforced a pattern: limited Western responses emboldened the Kremlin, laying the foundation for an even more audacious move.

That came in 2022, when Russia launched a full-scale invasion of Ukraine. Far more than a continuation of previous conflicts, this was a direct challenge to the post-Cold War security architecture in Europe and an unambiguous attempt to redraw borders through force. It marked Russia's most assertive effort yet to reverse NATO's expansion and reassert its position as a dominant power in the region—challenging not only Ukrainian sovereignty but the liberal international order itself.

The Road to Regional Hegemony

The war in Ukraine and the ongoing tensions in the Taiwan Strait, while ostensibly regional in nature, are in fact manifestations of a broader strategic objective shared by Russia and China: breaking through the geopolitical containment imposed by the United States and challenging the foundations of U.S. unipolarity. Russian President Vladimir Putin has repeatedly emphasized that the invasion of Ukraine is not merely a localized effort to block Kyiv's accession to NATO.[4] For him, it is a defining moment in the reassertion of Russian power and a direct challenge to the U.S.-led liberal international order.

The full withdrawal of U.S. forces from Afghanistan on August 30, 2021, was widely seen as a symbolic turning point. It not only marked the end of America's 20-year 'War on Terror' but also signaled the waning of U.S. global hegemony. Merely months later, by October 2021, Russia had reportedly finalized its decision to invade Ukraine. Around the same period, speculation emerged that Moscow was also eyeing Moldova,[5] and leaked U.S. intelligence in early 2023 suggested that Russia aimed to formally annex Belarus by 2030. Taken together, these developments point to a coherent strategic vision: in the aftermath of America's retreat from Afghanistan, Putin perceived a window of opportunity to implement his grand strategy—restoring Russia's regional dominance by reclaiming influence over Eastern Europe, Central Asia, and Southwestern Asia.

Putin's public rhetoric reinforces this interpretation. Since the war's outset, he has framed the conflict not only as a defense of Russia's national interests, but as a broader campaign to dismantle the U.S.-led global order. In numerous speeches and official pronouncements, he has insisted that the war in Ukraine will mark the end of U.S. unipolar dominance and the collapse of the liberal international order.[6] Echoing earlier Sino-Russian joint statements, Putin has repeatedly called for the emergence of a multipolar world—one in which the United States can no longer dictate the rules of global engagement unilaterally.

China, too, has long harbored ambitions to reshape the international system in its favor. During his visit to the United States in 2012, then–Vice President Xi Jinping famously remarked that the Pacific was "big enough to accommodate both great countries"—an implicit suggestion that the United States and China should share influence in the region. Washington, which has long viewed the Pacific as an "American lake,"[7] responded with the "Pivot to Asia" policy in 2011, aiming to reorient U.S. strategic focus toward the Asia-Pacific following years of entanglement in the Middle East. Undeterred, Xi continued to articulate China's vision of co-leadership in the Pacific. He reiterated the same message in conversations with Secretary of State John Kerry in 2013, at the U.S.–

China Strategic Dialogue in 2014, and again in informal discussions with President Barack Obama in 2015. By 2017, China's rise had reached a point where only the United States retained the capacity to challenge it directly, prompting speculation about a new bipolar world order—the so-called 'G2.' In 2018, Xi offered a clearer articulation of China's ambitions. Addressing a conference of overseas Chinese diplomats, he proclaimed that the world was undergoing "a transformation not seen in a century" and that the 21st century would be defined by "great changes"—a clear allusion to Beijing's expectation that global power was shifting irreversibly in its direction. According to this vision, China would achieve preeminence by 2049, the centenary of the People's Republic of China.

By 2021, Xi's rhetoric had evolved further. In a summit with President Joe Biden, he no longer limited China's ambitions to the Pacific but declared that "the planet Earth is big enough" for two global powers. This shift in tone was widely interpreted as a direct challenge to U.S. global primacy, signaling that Beijing now saw itself not just as a regional peer, but as a global superpower in the making. Since the outbreak of the Ukraine war, Xi—like Putin—has repeatedly invoked the need for an "equal, orderly multipolar world," underscoring China's commitment to dismantling the U.S.-led international order and replacing it with a system more reflective of Beijing's values and strategic interests.

Ideological Drives

China and Russia's revisionist ambitions are driven not only by the hard calculations of realpolitik but also by deeply ingrained nationalist ideologies. Neither country currently possesses the capability to achieve global hegemony[8]; instead, their ideological narratives serve to justify and legitimize efforts to reassert dominance within their respective spheres of influence. These ideologies—*Sinocentrism* in China and *Eurasianism* in Russia—function as guiding myths that reinforce their domestic authorities and external ambitions alike.

1. China's Story

China's claim to regional hegemony is grounded in the ancient worldview of Sinocentrism—the belief that China is, and should be, the center of the world. This worldview is deeply embedded in Chinese identity and culture, reflected in the very name for China, 中國 (Zhōngguó), meaning 'Middle Kingdom.' According to this worldview, China is not only superior to all other nations in terms of culture, politics, and economic organization, but also in moral virtue.

The ideological underpinnings of Sinocentrism trace back to Confucianism, which places a premium on hierarchical order, moral leadership, and societal harmony.[9] In traditional Confucian thought, the emperor of China was regarded as the 'Son of Heaven,' bearing responsibility for maintaining cosmic and earthly order within the realm of Tianxia (天下)—"All-Under-Heaven." This worldview extended beyond China's borders through the tributary system, which established a regional order premised on Chinese moral and civilizational superiority and reinforced China's hegemony in East Asia for centuries.

For ethnic Chinese, overcoming this Sinocentric orientation is no easy task, as it remains deeply embedded in the national psyche through generations of cultural pride and historical memory. For many in China, there remains a shared conviction—explicit or implicit—that China rightfully belongs at the center of global affairs. This belief has been further fueled by modern Chinese nationalism, particularly the desire to avenge the 'Century of Humiliation' at the hands of Western and Japanese imperialism. The drive to reclaim China's historic glory has become central to the national project.

For the Chinese Communist Party (CCP), this nationalist fervor is an indispensable tool for legitimizing continued one-party rule. As China's basic material needs have been increasingly met, aspirations for greater political freedom have naturally followed. The CCP's answer has been to postpone full democratization by invoking the historical mission of national rejuvenation. The unspoken social contract between the Party and the people rests on a compelling promise: the restoration of China's rightful place as the world's central authority.[10] If global supremacy remains out of reach, regional hegemony in East Asia is viewed as an acceptable alternative.

The 2008 global financial crisis marked a turning point in China's trajectory. As the United States reeled from economic turmoil and the world turned to Beijing for economic stability, Chinese leaders saw a validation of their model. With nearly double-digit annual growth rates, China not only weathered the crisis but played a key role in reviving the global economy. This moment of economic triumph fueled nationalist confidence. In 2009, then-President Hu Jintao declared that a "profound shift in the global balance of power" had occurred, signaling that China's moment on the world stage had arrived. Nationalist bestsellers like *Unhappy China* gained popularity, calling for China to shed its historical restraint and embrace its destiny as a hegemonic power.

In particular, Confucianism, once vilified during the Cultural Revolution, experienced a revival. Following the 2008 Beijing Olympics, China began re-embracing Confucian values—not just domestically, but as a normative framework for a new world order. Chinese intellectuals and policymakers began promoting the vision of a new Tianxia—a modern, global reinterpretation of Sinocentrism. This alternative to the U.S.-led liberal international order was presented as more harmonious, morally grounded, and respectful of civilizational diversity. In contrast to the perceived predation of Western imperialism, the Sinocentric order promised peace and global equilibrium under China's moral leadership.

Chinese theorists argue that this system is not hegemonic in the Western sense. Instead of a hierarchy of brute power, the Tianxia model is built on an 'authority hierarchy'[11] in which roles are defined by moral leadership rather than coercion.[12] They claim this model promotes order and harmony, preserving cultural pluralism while minimizing conflict. As the Pax Americana fades, they argue, a Pax Sinica can rise in its place—restoring a natural global balance with China at its apex.

2. Russia's Story

Russia's ideological framework for regional hegemony centers on Eurasianism, a geopolitical vision that emerged in the early 20th century. Unlike traditional Pan-Slavism, which emphasized ethnic unity among Slavic peoples, Eurasianism offers a broader civilizational identity—neither wholly European nor Asian.[13] It asserts that the Eurasian continent represents a unique cultural and geopolitical space, one distinct from and morally superior to the West. In its modern form, Eurasianism has been revived and popularized by figures such as Alexander Dugin, who has positioned it as an ideological alternative to Western liberalism and U.S.-led globalism.

At the heart of Eurasianism lies a belief in Russia's historical mission. As the heir to Kievan Rus, the Russian Empire, and the Soviet Union, Russia is portrayed as the natural leader of a multiethnic, Orthodox Christian Eurasian civilization. In this view, Western liberalism is not merely geopolitically hostile—it is culturally and morally decadent. To protect Eurasia's shared heritage and traditional values, Russia must reclaim its geopolitical sovereignty, restore its leadership over the region, and dismantle the unipolar, U.S.-centric world order.

President Putin has long echoed this worldview. In a widely circulated July 12, 2021 essay published on the Kremlin's official website, Putin argued that "modern Ukraine is entirely the product of the Soviet era," a legacy misunderstood or deliberately ignored by "leaders of modern Ukraine and their external 'patrons.'"[14] On February 21, 2022, just days before launching the full-scale invasion of Ukraine, he declared that Ukraine had "always been part of Russia," effectively denying its sovereignty. Similar statements have been made about Kazakhstan and other post-Soviet states, reflecting a broader strategic goal: the reintegration of the former imperial periphery under Moscow's leadership.

This vision was formally codified on March 31, 2023, when Putin incorporated Eurasianism into Russia's Foreign Policy Concept, enshrining it as the ideological foundation of Russian foreign policy.[15] From Moscow's perspective, Russia is not merely defending its borders but fulfilling a civilizational mission—restoring order to Eurasia, pushing back against Western encroachment, and paving the way for a new, multipolar global order.

Return of the Jungle

China and Russia have been relatively successful in legitimizing their hegemonic ambitions at home by appealing to nationalist sentiment. However, they have struggled to export these justifications beyond their borders—particularly to the neighboring states they seek to draw into their respective spheres of influence. In short, both powers have faced substantial resistance in persuading surrounding nations to accept the legitimacy of their regional dominance.

The rise of U.S. global hegemony not only facilitated the diffusion of liberalism as a normative international framework—one in which all nations are, at least in principle, sovereign equals[16]—but also disrupted the traditional geopolitical hierarchies maintained by regional powers. In the post-Cold War era, many smaller states proactively embraced this shift, seizing the opportunity to assert greater autonomy from their former imperial or regional patrons. As a result, efforts by once-dominant empires to reestablish control over their historic peripheries have met with persistent local opposition—resistance that is unlikely to fade unless the economic and security burdens of independence become untenable.

It is axiomatic that all states, regardless of size, value their national autonomy. Once their security and material well-being are reasonably secured, they tend to pursue greater independence. Conversely, this dynamic also suggests that the hierarchical order envisioned by China or Russia may become more palatable—at least to states facing acute threats to their survival or stability. History has repeatedly shown that nations are often willing to sacrifice a measure of autonomy in exchange for security and economic relief—a trade-off that underpinned many imperial systems throughout history.

At its core, the international order proposed by China and Russia seeks to dismantle the normative legacies of liberal internationalism and revive a world order reminiscent of pre-modern, hierarchical power politics. Yet the deeper concern is not simply the return of an "old system of the jungle"—but the reemergence of the "jungle" itself.

If global affairs indeed devolve into a more anarchic and competitive landscape, then even seemingly outdated or illiberal models of order may begin to appear as viable—perhaps even attractive—alternatives to many states.

Endnotes:

1 During the Cold War, the United States supported China's admission to the United Nations and its permanent membership on the Security Council as a counterbalance to the Soviet Union. However, Washington remained lukewarm regarding China's accession to the GATT and later the WTO. For 15 years, China struggled to gain entry into the global trading system, and it was only after securing U.S. approval that it finally joined the WTO. To assuage American concerns, then-President Jiang Zemin undertook an extensive charm offensive to cultivate a favorable image of China. During his 1997 visit to the U.S., he donned a British-style tricorn hat, engaged in candid discussions with American university students on sensitive topics such as Tibet, Taiwan, and the Tiananmen Square incident, and even used song and dance as diplomatic tools. While every Chinese leader since Deng Xiaoping had pursued strategic diplomacy, Jiang Zemin's efforts stood out as a particularly masterful display of statecraft, ultimately securing China's integration into the global economic order.

2 Since the Chinese Communist Party, led by Mao Zedong, defeated Chiang Kai-shek's Kuomintang in 1949, Taiwan has remained a central issue for China, with reunification as a core national objective. The Taiwan Strait, a mere 130 kilometers (80 miles) wide, separates mainland China from Taiwan but has long been patrolled by the U.S. Navy's Seventh Fleet, which oversees operations across the Asia-Pacific. China attempted military provocations against Taiwan in 1955, 1958, and 1996, but each time, its actions were deterred by the formidable presence of the Seventh Fleet. Even during a missile demonstration in the Taiwan Strait in 1996, China was forced to halt its provocations when a U.S. carrier strike group was rapidly deployed to the region. These setbacks prompted China to accelerate its military buildup. In the early 1980s, China outlined a strategic maritime framework known as the 'chain of islands' to assert control over its coastal waters. The first island chain, which includes Taiwan, represents China's ambition to dominate the East and South China Seas. Once secured, Beijing envisioned extending its reach to the 'second island chain,' a maritime expanse stretching from the Japanese archipelago and the Nansei Islands to the Philippines and the Malacca Strait, ultimately challenging U.S. dominance in the region. Until around 2010, however, the prevailing consensus was that China remained incapable of directly confronting the Seventh Fleet in the Taiwan Strait, even in its own maritime backyard. This was evident in November 2010 when the U.S. dispatched the USS George Washington aircraft carrier to the Yellow Sea in response to North Korea's artillery attack on South Korea's Yeonpyeong Island. Despite strong protests, China could do little militarily to counter the U.S. deployment. This underscored the continued disparity between Chinese and U.S. naval power. However, 2010 marked a turning point. Later that year, China's deployment of the DF-21D anti-ship ballistic missile in the South China Sea fundamentally altered the maritime balance of power, signaling a new phase in China's military capabilities and its growing ability to challenge U.S. naval supremacy.

3 For Russia, NATO's eastward expansion has long been perceived as the result of a calculated Western strategy reinforced by propaganda. However, many former Soviet

satellite states and republics that joined NATO have explicitly stated that their decision was driven by a sovereign desire to break away from Russia's sphere of influence. If Russia seeks to reassert itself as the dominant power in Eurasia, its leadership must critically examine why these former Soviet republics and satellite states have consistently sought alignment with the West, even at the cost of antagonizing Moscow. That said, just as much of Europe has historically viewed Russia as a geopolitical threat, Russia, too, has regarded Europe and the broader West as an existential danger. From facing invasions by Napoleon and Hitler to enduring a half-century-long Cold War with the United States, Russia's strategic outlook has been shaped by repeated confrontations with Western powers. Scholars like John Mearsheimer, a leading proponent of offensive realism, have long warned that NATO's expansion—particularly Ukraine's pursuit of membership—could provoke a full-scale Russian invasion. British foreign policy expert Tim Marshall, in his book Prisoners of Geography, also predicted that Ukraine's attempt to join NATO could lead to war, arguing that great powers confronted with perceived existential threats are likely to resort to military force.

4   Since losing Crimea in 2014, anti-Russian sentiment and fears of further aggression surged among the Ukrainian population, making NATO membership a national priority. In February 2019, Ukraine amended its constitution to explicitly mandate efforts toward joining both NATO and the European Union. When the pro-Western Volodymyr Zelenskyy was elected president later that year, Russia's concerns intensified. As Ukraine under Zelenskyy began actively discussing NATO accession, Moscow started preparing for war. Both the United States and Western Europe were acutely aware of the situation. In February 2022, French President Emmanuel Macron traveled to the Kremlin for direct talks with President Vladimir Putin, while NATO and the U.S. issued multiple statements attempting to reassure Russia. Zelenskyy himself hinted in mid-February 2022 that Ukraine's NATO membership was becoming increasingly unlikely. According to a Reuters report, a written instrument reflecting Ukraine's willingness to forgo NATO membership was even under negotiation, though the Kremlin later denied this claim. If Russia's primary objective in invading Ukraine had been solely to halt NATO's expansion, then the timing of the invasion—despite signs that Ukraine's accession was unlikely—becomes difficult to explain. A Washington Post investigation, citing U.S. intelligence reports, revealed that Russia had already formulated a concrete invasion plan by at least October 2021, months before the final pre-war diplomatic efforts. In sum, while Ukraine's NATO aspirations may have been one of several contributing factors, they were likely not the decisive reason behind Russia's decision to launch a full-scale invasion in February 2022.

5   In February 2023, Moldovan President Maia Sandu officially confirmed that Russia was actively working to overthrow the Moldovan government.

6   Throughout 2022, at major international forums such as the St. Petersburg International Economic Forum in June and the Moscow International Security Conference in August, President Vladimir Putin repeatedly asserted that the U.S.-led unipolar system was nearing its end. He proclaimed that Russia, alongside its allies, would

play a leading role in shaping an emerging multipolar international order. This rhetoric continued into 2023; during a meeting with African leaders in August, Putin once again emphasized the necessity of dismantling U.S. unipolar dominance and establishing a multipolar world system. These statements are just a few among many instances in which Putin has publicly framed Russia's geopolitical ambitions in direct opposition to U.S. global primacy.

7   The Pacific and Atlantic Oceans have long functioned as the twin pillars of American global hegemony. As early as 1945, the Institute of Pacific Relations published a report in the Far Eastern Survey emphasizing the strategic necessity of making the Pacific an "American lake." This idea was later reinforced by President Dwight D. Eisenhower in 1954, when he explicitly stated that the United States must ensure that the Pacific remains an "American lake." See among others, Eleanor Lattimore, "Pacific Ocean or American Lake?" Far Eastern Survey Volume, 14, Number 22 (7 November 1945), pp. 313-316; Pacific Historical Review, Volume 55, Number 1 (February 1986).

8   Becoming a global hegemon requires at least three key conditions: first, achieving overwhelming superiority in power, decisively outstripping all rivals; second, gaining universal recognition as the dominant power by all other nations; and third, establishing a global order under its leadership. The United States met all three conditions at the end of the Cold War. It emerged with an unrivaled level of national power, held the prestige of being the victor in the global ideological struggle, and was well positioned to expand its Cold War-era order into a truly global system. By contrast, even if China or Russia were to surpass the United States in raw power, achieving full-spectrum dominance would be an immense challenge. As a result, they would struggle to gain universal recognition as the world's hegemon. Moreover, neither country has put forth a compelling vision for an international order capable of integrating the entire world, particularly liberal democracies.

9   In this context, Confucius' Zhengming (正名) theory, which laid the foundation for Confucianism, offers a relevant perspective. The principle of jun jun, chen chen, fu fu, zi zi (君君臣臣父父子子) emphasizes that every individual must faithfully fulfill their inherent roles. At its core, Zhengming asserts that rulers, by virtue of their position, have an obligation to govern with virtue (de, 德) and propriety (li, 禮). However, the broader Confucian philosophy extends this idea to all members of society, advocating for harmony and order through the fulfillment of one's natural roles and duties.

10 For the Chinese Communist Party and many Chinese citizens, overcoming the 'century of national humiliation' and achieving the 'great rejuvenation of the Chinese nation' is often seen as a more fundamental goal than even economic development. This historical mission, deeply ingrained in China's national consciousness, serves as a driving force behind its domestic policies and assertive foreign strategy. Economic growth, while crucial, is ultimately viewed as a means to an end—one that enables China to reclaim its perceived rightful place as a global power and undo the injustices of the past. This sentiment is well articulated in Peter Hays Gries' China's New Nationalism: Pride, Politics, and Diplomacy (University of California Press, 2004), where he highlights

how nationalism, rooted in historical grievances, plays a central role in shaping modern Chinese political and social objectives.

11 However, this Confucian-based distinction raises several critical questions. First, even if the Tianxia framework claims to be based on authority rather than raw power, it still embeds power-based hierarchies within its structure. Rather than being a true alternative to Western hegemony, it is simply a competing hierarchical vision. More importantly, whereas Western power hierarchies emerge organically from material capabilities, the Chinese authority hierarchy is rigidly structured with China at the top, reinforcing an implicit normative order. This means that even if one accepts the premise that Tianxia offers a more harmonious framework than the Western-led system, its predefined role assignments effectively create class distinctions among nations, with China as the inherently dominant authority. In other words, as long as the Tianxia system is perceived as a normative hierarchy rather than an evolving power dynamic, it ultimately functions as a class-based model of international relations, one in which China maintains permanent primacy.

12 유희복, 「국제질서의 다면성과 '자유주의 국제질서'의 미래: 중국의 시각을 예로」, 『아태연구』 제4호. (2018) pp. 129-169, pp. 153-154.

13 The concept of 'Eurasia' is often traced back to Halford Mackinder, who described Europe and Asia as a single, interconnected landmass he called 'Euro-Asia.' 김동기, 『지정학의 힘: 시파워와 랜드파워의 세계사』 아카넷 (2020), p. 46. However, as a geopolitical construct, 'Eurasia' extends beyond mere geography; it represents a politically and socially defined region subject to varying scholarly interpretations. According to its broadest geographical definition, Eurasia includes not only Northeast Asia but also Southeast and South Asia. In geopolitical discourse, however, 'Eurasia' is often more narrowly defined to encompass Russia, Central Asia, Southwest Asia, and Eastern Europe—regions historically linked to the former Soviet sphere. (See Britannica's definition of 'Eurasia' for reference).

14 Article by Vladimir Putin, "On the Historical Unity of Russians and Ukrainians," Official website of Kremlin (last visited on March 25, 2025).

15 See "The Concept of the Foreign Policy of the Russian Federation," Decree of the President of the Russian Federation, No. 229, March 31, 2023, para. 4 ("More than a thousand years of independent statehood, the cultural heritage of the preceding era, deep historical ties with the traditional European culture and other Eurasian cultures, and the ability to ensure harmonious coexistence of different peoples, ethnic, religious and linguistic groups on one common territory, which has been developed over many centuries, determine Russia's special position as a unique country-civilization and a vast Eurasian and Euro-Pacific power that brings together the Russian people and other peoples belonging to the cultural and civilizational community of the Russian world").

16 Of course, like China and Russia within their respective spheres of influence, the U.S. retained a sense of superiority over other nations, exemplified by the concept of

American exceptionalism. Implicit hierarchies existed in almost all aspects of international relations, with the U.S. at the top. However, rooted in liberalism, the U.S. could not openly promote a class-based hierarchy. Many international institutions shaped under U.S. leadership, such as the UN and its affiliated organizations, operated on a one-state, one-vote system— although in some cases, such as the IMF, the U.S. favored a quota (equity)-based voting structure.

CHAPTER 12

THE END OF THE UNIPOLAR MOMENT
: THE DAWN OF A NEW ERA

Мы уверяемся, что мир всё более и более объединяется,
образуя братское общение,
благодаря сокращению расстояний,
передаче мыслей через воздух.
Увы, не верьте в такое единение людей.

We are told that the world is growing ever more united,
that it is being shaped into a brotherhood by the shrinking of
distances and the transmission of thoughts through the air.
But alas, do not believe in such a union of mankind.

Fyodor Dostoevsky (in The Brothers Karamazov)

The decline of U.S. global hegemony can be traced to three interrelated causes. First is the relative diminution of American power, which has weakened the structural underpinnings of the unipolar system. Revisionist states such as China and Russia have capitalized on this shift, seeking to supplant unipolarity with a more traditional multipolar order. Second is the evolving identity and sentiment of the American public regarding the United States' role in the world. As the costs of global leadership have grown more apparent, public appetite for sustaining the burdens of hegemony has diminished. Third—and closely intertwined with the first two—is the erosion of U.S. hegemonic legitimacy, which once rested securely on the normative appeal of the liberal international order. As that ideological foundation has come under increasing strain, so too has the global consensus underpinning American leadership.

Waning U.S. Dominance

For much of the post–Cold War era, the United States stood as the only nation consistently capable of forging international consensus on major global challenges. Under American leadership, international cooperation flourished across a wide array of domains—from overarching concerns such as free trade, peacekeeping, WMD nonproliferation, and human rights promotion, to more technical issues including intellectual property protection, internet governance, and cybersecurity. This ability to marshal global consensus across such diverse and complex issues was a hallmark of U.S. hegemony.

One of the clearest indicators of its decline is the growing paralysis of the UN Security Council. While the Cold War often saw the Council gridlocked by U.S.-Soviet rivalry, the post–Cold War period marked a shift: the Security Council emerged as a key mechanism for enforcing global stability. It authorized interventions, led peacekeeping operations, and took decisive action on terrorism and nuclear proliferation. Crucially, even when resolutions ran counter to the interests of China or Russia, they rarely exercised their veto power against U.S.-led initiatives[1]— underscoring the uncontested nature of American primacy at the time. However, since 2022, amid Russia's war in Ukraine and intensifying U.S.–Russia–China tensions, the Security Council has become increasingly paralyzed[2]—a visible sign that U.S. hegemony is no longer unchallenged.

The Global Strategic Competition

The decline of American power alone would not have necessarily led to the weakening of the liberal international order, so long as no alternative power could shift the system's gravitational center. In this sense, the relative decline of U.S. hegemony is primarily a consequence of China's rise as a global superpower. The liberal international order was predicated on unipolar dynamics, and China's emergence as a G2 power has fundamentally altered this equation.

1. Trade Disputes

The U.S.–China strategic rivalry formally began in 2017 during President Trump's first term, with the initiation of a trade war. At the time, many dismissed it as a reaction to the persistent U.S. trade deficit with China. Likewise, the U.S. blockade of appointments to the WTO Appellate Body was widely interpreted as frustration with the institution itself.[3] Observers assumed that once Trump's "aberrational" presidency ended, the situation would normalize. But the Biden administration continued and deepened the confrontation, signaling that the trade war was merely the opening salvo in a broader hegemonic contest between two superpowers.

For decades, the United States was the world's top importer and exporter of goods and the leading exporter of services, supported by its technological and industrial prowess. However, the spread of free trade—characterized by tariff reductions and non-discrimination—transformed the U.S. into a persistent net importer. While a surplus in services helped offset the goods deficit, the U.S. last recorded an overall trade surplus back in 1975. Still, Washington supported multilateral trade, not merely for economic reasons but as a pillar of liberal international order.[4]

In theory, free trade promotes comparative advantage: developing countries specialize in labor-intensive goods before transitioning to heavy industries, while developed countries focus on high-tech exports.[5] Many developing nations have adopted government-led export strategies while shielding domestic markets—practices the United States has largely tolerated. China, however, presented a more complex challenge.

China's vast economic potential and state-controlled market had already raised concerns before its accession to the WTO. Recognizing China's non-market economy, WTO members required additional commitments upon its entry, yet these proved insufficient. Despite WTO safeguards, China's accession in 2001 triggered an export surge that devastated U.S. manufacturing. The bilateral trade deficit ballooned from $83 billion in 2001 to $418.2 billion by 2018. China's state-led strategy and technological catch-up, enabled by massive trade surpluses and foreign investment, drew accusations of unfair competition, particularly for subsidized exports and coerced technology transfers.[6]

2. Technological Competition

The conflict soon expanded beyond trade. In late 2018, U.S. sanctions on Huawei marked the beginning of a technological cold war. Washington cited national security risks, accusing Huawei of data theft and ties to Beijing. China condemned the move as an attempt to block its progress in semiconductors and information technology. The dispute quickly broadened to include artificial intelligence (AI) and other advanced sectors. The U.S. began restructuring global supply chains to exclude China, forming economic alliances aimed at curbing Beijing's technological influence.

China, however, is unlikely to be easily contained. Long seen as the "world's factory," a low-cost subcontractor serving Western economies, China began shifting its industrial identity in 2013 when President Xi Jinping declared independent innovation a national imperative.[7] Two years later, the 'Made in China 2025' initiative outlined ambitious targets for domestic production in ten key sectors, from next-gen IT to robotics.[8] China's transformation has been remarkable. R&D spending soared from $33.1 billion in 2000 to over $700 billion by 2022. Its share of global high-tech exports climbed from 31.4% in 2018 to nearly 40% today.

Throughout history, great powers have cemented their dominance by leading the technological revolutions that defined their eras—from harnessing natural energy to steam power, internal combustion, and then electricity. Such technological dominance was long held by the United States. Today, as the Fourth Industrial Revolution unfolds, emerging technologies—AI, big data, the 'Internet of Things (IoT),' biotechnology, quantum computing, space technology, and robotics—are reshaping global power structures. China is uniquely positioned to leapfrog older industrial powers. The 'Wandao Chaoche' (弯道超車) strategy—or "overtaking on a curve"—exploits disruptive transitions to bypass established hierarchies. The electric vehicle (EV) sector is a case in point: as internal combustion becomes obsolete, China has surged ahead in both vehicle production and battery innovation. Except for Tesla, few foreign firms can now compete with China's domestic EV giants.

Military power is also being reshaped. Hypersonic missiles and drone warfare are eroding U.S. naval superiority, challenging the effectiveness of aircraft carriers—the linchpin of American maritime dominance. As China races ahead in defense technologies, the traditional foundations of U.S. military supremacy are coming under increasing pressure.

The U.S.-China tech competition and the broader realignment of international influence will hinge on mastery of the newly emerging innovations that will ultimately determine the next era of economic, military, and geopolitical leadership.

3. The Strategic Recalibration of Middle Powers

Over the past three decades, nearly every nation—save those isolated from the liberal order such as North Korea, Iran, and Syria—was compelled to accept U.S. global leadership. This widespread acquiescence stemmed from America's unrivaled ability to shape the global agenda. But as its dominance wanes and new power centers emerge, cracks are appearing in this consensus.

China's ascent is prompting states to diversify their alignments and reduce dependency on Washington. With Beijing redefining itself as a viable alternative, countries have greater latitude to pursue 'strategic hedging' and maximize their national interests. For many authoritarian regimes, China is an especially attractive partner. Unlike the U.S., which has a history of tying aid and cooperation to democratic norms, China's doctrine of non-interference provides domestic political insulation. Saudi Arabia exemplifies this shift. Once a linchpin of the U.S.-led petrodollar system, Riyadh has deepened ties with Beijing, especially after tensions with Washington over human rights during the Biden administration. Simultaneously, BRICS nations—including China, Russia, and Brazil—are promoting alternatives to the U.S.-dominated SWIFT system and global dollar dependence.

These developments reflect a deeper transformation: the slow but steady erosion of U.S. global hegemony. While Washington still commands systemic influence, China's gravitational pull is reshaping international alignments. The world is entering a prolonged period of contestation over the future of global order—one marked not by American primacy, but by strategic fluidity and multipolar competition.

The Internal Reckoning: America's Waning Appetite for Hegemony

The decline of U.S. hegemony is not solely the result of rising revisionist powers like China; it is also rooted in internal transformations within the United States itself.

Had Washington been willing to shoulder the burdens of global leadership for a few more decades, it might have prolonged its dominance. But the United States has grown weary of the responsibilities that come with global stewardship. In a January 2025 interview, U.S. Secretary of State Marco Rubio remarked, "It's not normal for the world to simply have a unipolar power," signaling a broader acceptance of the return to multipolarity, in which multiple great powers shape the global landscape. Indeed, the unipolar moment that followed the Cold War was never destined to endure—it emerged from a unique and fleeting convergence of historical forces.

During the Pax Americana, the United States did not become the world's policeman by grand design. Rather, it assumed that role almost by default, as the Soviet Union collapsed and no credible challenger remained. Even at the height of its dominance, international relations scholars recognized that U.S. supremacy was a contingent, not permanent, condition. The post–Cold War push to universalize liberal democracy, driven by both neoconservatives and liberal internationalists, was justified as a moral mission and an ideological imperative. Yet two decades of costly military interventions and failed nation-building in the Middle East have exposed the limits of American overreach. Public support for foreign entanglements has plummeted, with growing disillusionment over the human and financial costs of sustaining global leadership. As the United States grapples with rising domestic constraints, its once-unquestioned international authority is visibly fraying.

An old Korean proverb observes: "Generosity comes from a full granary." In international politics, abundance breeds magnanimity. As America's economic preeminence wanes, so too does its willingness to underwrite the liberal international order. The structural shifts driving this retreat are profound. The U.S.-led system of free trade enriched multinational corporations and global financial elites, but it hollowed out domestic manufacturing. As industrial jobs vanished and inequality deepened, political resentment surged—culminating in the new political wave that brought Donald Trump to power in 2016.

The "Make America Great Again" (MAGA) movement encapsulates this broader realignment. At its core, MAGA is a backlash to globalization: a revolt against free trade, open borders, and multilateralism. It champions economic nationalism, technological dominance, military primacy, and an end to what it sees as foreign free-riding. The movement's enduring appeal lies in its promise to prioritize the interests of working-class Americans over those of global capital. This shift in political discourse has made the idea of maintaining global leadership appear increasingly misaligned with national interest. As a result, Washington is showing signs of disengaging from the very multilateral frameworks it once designed and led.

The logic of a hegemon—concerned with system-wide stability—differs fundamentally from that of a dominant power focused narrowly on maximizing its own advantage. In this evolving mindset, cumbersome international institutions are seen as liabilities. A more agile, bilateral approach—one that asserts U.S. interests unilaterally—may prove more attractive. As sustaining global hegemony grows increasingly untenable, the United States appears to be shedding the liberal internationalist belief that global leadership is inherently aligned with its own national interests.[9] In its place, a more pragmatic, realist approach is emerging—one that prioritizes short- to medium-term advantages over long-term system-building.[10]

Even among those in the U.S. who do not explicitly advocate isolationism, pressure is growing for a more restrained foreign policy. Whether the overtly transactional posture of the Trump years becomes the new norm, or whether future administrations pursue a recalibrated version of multilateralism, the trajectory of U.S. grand strategy remains in flux. In any case, if this inward turn continues, it will mark the end of America's role as steward of the liberal international order. Instead of upholding a rules-based system, the United States may settle into the role of a preeminent—but self-interested—global actor.

Despite these shifts, however, the United States still occupies a uniquely privileged position, bolstered by alliances with key regional powers that offer strategic leverage. A more nationalist approach would not necessarily erase America's global influence—but it will redefine the character of its leadership in a more contested, multipolar world.

The Legitimacy Crisis of Liberal Hegemony

The challenge that revisionist powers pose to the liberal international order has always gone beyond traditional realpolitik. At its heart lies a question of legitimacy—an issue inextricably linked to the perceived legitimacy of U.S. global hegemony.

True hegemony is not sustained by brute force alone; it is fundamentally relational. A hegemon must earn recognition of its authority. The United States acquired such status not merely through material dominance but by winning two world wars, rebuilding the postwar international system, and ultimately prevailing in the Cold War. After that, Washington reshaped the global order in its image—embedding liberal values, building institutions, and thereby cultivating a legitimacy that extended far beyond raw power.

In this sense, China's inability to fully supplant the United States is not simply a matter of limited military or economic capability. It also reflects the distinctive nature of U.S. global hegemony, which was based not only on power but also on a normative framework rooted in liberal ideals. By institutionalizing free trade, multilateral cooperation, and legal norms, the U.S.-led liberal international order provided positive-sum incentives for participation. Its durability stemmed from a global consensus that these principles offered a legitimate and effective model of governance. This deeply institutionalized international order gave U.S. leadership a moral and ideological appeal that no state—not even China—can replicate.[11] For many years, therefore, analysts assumed that in the absence of such an alternative, U.S. hegemony—and the order it upheld—would retain its legitimacy.

But that assumption is increasingly under strain. The legitimacy of the liberal order is now contested from within and without. Some of its pillars have already crumbled; others are visibly eroding.

As Washington redefines its global role, the era of multilateral free trade has faded. In its place, protectionism, strategic industrial policy, and bilateral deals have taken root. The abandonment of the 'most-favored-nation' principle[12] in favor of 'reciprocal tariffs'—a concept adopted during the second Trump presidency—marks a fundamental shift away from the liberal trading system the U.S. itself built. Free trade is not the only liberal ideal that the United States is abandoning. America's overall strategic choices now reflect a prioritization of national advantage over systemic stewardship. This realignment entails a departure from other core liberal values that once defined U.S. foreign policy: sovereign integrity, collective security, and the provision of global public goods. Security guarantees and development aid are increasingly contingent on immediate national benefit. In its place, a more transactional approach is taking hold.

Currently, the United States is repositioning itself not as the guardian of the international system but as one of several competing great powers—albeit the most powerful. This perceptual shift was succinctly captured by Singaporean Defense Minister Ng Eng Hen at the 2025 Munich Security Conference. Reflecting on the global upheaval catalyzed by the second Trump administration, he remarked that the United States had ceased to act as a source of "moral legitimacy" and had come to resemble "a landlord seeking rent."[13]

The Waning Ideological Appeal of Liberal Internationalism

In addition, the image of the United States as the global standard-bearer of progressive ideology—once hailed as the harbinger of humanity's rightful future—is facing growing challenges.

For nearly three decades, the U.S.-led liberal international order promoted a form of cosmopolitanism that disseminated liberal values across the globe. Anchored in the principles of individual liberty, human rights, and national self-determination, liberal internationalism reshaped traditional societies, influencing norms of governance and societal organization. This ideological expansion was not merely a byproduct of American power; it was a deliberate strategy to entrench a normative framework that came to be seen—by many—as synonymous with modernity and progress. In numerous societies grounded in religious or nationalist traditions, liberalism's ascendancy sparked friction, often clashing with deeply rooted cultural norms and worldviews.

The effects of this ideological diffusion have been profound. Across the world, growing numbers of people have demanded political freedoms, gravitating toward liberal democracy and rejecting authoritarianism. In places like Taiwan and South Korea, the fear of authoritarian encroachment has intensified popular identification with democratic values. National identity itself has, in many cases, become entwined with the defense of liberal democracy. Even in states where democratic institutions remain fragile, liberal democracy has often been perceived as the ultimate model of political development, reinforcing alignment with the U.S.-led liberal order. American hegemony, in this sense, was legitimized not only through its material power but also through its ideological allure.

Today, however, the legitimacy of liberal internationalism is fraying. Liberal democracy—once heralded as the "End of History"—is revealing deep internal vulnerabilities. Political polarization, ideological fragmentation, and the rise of identity politics have fractured democratic societies, exposing the fragility of their governance. Tribalism and populism have challenged the assumption that liberal democracy is inherently superior or stable. This erosion of internal cohesion has undermined the ideological foundation of U.S. leadership, calling into question its global normative authority.

In an effort to reaffirm U.S. global leadership, President Biden convened the inaugural 'Summit for Democracy' in December 2021, inviting more than 100 countries to recommit to democratic governance both at home and around the world. Subsequent summits in 2022, 2023, and 2024 sought to forge a coalition of democracies capable of countering authoritarian resurgence and reasserting the moral leadership of the liberal world. But these efforts have struggled to produce meaningful results. Democracy has proven to be a tenuous rallying point against authoritarian expansion.

According to *Freedom House*, political rights and civil liberties have continued to deteriorate worldwide, suggesting not a democratic resurgence but a retreat.[14] Far from being marginalized, authoritarian regimes now capitalize on the perceived dysfunctions of liberal democracies, positioning their own models as more stable, pragmatic, and effective. As cultural and political crises engulf many democratic societies, the global appeal of liberalism has weakened. What once stood as a universalizing ideology now faces growing skepticism—not only from authoritarian challengers but also from within the democratic world itself.

Endnotes:

1 From the mid-1980s, when the Cold War was clearly tilting towards the U.S., until its official end in 1991, both China and Russia generally refrained from using their veto power in the UN Security Council. From 1992 to the onset of the 2008 financial crisis, a time when the U.S. fully embraced its role as the global enforcer, the U.S. cast 13 vetoes, while China and Russia together used theirs only seven times over those 17 years. However, the geopolitical dynamics began to shift following the 2008 financial crisis. Between 2009 and the end of the Obama administration in December 2016, China and Russia exercised their veto power 11 times. Even then, they largely avoided direct confrontations with key U.S. strategic interests, opting instead to abstain, for example, on the resolution to establish a no-fly zone over Libya during its civil war. The significant shift occurred in February 2017. From then until September 2022, China and Russia employed their veto power 17 times. This trend was particularly stark between 2020 and 2022, with seven vetoes in just two years, showcasing a much more assertive stance in the Security Council and signaling an increasingly direct challenge to U.S. global influence.

2 The most compelling evidence of the United States losing its grip on the UN Security Council is its recent failure to secure additional sanctions against North Korea. Since 2006, following North Korea's missile tests and its initial nuclear test, the Security Council has passed over ten significant resolutions, starting with Resolutions 1695 and 1718, imposing sanctions. In 2013, Resolution 2094 banned the export of aviation fuel to North Korea, and by 2017, Resolutions 2375 and 2397 further tightened sanctions, including restrictions on oil and refined petroleum products, in response to North Korea's sixth nuclear test. Until 2017, both Russia and China had, at least officially, complied with U.S.-led sanction demands, taking symbolic steps like cutting off oil and petroleum exports post-resolution. However, 2022 marked a significant change; despite the escalating threat from North Korea's nuclear and missile programs, no new UNSC resolution to impose sanctions was adopted. The only resolution passed that year related to North Korea—Resolution 2627—merely extended the mandate of the panel monitoring Pyongyang's nuclear activities. In sharp contrast, the UN General Assembly, outside the veto power of the Security Council, overwhelmingly passed a resolution condemning North Korea's nuclear tests, with 179 member states voting in favor on October 28, 2022. This discrepancy starkly illustrates the increasing dysfunction within the Security Council, which now struggles to respond to critical global security issues. Since 2022, this dysfunction has only intensified, highlighting a clear shift in power dynamics within the UN and signaling a decline in U.S. influence. Without a dominant power steering the system, the UN Security Council has struggled to respond effectively even to lower-stakes security crises. A striking example occurred in Haiti in October 2022, when armed gangs seized control of the country's largest fuel depot, effectively paralyzing the nation. Unable to restore order, the Haitian government formally requested UN military intervention on October 7, but China and Russia blocked the effort. Only after UN Secretary-General António Guterres issued a direct humanitarian appeal did the Security Council manage to pass Resolution 2653 on October 21, imposing sanctions on gang leaders—yet military

intervention remained off the table. This paralysis is particularly striking when contrasted with the early 2000s, when U.S.-led liberal hegemony frequently saw proactive humanitarian interventions, often sparking controversy. The current reluctance to act underscores how dramatically the international order has shifted.

3 The belief that the liberal trading system facilitated China's rise became a core grievance fueling the U.S.-China trade conflict (although U.S. dissatisfaction with the WTO predates China's accession to a certain extent). Despite these concerns, the United States long upheld the WTO system, underpinned by the conviction that free trade is a cornerstone of the liberal international order. Historical lessons from the Great Depression reinforced Washington's opposition to protectionism, and the post-Cold War consensus viewed the triumph of free markets and open trade as a key pillar of U.S. global leadership. At the same time, however, the U.S. actively employed trade remedies—including anti-dumping duties, countervailing duties, and safeguards—as well as powerful bilateral instruments such as Voluntary Export Restraints (VERs), to shield domestic industries. VERs, in particular, served as effective tools for securing favorable outcomes through bilateral pressure. But with the establishment of the WTO, VERs were banned outright, and the use of traditional trade remedies became subject to stricter multilateral disciplines. Although the United States reaped substantial gains from WTO rules in areas such as services and intellectual property, its manufacturing base deteriorated rapidly in the decades following the WTO's launch. The economic decline of the Rust Belt became a visible and politically salient issue. In response, Washington increasingly turned to trade remedies it considered legitimate policy tools. However, the WTO's dispute settlement system consistently ruled against U.S. measures. By 2020, the United States had lost every WTO case it faced concerning safeguard measures, and suffered repeated defeats in anti-dumping and countervailing duty disputes. The problem was not that the WTO adjudicators discriminated against the United States, but rather that, as one of the most frequent users of trade restrictions, it was naturally the most frequent respondent in trade disputes. Still, the cumulative effect of these institutional constraints steadily eroded U.S. policymaking autonomy and undermined domestic confidence in the WTO. Most notably, despite over two decades of transformative shifts in the global economy, not a single amendment had been made to the WTO agreements—leaving American grievances to fester unresolved. The Appellate Body attempted to modernize the application of WTO rules through judicial interpretation. Yet Washington increasingly viewed such efforts as impermissible "judicial activism." Even so, until relatively recently, the United States continued to respect the WTO's authority—complying with rulings by repealing domestic legislation, such as the Byrd Amendment, or withdrawing contested trade measures. Over time, however, the twin pressures of industrial decline at home and China's meteoric ascent abroad exhausted American patience. By 2016, trade protectionism had already become a bipartisan consensus. Therefore, some considered Trump's rise to power to be merely an acceleration of a shift that was already underway. Indeed, both Democrats and Republicans were placing an increasing emphasis on protecting domestic industry in trade policy, and the U.S. boycott of the Appellate Body had already begun during the final years of the Obama administration.

4   Free market capitalism and trade liberalization were instrumental in securing America's victory in the Cold War against the centrally planned economies of the communist bloc. There was also a broad consensus that the protectionist policies during the Great Depression of the early 20th century had worsened the crisis. For example, President Franklin D. Roosevelt, along with his advisor Secretary of State Cordell Hull—known for developing the "Hull Formula" used in investor-state dispute settlements (ISDS)—firmly believed that protectionist measures, like the U.S. Smoot-Hawley Tariff, had both triggered and deepened the economic downturn. This conviction significantly shaped the approach of American policymakers for generations. In stark contrast to the Great Depression, where protectionism led to economic catastrophe, both the 1997 Asian financial crisis and the 2008 global financial crisis were ameliorated to some extent by free trade policies, further solidifying America's commitment to a liberal economic order.

5   Free trade enhances economic efficiency by allowing countries to specialize based on their comparative advantage—a principle first introduced by David Ricardo. This means nations should focus on producing goods for which they have the lowest opportunity cost, or the least sacrificed alternative. Specialization according to comparative advantage enables a more productive global allocation of resources and improves overall economic welfare. Take Vietnam, for example—a country with abundant farmland and low-cost labor. These advantages make it well-suited to produce labor-intensive crops like coffee. Meanwhile, Germany, with its advanced technology and skilled workforce, excels in manufacturing high-end machinery. Through free trade, Vietnam can export coffee and earn vital revenue, while importing sophisticated machinery from Germany at a lower cost than producing it domestically. Germany, in turn, benefits from cheaper coffee and can concentrate on its competitive industrial sector. This exchange benefits both sides: consumers enjoy lower prices, better quality, and more variety, while countries experience greater productivity and economic growth.

6   China's remarkable rise within the WTO framework largely stems from its vast economic potential and extensive human resources. However, over the last two decades, it has faced significant criticism, particularly from the United States, for not engaging in fair competition within the global trading system. In her September 2023 CSIS conference speech, the United States Trade Representative Katherine Tai characterized China's unfair trade practice as follows: "This is how certain Members are continuing to skew the playing field, strategically and systematically. They seek to dominate key industrial sectors, promote national champions and discriminate against foreign competitors, massively subsidize key sectors, and manipulate cost structures. And as they become dominant suppliers for many important goods and technologies, they create supply chain concentrations and vulnerabilities—which in turn become levers for economic coercion." See Simon Lester, "Katherine Tai on Chinese Non-Market Practices and WTO Dispute Settlement Reform," *International Economic Law and Policy Blog* (22 September 2023).

7   In 2013, President Xi Jinping, addressing the Chinese People's Political Consultative

Conference, declared: "If one country persistently lags behind another, the fundamental reason is that it has fallen behind in technology. China has no choice but to take the path of independent innovation."

8   China's 'Made in China 2025' initiative set a target of 70% domestic content in ten key sectors - including next-generation IT, advanced materials and robotics - by 2025. This signaled China's determination to move beyond low-cost manufacturing and directly challenge Western technological dominance.

9   Whether one views the U.S. with favor or critique, it is undeniable that over the last three decades, Washington has been held to a unique set of standards different from those applied to other major powers. If the U.S. were judged solely as another great power within an anarchic international system, the widespread disappointment over actions like the Iraq War under President George W. Bush, or the unilateralism during President Trump's tenure, would be less comprehensible. In reality, the global community has assessed the United States not merely on how effectively it navigates as a powerful state but on how responsibly it exercises its hegemonic influence. Even those who decry American exceptionalism have, paradoxically, expected the U.S. to indeed be exceptional.

10 A hegemonic power traditionally sustains its authority by managing the order and enforcing norms within its sphere of influence. In contrast, a dominant power focuses on securing unilateral advantages, selectively engaging with the region to maximize its own interests. This transition indicates that the United States is recalibrating its foreign policy, shifting from the resource-intensive task of maintaining a liberal international order to adopting a more pragmatic and self-serving strategy. This approach aims to preserve U.S. supremacy while shedding the responsibilities associated with global stewardship.

11 To emerge as a true global leader, China would need to articulate and export a compelling set of values, norms, institutions, and visions capable of securing broad international consent. Its inward-looking worldview, however, hampers Beijing's ability to articulate a universally attractive alternative.

12 The Most-Favored-Nation (MFN) principle ensures non-discriminatory trade practices among trading partners. As a cornerstone of trade liberalization, it not only promotes open markets but also acts as a safeguard against the formation of exclusive trading blocs, thereby reinforcing multilateral cooperation in both trade and international relations. Conversely, any erosion of the MFN principle increases the risk of economic fragmentation and encourages trade blocs that could undermine the foundations of multilateralism and weaken its role in global governance.

13 To put this comment in perspective, when Ng Eng Hen made his remark, the international news was saturated with the actions of the second Trump administration, including the imposition of various unilateral tariffs, bypassing NATO allies to negotiate directly with Russia about the Ukraine War, and demanding half of Ukraine's rare

minerals in exchange for previous military support. Additionally, President Trump had repeatedly voiced expansionist ambitions towards Greenland, Canada, and Panama. In particular, many commentators had compared the U.S.'s negotiation with Russia over Ukraine to the Munich Agreement of 1938, where Britain and France negotiated with Germany over Czechslovakia, ultimately allowing Germany to annex the Sudetenland without Czechoslovakia's direct participation in the discussions. The Czech and Slovak foreign ministers, however, rejected these parallels, arguing that the current situation is "completely different" because Ukraine "will and must be at the table."

14 See Freedom House, "Freedom in the World 2024: The Mounting Damage of Flawed Elections and Armed Conflict" (February 29, 2024). The Biden administration also introduced several other international initiatives centered on these so-called 'shared values' or 'like-minds' to build geopolitical partnerships aimed at curbing the influence of authoritarian states. Certain strategic alliances forged by the Biden administration—such as the Quadrilateral Security Dialogue (Quad) among the U.S., Japan, India, and Australia; the AUKUS security pact between Australia, the United Kingdom, and the U.S.; and the U.S.-Japan-South Korea Trilateral Pact—demonstrated notable resilience. The key to their success lay in the fact that their members had intrinsic geopolitical motivations to balance against regional authoritarian influence.

CHAPTER 13

A WORLD WITHOUT HEGEMON

> When environmental changes occur, individuals that are best adapted to the new conditions are more likely to survive and thrive.
>
> Charles Darwin
> (Adapted from The Origin of Species Chapter 4 "Natural Selection")

As the unipolar moment began to show signs of decline, some anticipated a shift away from U.S. dominance toward a more decentralized global system—a 'non-polar' or 'poly-nodal' world[1] in which no single state would hold primacy. In this envisioned order, power would be diffused among states, regional blocs, and even non-state actors. Ad hoc coalitions would tackle global challenges, supplanting rigid alliances and centralized authority. This vision rested on two key assumptions: first, that the United States would remain committed to the liberal order even as its dominance waned; and second, that rising powers such as China and Russia would not embrace reactionary nationalism. Both assumptions have proven false.

Rather than evolving into a cooperative, multilateral system, the international order is reverting to traditional multipolarity, marked by strategic rivalry and zero-sum competition. China and Russia have leaned into aggressive nationalism, while the United States has grown increasingly skeptical of the very liberal values it once championed.

The decline of the liberal international order is poised to trigger a worldwide resurgence of nationalism. Across the globe, nations are indeed turning inward, putting national identity before international cooperation. While each country's foreign policy will continue to reflect its unique geopolitical circumstances, this broader shift toward nationalist sentiment is likely to define the character of the emerging era.

1. United States: From Hegemon to the Most Powerful

At the center of this transformation stands the United States. What many initially saw as a historical anomaly—Donald Trump's election in 2016—has, with his return to power in 2025, revealed itself as a harbinger of a deeper shift in America's political trajectory. Trump's second presidency marks not merely a change in leadership but a turning point in how the U.S. engages with the world. In this world without a clear hegemon, the direction other major powers take will hinge on how the United States chooses to redefine its role in the decades ahead.

In a Hegemonic Vacuum

The erosion of U.S. global dominance has created a power vacuum, inviting the emergence of new hegemonic contenders. History suggests that great powers, when unrestrained, naturally seek regional dominance—an enduring principle rooted in realist logic. States with long-standing regional influence are now poised to reassert themselves as dominant actors within their spheres.

Optimistically, one might envision a world in which these potential hegemons mutually respect each other's spheres of influence, producing a stable 'balance of hegemony' in place of a global order. But history rarely supports this hope. Even when geography appeared to provide natural buffers, regional hegemons often found themselves on a collision course. Whenever their expansion led to geographical overlaps, rivalries were inevitable. And when these hegemonic rivalries erupted, they tended to persist for centuries. The Roman and Parthian Empires—later succeeded by the Sassanid Persians—were locked in continuous conflict for over 700 years. The Holy Roman and Ottoman Empires engaged in wars spanning nearly three centuries. Unified Chinese dynasties routinely clashed with northern nomadic empires over millennia. These enduring conflicts reveal a recurring pattern: when regional hegemons collide, strategic competition intensifies into prolonged confrontations, with only brief interludes of peace.

In the modern era, technological advances have exacerbated this problem by eroding traditional geographic constraints. Just as British Empire's naval and industrial superiority in the 19th century led to the subjugation of the Mughal Empire and Qing China, today's technological environment ensures that no region is truly insulated from external competition. Modern connectivity and global interdependence make it increasingly unlikely that great powers will confine their ambitions to their immediate peripheries. The United States, even if inclined toward strategic retrenchment, will continue to seek to dominate the Western Hemisphere. Meanwhile, China's Belt and Road Initiative stretches far beyond East Asia into Europe, Africa, and even Latin America. Russia is extending its reach not only into Central Asia and Eastern Europe, but also into Africa and beyond. These overlapping ambitions magnify the risk of strategic friction and geopolitical contestation.

Even the rise of regional hegemons is unlikely to unfold peacefully. No state can consolidate regional dominance without first neutralizing or absorbing its local challengers. As such, aspiring hegemons will first seek to eliminate or subjugate rivals within their spheres of influence, while secondary powers will respond by forming counterbalancing alliances. This dynamic will produce instability and conflict long before any new regional order can be established.

Unchecked regional hegemons also raise the specter of accelerated nuclear proliferation. Unlike in the 19th century, today's technology enables even isolated states to acquire nuclear capabilities. North Korea's nuclear success amid crippling sanctions illustrates this. Technologically advanced nations could arm themselves even more quickly. A U.S. retreat from global security guarantees would undermine the international community's ability to manage proliferation. In the face of the threat of subjugation by an unchecked neighboring power, more states may see nuclear weapons as the only viable safeguard, triggering a cascade of proliferation.[2]

In sum, as U.S. hegemony fades and the liberal order unravels, the world is entering a volatile multipolar era defined by resurgent great-power rivalry, expanding spheres of influence, and the convergence of nuclear, regional, and technological threats—posing an unprecedented challenge to global stability and the future of international order.

Trajectory of U.S. Foreign Policy

Any vision of a post-hegemonic world must begin with an assessment of U.S. foreign policy.

Once relieved of its hegemonic responsibility, the United States must confront the challenge of redefining its global role. Recent developments suggest a decisive break from the post-Cold War consensus. The first Trump administration marked a turning point, openly questioning the utility of existing international institutions. Washington began dismantling key elements of the liberal international order, including its commitment to the WTO and free trade. Despite rhetoric promising the restoration of multilateralism, in practice, the Biden administration preserved many of Trump's policies. It refused to revive the WTO Appellate Body and doubled down on industrial policies that would have previously been inconsistent with the WTO Agreement on Subsidies and Countervailing Measures. The liberalization agenda that once underpinned Pax Americana has now been replaced by strategic economic nationalism.

Looking forward, future U.S. administrations are likely to operate under the implicit assumption of declining American primacy. The focus will shift from global dominance to strategic repositioning. In a sense, the Biden and Trump administrations have pursued a similar overarching goal: to facilitate the United States' transition away from hegemonic leadership while maintaining its global preeminence. Central to this shift is the identification of China as the primary strategic competitor. The divergence lies in how each administration has approached this challenge. While abandoning free trade, Biden attempted to preserve a rules-based international order rooted in liberal democratic norms. In this context, Biden sought to leverage the U.S. alliance network—a key strategic asset that China lacks—to counterbalance Beijing. This approach aimed to maintain American leadership within a restructured global system, even if outright hegemony could no longer be sustained.

In contrast, the second Trump administration appears to have abandoned systemic leadership altogether. Its approach was shaped by a cost-benefit analysis that concluded the burdens of global structural dominance outweighed its benefits. Trump's vision favored a multipolar system in which great powers define and defend their own spheres of influence. Evidence of this shift includes his administration's interest in territorial acquisitions in Canada, Greenland, and Panama—moves aimed at deepening U.S. control over its hemisphere rather than projecting global leadership.

This forceful and at times abrupt withdrawal from systemic stewardship has triggered major disruptions. A deep rift has opened between proponents of the 'America First' doctrine and much of the international community—including U.S. allies and partners. Many Americans have come to see global engagement as a form of international free-riding, while U.S. allies and partners—accustomed to the implicit hegemonic bargain in which the U.S. provided global public goods in exchange for deference—now feel betrayed. Disillusioned, they are beginning to contemplate a once-unthinkable future: one in which they must balance between Washington and Beijing.

The primary beneficiary of America's retreat is China. Guided by its Sinocentric worldview, Beijing ultimately aspires to inherit global leadership. While military and economic power alone may not be sufficient to achieve this goal, systemic and structural influence offers an alternative pathway.

Despite its relentless pursuit of national rejuvenation and great-power status, Beijing officially maintains that it does not seek to challenge or replace the United States as the global hegemon. Nevertheless, it has shown a clear willingness to assume global leadership in specific domains—particularly free trade. During Trump's first presidency, when U.S. trade protectionism surged, Xi Jinping presented China as the new guardian of free trade and globalization. This narrative returned in 2025 following Trump's reelection and the imposition of a new wave of tariffs that destabilized global markets. Xi once again portrayed China as the defender of the liberal trading system, positioning Beijing as a credible alternative to a protectionist United States.

Free trade is not without flaws—especially for communities left behind by globalization—but it remains a system that delivers broad net benefits. Even amid intensifying strategic rivalry, many countries still have strong incentives to preserve a rules-based trading framework. The golden era of liberalization under U.S. leadership may be over, but a more pragmatic trade order could emerge. Such a system would retain many of the benefits of free trade—at least in non-sensitive sectors—while allowing for broader exceptions reflecting the realities of deglobalization and strategic competition. In this evolving architecture, protectionism may still remain the exception rather than the rule. If the United States chooses to step back from this space, the possibility of China stepping in as a structural leader cannot be discounted.[3]

To be sure, China lacks the soft power appeal that underpinned U.S. leadership during Pax Americana. Still, if Washington continues to abandon its leadership role while resorting to unilateralism and coercion, more states—facing an increasingly fragmented international landscape—may turn to Beijing as a counterbalance.

Complexities of Realist U.S. Foreign Policy

A growing sentiment within U.S. foreign policy circles suggests an increasing willingness to accept multipolarity. But this is far from the final chapter. From this juncture, multiple pathways remain open—each with the potential to reshape the global order.

One possibility is that the United States fully embraces multipolarity and begins acting as a traditional great power. The territorial instincts displayed during Trump's second term resembled 19th-century realpolitik. Historically, U.S. foreign policy in that era adhered to a dual logic: isolationism outside its immediate sphere of influence and active expansion within it. This brand of U.S.-style isolationism—dominant for much of American history—could once again define its diplomatic posture in the 21st century.

Yet history also warns that even if the U.S. attempts to retreat from global commitments, power shifts abroad may compel it to reengage. America's departure from isolationism in the 20th century was not voluntary. Despite its firm commitment to the Monroe Doctrine, the United States was compelled to enter World War I due to the escalating geopolitical turmoil in Europe. Afterward, Washington attempted to pull back again, only to be drawn into global conflict once more. Notably, had the U.S. adopted a more proactive foreign policy in the interwar period, the outbreak of World War II might have been averted.

Compared to the early 20th century, today's geopolitical landscape presents even greater challenges to such a binary foreign policy. In an era of unprecedented global interconnectivity, nearly every international development affects the United States in some way. While certain crises will demand immediate attention due to their strategic implications, even seemingly minor issues can accumulate over time, creating a 'salami-slice' effect. A purely reactive foreign policy would fail to address such gradual shifts until they escalate into full-fledged crises.

To navigate this complexity, the U.S. must articulate clear foreign policy standards that can guide the degree of its international engagement. In a January 2025 interview, Secretary Rubio summarized the guiding principle: "Where our interests align, that's where you have partnerships and alliances; where our differences are not aligned, that is where the job of diplomacy is to prevent conflict while still furthering our national interests." This reaffirmation of national interest as the bedrock of U.S. foreign policy raises a critical question: What exactly constitutes the U.S. national interest?

A foundational element of national interest is the concept of 'vital interests,' which evolve in response to shifts in national power and the international environment. During the Cold War, Washington prioritized the defense of allies as part of the broader ideological struggle against communism. Containing Soviet influence was considered essential to U.S. security, spurring expansive foreign aid initiatives like the Marshall Plan and widespread military support for anti-communist regimes.

Following the Soviet Union's collapse, the United States emerged as the world's only superpower. In the absence of a great-power rival, Washington pivoted toward shaping a liberal global order. In this unipolar moment, U.S. foreign policy emphasized value-driven engagement—advancing democracy, human rights, and environmental goals. The Clinton administration's interventions in Rwanda, Somalia, Haiti, and Bosnia were less about great-power rivalry and more about humanitarian ideals. These priorities were codified in U.S. foreign aid laws that emphasized ethnic and religious harmony, gender equity, and anti-discrimination. Edwin Feulner, founder of the Heritage Foundation, captured this broader ethos by defining U.S. vital interests as "issues that could decisively impact the security and economic *future* of the United States and its citizens."[4] By 1998, an official U.S. national interest report outlined five core priorities for the 21st century: (i) preventing WMD attacks against the U.S. and its forces; (ii) ensuring the survival of U.S. allies and a stable global order; (iii) deterring hostile powers near U.S. borders; (iv) sustaining the functionality of key global institutions; and (v) building constructive ties with potential adversaries.[5] These goals drove policies aimed at managing nuclear proliferation, integrating China into the global system, and discouraging Russia from regressing into authoritarianism. Maintaining U.S. leadership remained central to strategy.

This debate over national interest extended into the 2000s. The George W. Bush administration, especially its neoconservative wing, responded to the 9/11 attacks by embracing an even more assertive, values-based foreign policy. Justified by concerns over WMDs and democracy promotion, U.S. military interventions expanded. Neoconservatives argued that America's security required the global spread of human rights—including protections against racial, religious, and gender discrimination—alongside initiatives to address transnational threats like climate change.[6]

Realists, however, remained deeply skeptical. They rejected the notion that exporting liberal values constituted a vital national interest, dismissing it as "self-image preening." For realists, U.S. grand strategy should center on existential threats, not ideological crusades. They warned that embroiling America in complex foreign entanglements for moral reasons was both unnecessary and self-defeating.[7]

With the decline of U.S. unipolarity, American global priorities are gravitating toward more realist principles. Many of the vital interests that once shaped U.S. engagement now appear obsolete. Increasingly, U.S. foreign policy is driven by pragmatic cost-benefit analyses. Calls for Washington to behave as "one of them" rather than "the one" are growing louder. Given its vast power, a multipolar world is not necessarily a nightmare for the United States—it is a reality to which it can adapt. This shift raises a fundamental question: Will the United States transform into a traditional great power, unmoored from liberal values and moral obligations? For now, the answer appears to be 'no.'

American foreign policy has long been rooted in the ideology of exceptionalism, which has propelled the country to pursue liberal ideals in international affairs. Certainly, the failures of the 'War on Terror' have deeply shaken the belief in universal values. Yet, American exceptionalism itself endures. Even Donald Trump, under the banner of "Make America Great Again," invoked the notion of America's Manifest Destiny during his second term. However, his interpretation deviated sharply from the liberal vision that had underpinned 20th-century U.S. leadership. His foreign policy reflected a 19th-century power-politics mindset rather than a commitment to spreading democracy.

Trump pressed Canada—a core Five Eyes ally—to consider becoming the 51st U.S. state, encouraged Denmark to sell Greenland, redefined the Gulf of Mexico as an exclusively American zone, and pressured Panama over control of the Canal. He appeared to take these proposals seriously. He also bypassed NATO allies to pursue direct negotiations with Russia over Ukraine, disregarding Kyiv's security concerns. These moves echoed the actions of 19th-century great powers far more than those of a liberal hegemon. In effect, Trump's version of 'American exceptionalism' reduced it to a belief in the inherent superiority of the United States—

an ideology indistinguishable from conventional nationalism. But nationalism is not exceptional; it is universal. If American exceptionalism, stripped of its liberal aspirations, devolves into mere nationalism, then U.S. foreign policy risks becoming indistinct from the realpolitik strategies of traditional great powers. History demonstrates that in multipolar systems, nationalism often becomes the principal engine of great-power behavior. If nationalism replaces liberal ideals as the ideological core of U.S. strategy, the world may witness a full reversion to traditional multipolar competition—with consequences history has already made clear.

Yet the United States faces unique constraints. Unlike most great powers, it lacks a unifying ethnic identity or foundational mythology. Built by settlers and sustained through immigration, the U.S. is arguably the most ethnically and culturally diverse society in history. In this sense, it is an empire in modern form. Empires need more than military might or economic prosperity to sustain themselves—they need cultural cohesion and a shared identity. The United States binds itself not just through force, but through common values: liberty, freedom, and a political culture rooted in liberalism.[8] These values, deeply embedded in American society, act as constraints against fully abandoning idealistic commitments for raw power politics.

Consider this: no matter how strategically advantageous it might appear from a realist perspective, it would be virtually impossible to persuade the American public to support the military conquest of Canada or Greenland. That is, unless the foundational values of the republic were fundamentally altered. Such a transformation is not inconceivable; political and cultural fragmentation could eventually erode these principles. But for now, substantial limits remain on how far U.S. foreign policy can deviate from its liberal roots.

In short, while the United States may step back from its role as global steward, it will still distinguish itself from authoritarian great powers. It will continue to play a leadership role—though not as a global policeman—in addressing crises abroad. U.S. history offers ample warning about the dangers of failing to address threats early. This legacy suggests that even in a post-hegemonic era, Washington will remain committed to preventing developments that could endanger its security. This, at least, offers hope that the world will not fully revert to the anarchic conditions of the pre–World War era.

The Future of U.S. Foreign Policy and a More Volatile World

Even without global hegemony, the United States will retain significant capacity to shape regional power dynamics, particularly in strategic vacuum zones. It will thus remain the most influential actor in the international system.

In the absence of hegemonic responsibility, however, Washington is likely to grow more reluctant to shoulder the burdens of stability in regions not central to its national interests. Even where vital interests are implicated, U.S. involvement will increasingly hinge on pragmatic cost-benefit calculations. How the United States responds to the rise of regional hegemons will depend on context: the administration in power, domestic sentiment, economic and military capacity, and the nature of the emerging threat.[9]

In a truly multipolar world, where even the United States will have to practice more measured statecraft, its policymakers will come to view allies as indispensable strategic assets. Effective diplomacy will require cooperation with trusted partners. Accordingly, Washington is likely to adopt a balancing strategy—supporting regional powers to counterbalance rising challengers rather than relying on direct intervention.[10] In situations where neighbors cannot contain an aspiring hegemon alone, the U.S.—though no longer a global hegemon—may still act as an offshore balancer, ensuring no single power dominates its region. This function will help sustain America's role as the most consequential global actor, even in a post-unipolar age.

The true test will arise when indirect balancing no longer suffices. If direct U.S. intervention becomes necessary to prevent the rise of a regional hegemon, the scope of that commitment will determine whether Washington remains a central pillar of global security or recedes into a more constrained role. Meanwhile, any erosion in the credibility of U.S. deterrence will only deepen uncertainty—inviting miscalculation and heightening the risk of conflict.

2. Russia & China
: Rivals and Partners

The relationship between China and Russia is defined by a delicate balance of strategic cooperation and historical rivalry. To understand this dynamic, consider two hypothetical extremes.

In the first scenario, the United States continues to serve as global hegemon, actively defending the liberal international order. Under this condition, China and Russia are likely to maintain their strategic partnership, united by a shared interest in countering U.S. influence, securing strategic autonomy, and advancing a multipolar world.

In the polar opposite scenario, imagine a full-scale American retreat into a neo-Monroe Doctrine—withdrawn from both the Pacific and Atlantic, with strategic assets pulled back to Hawaii and Puerto Rico, respectively, and a complete disengagement from Eurasia. Without the unifying pressure of a common adversary, the rationale for China-Russia cooperation would weaken. Instead, their latent geopolitical competition would likely re-emerge, casting them as each other's primary rivals.

Reality, of course, lies somewhere between these extremes. Accordingly, the China-Russia relationship will continue to oscillate between cooperation and competition, shaped by broader shifts in the global balance of power.

Story of the Two Giants

Despite current alignment, the China-Russia relationship is rooted in centuries of rivalry. Their first significant clash dates back to the 17th century, when Russian explorer Yerofey Khabarov crossed the Amur River into Qing-controlled Manchuria. The resulting military confrontations culminated in the 1689 Treaty of Nerchinsk, which established a formal border. Yet tensions persisted, especially during the late Qing period, when a weakened China faced aggressive expansion by imperial powers—including Russia. Capitalizing on China's vulnerability following the Opium Wars, Russia annexed vast territories in the Far East through the Treaty of Aigun (1858) and the Convention of Peking (1860).

Even during the Cold War, ideological alignment under communism failed to suppress their geopolitical rivalry. As usual, realpolitik prevailed. The most striking episode was the 1969 Sino-Soviet border conflict, fought over territory Russia had taken under the Treaty of Aigun. This incident underscored the enduring importance of geography and historical memory over ideology.

Following the Soviet Union's collapse in 1991, the power dynamic shifted once more. A diminished Russia regarded China's rapid rise with increasing apprehension. Alexander Dugin, a key architect of neo-Eurasianism, even proposed a strategy to redirect China's ambitions southward—and ultimately divide China—as a way to preempt a future confrontation.[11] This reflected a deeper strategic anxiety: for both powers, geographic proximity made long-term competition unavoidable. While their current partnership serves mutual interests, history suggests their trajectories remain divergent. Whether they are allies of convenience or rivals-in-waiting, the tension between cooperation and competition continues to define their relationship.

Before the war in Ukraine, Russia sought to deepen ties with China while maintaining a careful balance in its relations with both Beijing and Washington. Its participation in the China-led Shanghai Cooperation Organization (SCO) signaled a willingness to coordinate against U.S. influence. However, on matters of regional security, Russia relied primarily on its own framework—the Collective Security Treaty Organization (CSTO)—rather than deferring to China's growing presence in Central and Southwest Asia.

This wariness also shaped Moscow's approach to sensitive geopolitical issues. In a June 2021 interview with *NBC*, President Putin sidestepped questions about how Russia would respond to a hypothetical U.S.-China conflict over Taiwan. Russia's ambassador to China, Andrey Denisov, similarly avoided offering a clear stance when interviewed by the Chinese state-owned *Global Times*. Implicit in their evasions was a strategic calculus: in the long run, China—not the United States—was seen as the more plausible competitor.

By 2021, Chinese public discourse and academic discussions increasingly raised questions about Russia's Far Eastern territories, which had been seized during the 19th century. Western analysts also speculated that demographic and economic trends could make Chinese expansion into the Russian Far East likely. Although both Moscow and Beijing dismissed such concerns, the underlying facts were difficult to ignore. The Russian Far Eastern Federal District, encompassing 40% of Russia's landmass, housed only 8 million people. In contrast, China's neighboring provinces—Heilongjiang, Jilin, and Inner Mongolia—boasted populations of 40 million, 25 million, and 24 million, respectively, and cross-border integration continued to accelerate.

Meanwhile, China expanded its influence beyond the Far East, aggressively consolidating its presence in Central Asia—long considered Russia's historical backyard—through the Belt and Road Initiative. These trends fueled Russian unease, even as both sides maintained the façade of strategic harmony.

Moscow avoided committing to a formal alliance with Beijing, preferring a transactional partnership that allowed for flexibility. This hesitation was mutual. Before the Ukraine war, China had formally designated 14 countries as strategic partners aligned with its interests—yet neither Russia nor North Korea made the list. Despite growing cooperation, Moscow remained conspicuously absent from China's inner circle.[12]

As the Biden administration pivoted to great power competition with China, Beijing began to more actively embrace its partnership with Russia. Following a 2021 summit between their leaders, *Global Times* warned the United States that "threatening and pressuring a superpower is a bad choice" and that "turning two of them into enemies is especially unwise." The publication acknowledged America's strategic advantages but dismissed the idea that Washington could prevail by containing both China and Russia at once. In early 2022, Chinese Foreign Minister Wang Yi echoed this sentiment, stating that "if China and Russia stand shoulder to shoulder, the United States cannot win."

Still, even amid this rhetorical solidarity, Russia remained focused on safeguarding its influence in Central Asia, Southwest Asia, and Eastern Europe—quietly working to preserve a regional balance of power that limited China's encroachment. The outbreak of the Ukraine war, however, would soon upend this fragile balance.

The Case of Russia

Undoubtedly, the most pressing challenge facing Russia today is the war in Ukraine and its aftermath. While the conflict has reshaped global power dynamics and tested U.S. influence, it has also exposed the limitations of Russia's military and economic capabilities.

1. Development of the War

Moscow's initial miscalculation proved costly. Expecting a swift victory akin to its 2014 annexation of Crimea, Russia launched a blitzkrieg-style offensive aimed at toppling the Ukrainian government. Instead, it encountered fierce resistance. President Volodymyr Zelensky's decision to stay and lead the defense became a turning point, galvanizing Ukrainian resolve and prompting massive Western military aid.

Despite Russia's overwhelming firepower, Ukraine succeeded in blunting the initial invasion. By mid-2022, Russia had transitioned to a strategy of attritional warfare, relying heavily on massed artillery to wear down Ukrainian forces. That summer, as Russia made incremental gains, Foreign Minister Sergei Lavrov declared regime change a formal objective, asserting that Russians and Ukrainians would "live together in the future." Yet Western support once again proved pivotal. In late 2022, Ukraine launched successful counteroffensives in Kharkiv and Kherson, forcing Russia into strategic withdrawals to preserve its forces. In response, Moscow redeployed its troops to eastern and southern Ukraine, constructing fortified defensive lines to prevent further Ukrainian advances. In September 2022, Putin announced a partial mobilization of 300,000 troops. Simultaneously, Russia held staged referendums in occupied territories to justify their annexation, echoing its 2014 playbook in Crimea.

Reinforced by new recruits, Russia launched a large-scale winter offensive, though Ukrainian forces largely held their ground. In June 2023, Kyiv initiated its long-anticipated counteroffensive, driven by political urgency. With Western support beginning to show signs of fatigue—and the 2024 U.S. presidential election looming—Ukraine faced pressure to demonstrate progress. However, Russia had by then deeply entrenched its positions in eastern Ukraine, laying down extensive trench networks, minefields, and layered defenses. The counteroffensive soon stalled, and Ukrainian forces, having lost momentum, began to struggle against mounting Russian pressure. The West was forced to confront an uncomfortable truth: a decisive Ukrainian military victory was increasingly out of reach.

By 2025, following President Trump's re-election, U.S. pressure on Ukraine to negotiate intensified. Although Ukrainian morale remains high, Kyiv's ability to continue the war without robust U.S. support has become untenable. Europe, while more directly threatened by Russian aggression, cannot replace Washington as Ukraine's principal backer. Meanwhile, with battlefield momentum shifting, Russia approaches negotiations from a position of relative strength.

2. Russia's Challenges

As a result of the war, Moscow has consolidated substantial territorial gains, incorporating resource-rich areas and strategic industrial hubs, while retaining control over millions of pro-Russian inhabitants. Despite such gains, Russia's ability to sustain a prolonged conflict remains uncertain. The war has created profound long-term challenges, and failing to conclude it swiftly could cripple Moscow's broader geopolitical ambitions.

Russia's vast geography and abundant natural resources have proven resilient in a war of attrition. Expanded trade with China, India, and other non-Western partners has offset the effects of Western sanctions. Yet sustaining a war economy requires eventual recalibration; postponing economic normalization will only deepen future dislocation.

The human cost is equally alarming. Russia was already facing a demographic crisis prior to the invasion, and prolonged fighting has compounded the issue. While casualty estimates vary, the number of Russian troops killed or wounded likely exceeds several hundred thousand. To contextualize: in the early 2000s, Russia recorded approximately 1.2 million births annually—half of them male. Given these figures, the war's demographic toll is irreversible.

Geopolitically, Russia now faces deepened isolation along its western flank. Ukraine, once home to a sizeable pro-Russian constituency, has become a hardened adversary.[13] Europe—formerly reliant on Russian energy and largely deferential to U.S. leadership—has decisively pivoted. The accession of Sweden and Finland into NATO has tightened the alliance's grip on the Baltic Sea and northern maritime routes.[14] Even in Central Asia, long regarded as Moscow's strategic sphere, Russian influence has come under strain.[15]

More pressing still is Russia's growing dependence on China. As Europe decoupled from Russian energy, China emerged as Moscow's largest economic partner and critical supplier of dual-use goods, including semiconductors and other military-adjacent technologies. By mid-2023, China's overall exports had declined 5% year-on-year, yet exports to Russia surged by more than 70%. In April 2023, CIA Director William Burns warned that Russia risked becoming China's "economic colony." Indeed, as Western companies exited the Russian market, Chinese firms swiftly filled the vacuum—even in sectors of strategic sensitivity.

One of the most striking developments occurred in May 2023, when Russia granted China access to the port of Vladivostok—a territory ceded by the Qing Dynasty under the 1860 Convention of Peking. Ostensibly, the agreement aimed to streamline trade for China's northeastern provinces, offering a direct maritime outlet in place of overland routes exceeding 1,000 kilometers. Given China's prior unsuccessful efforts to secure North Korean port access (in Rajin and Chongjin) in the 2010s, Vladivostok indeed represented a major strategic breakthrough. Yet the implications extend far beyond trade. For China, access to Vladivostok provides a critical node in bypassing U.S. maritime containment. For Russia, however, it risks relinquishing a vital military asset. Even temporary concessions in such a sensitive region could lay the groundwork for long-term tensions.

As China's influence expands in Russia's Far East, latent historical grievances could resurface—especially given the demographic and economic asymmetry between the two nations. While the Sino-Russian relationship is currently defined by pragmatism, the growing imbalance risks reducing Moscow from equal partner to junior appendage.

Still, like China, Russia plays the long game. Its actions are shaped not only by Eurasianist ideology but also by hardheaded geopolitical calculation. As the war in Ukraine nears a conclusion, Moscow will likely seek to recalibrate its relations with both the West and China. Despite frequent portrayals of post-2022 Russia as Beijing's subordinate, the Kremlin will aim to rebalance its external dependencies once the conflict subsides.

At the same time, Russia is unlikely to allow itself to be used against China in the way that the U.S. once exploited the Sino-Soviet split during the Cold War. China and Russia offer one another complementary strengths: the former brings scale, technology, and manufacturing; the latter supplies energy, raw materials, and food. In contrast, U.S. foreign policy continues to shift with each administration. One may undermine NATO; the next may double down on transatlanticism. Against this backdrop, sustained Sino-Russian cooperation will remain central to countering U.S. influence—particularly if Putin pursues further territorial ambitions in Eastern Europe.

3. Russia's Future

Russia's likely de facto victory in Ukraine will ignite a powerful surge of nationalism. Long governed by a conservative, hierarchical political culture with limited tolerance for dissent, Russia has functioned as a de facto authoritarian state despite nominal democratic institutions.

Even so, liberal voices persisted in the years leading up to the war. In its early stages, limited opposition to the war remained visible. On the day of the invasion—February 24, 2022—Elena Kovalskaya, director of Moscow's Meyerhold Center, resigned, declaring, "It is impossible to work for a murderer and receive a salary from him." The theater itself publicly condemned the war. On February 27, Oleg Anisimov, a Russian delegate at a UN climate panel, issued a rare statement of dissent, apologizing "on behalf of all Russians" and calling the invasion unjustifiable. There have even been reports of open school debate about the war among students in Russia. Dissent also emerged from within the business elite: Mikhail Fridman of Alfa-Bank and Oleg Deripaska of Rusal expressed opposition to the war, with Oleg Tinkov, founder of Tinkoff Bank, calling it "senseless." Protests erupted in major cities.

But this brief window of dissent was swiftly slammed shut. Putin called for a purge of "traitors," resulting in mass arrests, exile of opposition leaders, and the rapid collapse of the anti-war movement. Nationalist rhetoric filled the void. As the war dragged on, public discourse became increasingly radicalized. A perceived victory will only supercharge this trend.

In Russia's official narrative, the war has always transcended Ukraine—it is framed as a civilizational struggle against the West. A military triumph, therefore, will be cast as a defeat of the West itself. In this ideological climate, the resurgence of Eurasianism is all but assured. This points to a deeply concerning conclusion: Russian expansionism is far from over. Moscow's confrontation with the West is likely to intensify. At the same time, to assert dominance across Eurasia, Russia will attempt to reestablish hegemony in Central Asia—potentially bringing it into quiet but growing competition with China, which has steadily expanded its influence in the region.

Still, a new military campaign in the near term would be unwise. The Ukraine war has exposed Russia's limitations, emboldened Ukrainian nationalism, accelerated European rearmament, and strained Russia's economy and demographics. Moscow must now rebuild its military, stabilize its economy, and recalibrate its relations with both China and its Eurasian periphery.

Despite its territorial expanse and resource wealth, today's Russia is not the Soviet Union. It cannot sustain Cold War-style rivalry against a united Europe with four times its population and over ten times its economic size. A more viable path lies in consolidating influence within Eurasia and reshaping the global order through institutions such as BRICS, outreach to the Global South and engagement with any receptive U.S. administration. Only in such a transformed international system—where Eurasianism can flourish independent of Western dominance—would Russia have the strategic space to define its long-term future.

But if a postwar Ukraine remains weak and under-defended, Putin may once again be tempted. Conversely, a robust Ukrainian military, backed by a rearmed and resolute Europe, may yet serve as the ultimate deterrent.

The Case of China

China understands that the United States now regards it as a hegemonic rival—a perception reinforced by a bipartisan consensus in Washington that ensures sustained pressure on Beijing. Without acceding to American demands, China remains steadfast in its pursuit of strategic ascent. This rivalry is poised to endure for the remainder of the century, manifesting across multiple domains: military, technological, economic, and the structural governance of the international system.

This hegemonic contest is unlikely to find resolution absent a decisive victory by one side or a transformative event that fundamentally reshapes the balance of power. In the absence of capitulation, the competition may persist for decades. Alternatively, a single momentous development—such as a successful Chinese occupation of Taiwan despite U.S. opposition—could redefine both the global and regional orders.

1. Taiwan Strait Confrontation

During the era of Pax Americana and China's integration into the multilateral trading system, cross-strait relations remained relatively stable. This equilibrium was particularly evident following the 2008 election of Ma Ying-jeou, the Kuomintang candidate favoring closer ties with Beijing. His presidency ushered in a period of détente, characterized by robust bilateral trade and cultural exchanges. Optimism about eventual unification under the 'one country, two systems' framework grew, wherein Taiwan's capitalist system would coexist alongside China's communist regime—modeled after Hong Kong's governance.

However, by 2010, as China aggressively pursued its "great power ascendance" (大國崛起), skepticism in Taiwan intensified. Growing doubts emerged over the viability of peaceful coexistence under such an arrangement, particularly regarding Beijing's willingness to uphold its promises. A significant portion of Taiwan's population increasingly identified as Taiwanese rather than Chinese, elevating their distinct national identity above pan-Chinese nationalism.

This identity shift crystallized in the 2016 election of Tsai Ing-wen, a Democratic Progressive Party (DPP) candidate advocating for Taiwanese sovereignty. Under her leadership, cross-strait relations deteriorated. Tensions escalated further in 2019, when Beijing's crackdown on Hong Kong's pro-democracy protests provoked strong anti-China sentiment in Taiwan, reinforcing fears that a similar fate could befall the island. Consequently, the 'one country, two systems' model lost all political credibility.

A major inflection point arrived in July 2022 with U.S. House Speaker Nancy Pelosi's visit to Taiwan. In response, China challenged the longstanding de facto median line in the Taiwan Strait through intensified military activity. The People's Liberation Army (PLA) began routinely breaching the line, confronting Taiwanese forces directly. As incursions escalated, U.S. President Joe Biden reiterated—his fourth such statement since August 2021—that the United States would defend Taiwan in the event of a Chinese invasion. Undeterred, Beijing intensified its provocations, including a surge in PLA aircraft entering Taiwan's Air Defense Identification Zone (ADIZ), culminating in December 2022 when a nuclear-capable H-6 bomber penetrated the zone. Shortly thereafter, the PLA conducted military exercises simulating a blockade of Taiwan—widely seen as rehearsals for a future invasion.

CIA Director William Burns later revealed that Xi Jinping had instructed the PLA to be ready for an invasion by 2027, coinciding with the PLA's centenary and the end of Xi's third term. At the March 2023 National People's Congress, Xi reaffirmed that "complete reunification of the motherland is an inevitable requirement for the great rejuvenation of the Chinese nation." Taiwan's Mainland Affairs Council firmly rejected this assertion, reiterating that only Taiwan's 23 million people could determine their future. The following month, Xi visited the PLA Southern Theater Command Navy, urging "innovation in combat concepts and methods" and more "real combat training." By May 2023, Beijing had officially directed preparations for "the worst and most extreme scenarios."

Beijing now faces two potential paths to incorporate Taiwan: political integration or military annexation. The former would require a pro-Beijing administration in Taipei, legitimized by a national referendum. Such an outcome would severely constrain U.S. intervention, enabling China to achieve unification without conflict. However, the erosion of trust following Beijing's handling of Hong Kong, its persistent military threats, and the domestic unrest symbolized by the 2022 'white paper protests' against Zero-COVID policies have made such a political outcome highly unlikely.[16] Taiwanese public opinion overwhelmingly rejects unification under Beijing's terms. This leaves military annexation as China's most feasible option in the near term.

The United States plays a pivotal role in deterring this scenario.

Should Washington concede regional hegemony in the Taiwan Strait and South China Sea, China's maritime dominance would rapidly expand across the First Island Chain. Not only would Taiwan fall under Chinese control, but so too could much of Southeast Asia's maritime domain.[17] From there, Beijing would shift its strategic focus to the Second Island Chain. If China successfully projects power beyond Japan and the Philippines to encompass Guam, it would bring the Western Pacific under its sphere of influence. The South Pacific would be the next target, where China's Third Island Chain strategy seeks to project power into waters near Hawaii—effectively dividing the Pacific with the United States. This would constitute a decisive hegemonic victory for China. Yet, such ambition demands more than an Anti-Access/Area Denial (A2/AD) strategy; it requires a true blue-water navy capable of challenging U.S. maritime supremacy on the open seas. Though originally envisioned for 2040, China remains committed to achieving this by 2049. The rapid expansion of its fleet—including destroyers, cruisers, and aircraft carrier strike groups—reflects this long-term aspiration.

In contrast, the U.S. strategy centers on containing China within the First Island Chain. While American administrations may vary in tone, Taiwan remains the linchpin of Washington's containment posture in the Western Pacific. The Taiwan Strait connects the South China Sea to the south and the East China Sea to the north. If Taiwan were to fall, the defensive line would shift southward, placing Guam and the Philippines on the frontlines. Given the limited military capacity of Southeast Asian states, Australia would be compelled to shoulder a heavier security burden. The AUKUS pact—entailing U.S. nuclear submarine sales to Australia and joint hypersonic missile development—underscores this reality. Similarly, a breach in the East China Sea would place U.S. forces in Japan and South Korea at the forefront. Despite the advanced military capabilities of Japan and South Korea, the most effective U.S. strategy for securing East Asia and the Western Pacific remains deterring Chinese expansion through the defense of Taiwan.

2. Cross-Strait Crisis Control

China's authoritarian structure, centered around Xi Jinping, concentrates power to a degree that invites risk. Unchecked authority can distort information flows, introduce confirmation bias, and lead to strategic miscalculations. Avoiding war in the Taiwan Strait therefore demands a multifaceted strategy grounded in prudence.

U.S. defense circles have repeatedly warned of a potential Chinese invasion by 2027. Meanwhile, Beijing has insisted that any formal move toward Taiwanese independence would provoke immediate military action. The United States views China as preparing for military unification with Taiwan, while Beijing sees Washington's actions as part of a broader containment effort, with Taiwan as the pivotal fulcrum. Mutual distrust, misperception, and self-reinforcing narratives heighten the risk of cold rivalry escalating into hot war.

History teaches that wars often stem from miscalculation. But as the 1962 Cuban Missile Crisis demonstrated, timely communication can prevent catastrophe. The same principle applies to the current U.S.-China-Taiwan triangle. Open and consistent lines of communication among all three parties are essential to avoid spiraling misunderstandings.

While Taiwan's right to self-determination must be respected, strategic realism dictates restraint. In liberal democracies, political power shifts with elections, and losing parties have the opportunity to recover. In authoritarian systems, however, regime survival is paramount and closely intertwined with nationalistic imperatives. For the Chinese Communist Party (CCP), legitimacy rests on fulfilling the nationalist 'Chinese Dream.' Any overt challenge to the 'One China' principle undermines the regime's authority. Thus, a formal declaration of independence—or even the perception of a move in that direction—represents a red line that could trigger military retaliation by China. If Taiwan avoids crossing this threshold, Xi and the CCP retain political flexibility. As Carl von Clausewitz noted, "war is merely the continuation of politics by other means." So long as Beijing sees no political imperative for conflict, the likelihood of war decreases. Effective crisis management therefore requires presenting China with diplomatic alternatives that render military escalation unnecessary.

That said, deterrence remains central to maintaining regional stability. Even if Taiwan avoids crossing China's red lines, domestic pressures or Xi's personal ambitions could prompt military action. To counter this, both Taiwan and the United States must maintain a robust military posture. In March 2023, U.S. Joint Chiefs of Staff Chairman General Mark Milley emphasized that maintaining overwhelming military superiority is the best deterrent against Chinese aggression. A failed invasion would jeopardize CCP rule—making Beijing unlikely to act unless assured of success. Accordingly, Washington and Taipei must build their military strength in the Taiwan Strait and South China Sea, ensuring that the risks of conflict far outweigh any perceived benefit for CCP.

Deterrence must also operate in the economic realm. Russia's war in Ukraine has demonstrated the costs of military aggression. Ukraine's resistance—bolstered by Western military aid—and the resulting economic isolation of Russia have served as a cautionary tale. China, far more integrated into the global economy than Russia, is especially vulnerable to sanctions and capital flight. Its ongoing economic slowdown makes the potential fallout from conflict even more daunting. Emphasizing these economic risks is a vital component of effective deterrence.

Most importantly, the credibility of U.S. security commitments plays a pivotal role. Increasing unpredictability in American foreign policy has raised questions about alliance reliability. Any ambiguity regarding Washington's commitment to Taiwan could embolden China. Historians often cite the exclusion of South Korea from the U.S. defense perimeter in Secretary of State Dean Acheson's 1950 speech as a factor that emboldened North Korea's invasion months later. Similarly, perceived wavering on Taiwan could invite Chinese escalation. Credible U.S. commitments are essential to avoiding such miscalculations.

While these deterrence measures can help preserve the current uneasy equilibrium, they remain stopgap solutions. A long-term resolution to the Taiwan crisis remains elusive. Though the current standoff may hold, the risk of conflict endures unless both sides engage in careful crisis management and sustained diplomatic dialogue.

As history suggests, progress will likely require steady diplomacy, not dramatic breakthroughs. Notably, many Taiwanese still continue to identify, at least partially, as Chinese. This cultural affinity, while a source of friction, also offers a foundation for future reconciliation. If reunification is ever to occur, it must be voluntary—preserving a shared heritage rather than forcing an artificial political union. Avoiding an imposed timeline for action is therefore essential. The key to peace lies in patience, diplomacy, and the foresight to prevent short-term ambition from destroying long-term possibilities.

3. Confused Liberal Democracies
: Amidst Lost Leadership

The concept of 'liberal democracy' is inherently contested and lacks a universally accepted definition, making it difficult to quantify its global prevalence. Depending on criteria used—such as the extent of civil rights, rule of law, separation of powers, and protection of minority rights—estimates of the number of liberal democracies range widely, from about 30 to over 80 countries. Despite these definitional ambiguities, the 2024 Freedom House report marks an eighteenth consecutive year of global democratic decline.[18] In essence, only a relatively small group of Western nations and a few developed East Asian countries consistently meet the threshold for liberal democracy today.

This limited cohort, under U.S. leadership, has played a central role in shaping and sustaining the post-World War II international order. They not only have subscribed to the normative pillars of the liberal international order, but also supported the U.S. global leadership. Thus, when the principal architect of the order begins to withdraw—emphasizing national self-reliance over global stewardship—its dependents face predictable disorientation.

Eroding Liberal Ideals and Resurgent Nationalism

The erosion of liberal values—once the bedrock of democratization and globalization—has coincided with a resurgence of nationalism in many democratic states. This trend, coupled with intensifying multipolar competition, risks reinforcing exclusionary ideologies and adversarial politics, potentially triggering long-term crises of national identity.

History underscores liberalism's enduring ideological appeal. The end of the Cold War signaled liberalism's victory over communism, and the subsequent 'unipolar moment' briefly suggested its global dominance. Authoritarian regimes such as Russia, China, Iran, and North Korea, continue to treat liberal values as existential threats. These governments often perceive liberalism's cultural and ideological influence as more destabilizing than military pressure. It is telling that only near-total isolation, as seen in North Korea, has proven effective in resisting its normative reach.

Recognizing liberalism's enduring influence, the Biden administration sought to rebuild a coalition of democracies to counter the resurgence of authoritarianism. While this effort did not result in a formal democracy-versus-autocracy bloc, the prospect of such alignment—reminiscent of a new Cold War—briefly offered a moment of potential ideological consolidation. However, Washington's embrace of an America First doctrine has fractured this continuity.

As the U.S. appears to embrace its own version of multipolarity, even its closest allies—long aligned with American strategy—are now compelled to chart independent courses in an increasingly fragmented geopolitical landscape. As a result, the era of reflexive alignment with American leadership is over.

Revisionist Momentum

Authoritarian powers have moved swiftly to fill the vacuum left by U.S. retreat. China has softened its aggressive wolf warrior rhetoric, presenting itself as a more stable and predictable alternative to the volatile American superpower—or at least as a proponent of reduced dependence on the U.S. Russia, capitalizing on its Eurasian geography, simultaneously invokes the legacies of Soviet socialism and traditionalist values—often couched in racialized and religious terms—while positioning itself as an opponent of Western imperialism. This dual messaging resonates across diverse regions and ideologies.

In contrast, the U.S. has shifted away from universalist rhetoric. Within the new U.S. narrative, authoritarian challenges are viewed as external and peripheral, not intrinsic to America's national interest. This framing also casts the U.S. as a unilateral benefactor, with the international community a passive recipient of its largesse. Yet, in reality, liberal democracies have long functioned as strategic outposts constraining authoritarian advances in ways directly or indirectly aligned with U.S. interests. NATO members contain Russian influence in Europe; East Asian allies balance China's power in the Pacific. U.S. military deployments in these regions reflect mutual security calculations—not mere acts of generosity.

At the heart of this debate lies a pivotal question: Is the U.S. security architecture a benevolent gift or a shared strategic imperative? How Americans answer this question will likely shape the future alignment of liberal democracies in an increasingly volatile world.

Liberal Democracies in a Fractured Future

As global uncertainty deepens, the need for a multidimensional alliance among liberal democracies—a latticework of interlocking partnerships—has never been more urgent. Yet significant doubts remain as to whether these states, grappling with divergent national interests and fraying ideological unity, can forge genuine cohesion grounded in democratic values.

Liberal democracies now stand at a historic crossroads. They retain the capacity to revitalize liberal cohesion by reimagining democratic governance in response to existential threats—climate change, technological disruption, authoritarian resurgence—within a post-hegemonic framework. The Cold War proved their ability to coordinate around shared ideals and strategic necessity. Today, their survival as a coherent bloc will depend on reconciling principled commitments with geopolitical pragmatism. The alternative is a descent into fragmented transactionalism. This would not only dilute liberalism's moral authority but also cede the strategic initiative to regional powers operating under multipolar logic. If nationalist currents within liberal democracies intensify—and if normalized transactional engagement with authoritarian regimes continues—the liberal international order may unravel completely.

Such a rupture would mark a decisive end to the postwar era, and a profound reconfiguration of the global architecture liberalism helped build.

1. Europe

Europe has long been a continent marked by perpetual conflict. Following the fall of the Roman Empire, various ethnic groups and emerging states engaged in near-constant warfare for over a millennium. Europe's internal strife further intensified during the Age of Exploration, the Industrial Revolution, and colonial imperialism—culminating in two world wars. After World War II, however, Europe quietly relinquished its global hegemony. Having once dominated the world through innovation and military power, Europe was left devastated. Confronted with the reality of subordination to the United States and the Soviet Union, it sought a path to autonomy through integration.

In 1946, as the Cold War began to unfold, Winston Churchill delivered his famous "United States of Europe" speech, advocating for continental unity as a means to preserve autonomy in a world shaped by rising superpowers. This vision eventually materialized in the form of the European Union (EU),[19] which achieved monumental success in fostering economic cooperation and political stability.[20]

Yet idealism alone did not bring about this transformation. European integration was largely made possible through American involvement. U.S. military power and economic aid—particularly through the Marshall Plan and NATO—secured Europe's peace from both external threats and internal divisions. These efforts enabled Germany to reunify and reindustrialize, France to reassert its global position, and the Great Britain to stabilize its postwar economy. In essence, it was U.S.-European cooperation that laid the foundations for the EU, transforming a war-torn continent into a cooperative bloc grounded in liberal ideals. Today, however, the United States is scaling back its role in European security, forcing Europe to confront a new era of strategic uncertainty. Without consistent U.S. leadership, European states must recalibrate their security, economic, and political strategies.

Europe's ongoing challenge is twofold: internal fragmentation and external opportunism.

Internally, nationalism is straining the cooperative spirit that underpinned postwar integration. Nationalist movements across the continent are calling for stronger borders and the primacy of national sovereignty—undermining the EU's emphasis on shared governance.[21] This struggle pits national self-determination against the vision of a borderless liberal community.[22]

The EU has already weathered several existential crises in the 21st century, including the Eurozone crisis in 2009[23] and Brexit in 2016. The rise of far-right parties across member states has further fueled speculation about potential disintegration. Were it not for the Ukraine War in 2022—which unexpectedly reignited a sense of European unity—the EU might already be on a path toward fragmentation.

Externally, authoritarian powers are exploiting this flux. Russia, leveraging its energy dominance and appeal to traditionalist values, courts European states skeptical of liberal norms. Meanwhile, China targets trade-dependent economies unsettled by U.S. unpredictability, presenting itself as a stable economic partner. NATO remains a critical deterrent to Moscow's ambitions, but its effectiveness depends on sustained U.S. commitment—an increasingly uncertain proposition.

Europe's response has been uneven. Each EU member pursues its own strategic agenda, often at the expense of continental unity. Reconciling these divergent interests into a coherent strategy remains an immense challenge. During the Cold War, U.S. leadership compelled European unity. In the post-Cold War era, Europe outsourced its security to the U.S., relied on Russian gas for energy, and enjoyed the benefits of affordable Chinese goods.[24] Unburdened by geopolitical pressures, Europe pursued the 'European Dream'—a liberal, supranational ideal centered on social welfare and integration.[25] But looking ahead, Europe's inevitable expansion of defense spending will likely divert resources away from its social-democratic priorities. This shift could gradually erode the liberal values that have long underpinned its political and economic identity. The essential question is whether Europeans will continue to pursue the so-called 'European Dream' amid growing geopolitical and economic headwinds.

As Europe navigates a multipolar world, its future hinges on its ability to adapt. A stronger and more unified Europe could modernize postwar liberal ideals to meet contemporary challenges. It could deepen ties with democratic partners—such as Canada, Australia, New Zealand, South Korea, Japan, or the United States (for that matter)—to sustain a liberal global order. Alternatively, persistent nationalism and increasingly transactional relations with authoritarian states could erode Europe's collective influence, reducing its states to individual actors in a fragmented global landscape.

2. East Asia

As the United States recalibrates its global role, East Asia's leading democracies—South Korea, Japan, and Taiwan—are emerging as pivotal actors in an evolving international order. Long embedded within the U.S.-led liberal system, these nations now face a defining challenge: Can they sustain democratic governance and open markets in a multipolar world, or will shifting power dynamics compel new strategic compromises?

Since World War II, these states have flourished under American leadership. Their economic rise and democratic consolidation were underwritten by U.S. security guarantees and access to global markets. Japan rebuilt from the ashes of war into an economic powerhouse under a U.S.-drafted pacifist constitution, protected by American troops.[26] South Korea transitioned from dictatorship and poverty to a thriving democracy and technological leader, bolstered by U.S. support against North Korean aggression.[27] Despite longstanding tensions with Beijing, Taiwan has emerged as a semiconductor powerhouse with a resilient democracy that relies on American arms and economic ties. Their stability and prosperity have been deeply intertwined with U.S. strategic dominance in the Western Pacific.

For decades, these nations formed a key pillar of Pax Americana, reinforcing regional stability through military alliances and economic interdependence. U.S. bases in Japan and South Korea deterred regional threats, while open markets positioned them as critical nodes in a U.S.-backed global economy. This alignment delivered decades of peace and growth, largely insulated from large-scale conflict.

Today, however, America's shifting global posture introduces new uncertainty. President Trump's assertion that distant conflicts are not central to U.S. interests—and his transactional approach to alliances—undermined long-standing assumptions about American reliability. This has forced East Asian democracies to reconsider their strategic dependencies and recalibrate both their security and economic policies.

At the same time, regional tensions are rising. Economic friction with China—manifested through supply chain vulnerabilities, export controls, and coercive trade practices—complicates their external balancing acts. Longstanding territorial disputes, such as those between Japan and China in the East China Sea, add to the volatility. These democracies must now strike a precarious balance: maintaining diplomatic stability while enhancing deterrence. The larger question looms—can liberal democratic values endure in a region increasingly shaped by authoritarian capitalism, or will security imperatives and economic pragmatism dilute their liberal commitments?

Responses vary. Japan is expanding its defense capabilities and deepening ties with partners like Australia and India, seeking a larger role in regional security while cautiously redefining its pacifist doctrine. South Korea walks a delicate line—enhancing military readiness and alliance coordination while preserving its economic entanglement with China. Taiwan, under unrelenting pressure from Beijing, is doubling down on its democratic identity and global outreach, though its survival ultimately hinges on continued external support.

This strategic recalibration reflects a broader reality: with U.S. leadership in flux, East Asian democracies are pursuing greater self-reliance and exploring new multilateral frameworks. Japan and South Korea are engaging more actively with ASEAN and regional security initiatives, while Taiwan is diversifying its trade relationships to reduce dependence on any single power. While these nations remain vital to U.S. interests—particularly in efforts to contain China's influence—the benefits of alignment are increasingly asymmetric, as Washington prioritizes domestic concerns and global restraint.

East Asia's democracies now stand at a historic crossroads. A sustained U.S. disengagement could push them toward accommodation with regional powers, potentially softening their liberal commitments in exchange for stability. Alternatively, they may forge a more cohesive democratic coalition—leveraging their technological and economic strengths to preserve liberal norms and counter authoritarian momentum.

Their choices will not only shape the future of the Indo-Pacific but also determine whether liberal democracy remains a defining force in the region—or recedes in the face of a more fragmented, pragmatic realignment.

3. Five Eyes

The Five Eyes alliance—comprising the United States, Great Britain, Canada, Australia, and New Zealand—remains the world's most enduring and comprehensive intelligence-sharing network. Its origins lie in secret wartime cooperation between British and American code-breakers at Bletchley Park in 1941, predating even the U.S. entry into World War II. This collaboration was formalized with the UKUSA Agreement in 1946 and later expanded to include Canada (1948), Australia, and New Zealand (both in 1956), forging a unique Anglosphere coalition grounded in shared language, history, and strategic values.

For decades, the Five Eyes symbolized the cohesion of liberal democracies under U.S. leadership.[28] The United States provided the military and technological backbone, while each partner played a vital regional role: Britain served as a European conduit, Canada oversaw Arctic and North Atlantic domains, Australia monitored Asia, and New Zealand covered the South Pacific. Collectively, they countered Soviet influence during the Cold War, tracked global terrorism in the post-9/11 era, and reinforced the U.S.-led international order.

Yet today, the alliance faces growing strains. America's inward turn and increasing focus on domestic challenges have unsettled long-standing assumptions about its commitment to global leadership. Britain is recalibrating its global role amid the realities of Brexit and the war in Ukraine. Canada, economically intertwined with China, faces difficult trade-offs. Australia confronts Beijing's assertiveness in the Indo-Pacific, while New Zealand—traditionally more restrained in security affairs—is reassessing its Pacific strategy in the face of intensifying great-power competition.

Recent developments have tested the alliance's cohesion. In early 2025, reports that Washington was considering expelling Canada from the Five Eyes, despite strong denials from senior U.S. officials, raised concerns about the future of the alliances. While there is no confirmed evidence that the U.S. actually sought Canada's removal from the alliance, such an episode highlights fears of a potential erosion of the mutual respect and solidarity that have long defined the Five Eyes framework.

Despite these tensions, adaptation is underway. Britain and Australia have deepened trilateral defense ties with the U.S. through the AUKUS pact, aimed at enhancing deterrence in the Indo-Pacific. Canada is reinforcing Arctic defense coordination with the United States while maintaining its multilateral posture. New Zealand is cautiously broadening its security partnerships across the Pacific. While intelligence-sharing remains robust, strategic cohesion is increasingly strained as each member recalibrates in response to regional pressures.

The Five Eyes now stands at a crossroads: preserve its foundational pluralism and shared liberal ethos, or drift toward fragmented, interest-driven realignment. Continued U.S. retrenchment could prompt members to pursue pragmatic accommodations—such as Australia's deepening trade with China or Canada's regional prioritization—that risk diluting the alliance's ideological coherence. Alternatively, the network could evolve, adapting its Cold War-era unity to confront modern challenges like cyber threats, disinformation, climate security, and strategic competition, potentially by broadening cooperation with other democratic partners.

Ultimately, the future of the Five Eyes will hinge not on American leadership alone, but on the collective political will of its members to maintain strategic alignment. Whether the alliance adapts or fragments will serve as a bellwether for the viability of liberal alliances in an increasingly multipolar and contested global landscape.

4. The Global South
: A Renewed Geopolitical Middle Ground

The term Global South once denoted nations in the Southern Hemisphere—a geographic reference still broadly applicable, encompassing Latin America, Africa, the Middle East, Central Asia, the Indian Ocean region, Southeast Asia, and the South Pacific. Yet in contemporary discourse, the Global South has evolved beyond geography to reflect a shared geopolitical and geo-economic identity.[29]

Initially used to distinguish developing economies from the industrialized Global North, the term gained traction as a framework for categorizing countries by income level, industrial capacity, and historical experience. Many states in the Global South remain less than fully industrialized. But just as defining is their historical disposition toward non-alignment: rooted in the Cold War-era Non-Aligned Movement, these countries rejected alignment with either the U.S.-led liberal order or its ideological adversaries. As a result, the Global South occupies a complex, often intermediary position in global politics—neither wholly aligned with major power blocs nor entirely removed from them. This lens clarifies why Australia and New Zealand—despite their southern locations—are geopolitically aligned with the Global North, while countries like China, Russia, and Iran often sit outside the Global South framework due to their assertive power politics and alignment in global contests.

Growing Strategic Importance

The Global South's strategic profile is rising as the economic dominance of the Global North wanes. In the 1960s, the United States alone accounted for approximately 40% of global nominal GDP. By 1991, the G7 controlled over two-thirds of global output. Today, the U.S. share has fallen to around 25%, and the G7's combined share has dropped below 50%. Meanwhile, the Global South—home to over 70% of the world's population—is emerging as a vital engine of global economic growth, investment opportunity, and supply chain resilience.

Three main factors are driving the rise of the Global South.

First, the Global South's abundance of critical minerals—lithium, nickel, cobalt, and rare earth elements—makes it indispensable to the Fourth Industrial Revolution. Just as Middle Eastern oil reshaped 20th-century geopolitics, the lithium triangle of Latin America (Bolivia, Chile, and Argentina) is becoming a focal point of 21st-century competition. China has already secured strategic stakes in resource-rich regions, prompting the U.S. and EU to race for access.

Second, low-cost labor remains a major economic advantage. While China's rise as a manufacturing hub was fueled by cheap labor, rising wages have shifted global attention to new labor-rich economies. Although the era of unbridled offshoring has slowed, foreign direct investment remains a powerful driver of industrial development in the Global South.

Third, geopolitical neutrality enhances the Global South's bargaining position. Amid intensifying U.S.-China rivalry and the fragmentation of global supply chains, many Global South countries have chosen to avoid firm alignment with either superpower. By maintaining flexible diplomatic positions, many Global South states have increased their leverage. They engage in trade across all geopolitical factions, leverage strategic concessions, and actively resist binary geopolitical choices.

The Rise of Resource Nationalism

The liberal economic order is in retreat. Multilateral frameworks such as the WTO, ISDS, and the Washington Consensus—once established to constrain unilateral barriers to cross-border trade and investment—are weakening. This erosion has opened a strategic window for the Global South. In response, resource-rich countries in the Global South are asserting greater sovereignty over their development paths.

In particular, they are leveraging 'resource nationalism' not only to drive industrialization and escape the middle-income trap, but also to correct historical patterns of economic dependency rooted in colonial exploitation. Unlike previous industrial revolutions led by advanced economies and multinational corporations, today's transition is marked by a deliberate effort to localize value chains and retain greater economic benefits at home.

Latin America's "lithium triangle"—Bolivia, Chile, and Argentina—exemplifies this trend. Bolivia, for instance, has nationalized its lithium sector, prioritizing state control and forging partnerships with foreign firms only on its own terms, with the goal of developing domestic expertise and industrial capacity. Chile and Argentina have also moved toward greater state involvement, with Chile announcing plans to nationalize its lithium industry and Argentina debating the creation of a state-owned lithium company, although implementation varies by country. These nations are exploring the formation of a lithium cartel akin to OPEC, aiming for greater influence over pricing and technological advancement.

Indonesia, a leading nickel producer, offers a parallel example. The government's export bans on nickel, bauxite, and other minerals are designed to force domestic processing and move up the value chain (desirably to position itself as a global hub for electric vehicle batteries), challenging the multilateral trade rules and directly confronting China's dominance in mineral processing. President Joko Widodo's policies signaled a decisive push for strategic autonomy, with Indonesia envisioning a 'Nickel OPEC' through coordination with other major producers.

This new wave of resource nationalism is not just about controlling raw materials. Countries are increasingly seeking to develop downstream industries: Latin America aims to manufacture batteries and electric vehicles, Indonesia aspires to become an EV battery hub, and Zimbabwe has banned raw lithium exports to foster local production. As one Argentine official put it, "We don't want to sell lithium... We want lithium vehicles," capturing the ambition to capture more value domestically.

The weakening of the free trade order mean multinational corporations can no longer rely on a one-sided system; instead, they must negotiate directly with resource-rich states that now wield greater bargaining power. While this power is not absolute—given the global distribution of critical minerals—it marks a decisive break from the historical role of these countries as mere providers of raw materials.

In this evolving landscape, the Global South faces both opportunity and challenge. Fragmenting supply chains and rising protectionism among major economies have given resource-exporting nations newfound leverage. However, translating this temporary advantage into long-term economic and technological progress will require sustained investment, institutional capacity, and careful management of external partnerships. If successful, this moment could mark a fundamental reordering of the global economic hierarchy, with the Global South playing a far more assertive and independent role.

The Global South's Reckoning: Power Plays and National Dreams in a Multipolar Dawn

The Global South stands at a rare historical inflection point. As the old order recedes and global power becomes more diffuse, these nations have gained unprecedented leverage—economic, geopolitical, and ideological. Yet this shift is fraught with risk. The Global South is far from monolithic. While regional groupings like ASEAN offer some degree of coordination, the broader Global South lacks the institutional cohesion to act as a unified bloc. Resource wealth is unevenly distributed, and conflict-prone or governance-weak states remain vulnerable to marginalization or exploitation. Even for relatively stable, resource-rich nations, successful transformation is not guaranteed. Cheap labor alone cannot sustain long-term growth. Industrial upgrading requires investments in education, infrastructure, and technology—alongside stable governance and sophisticated diplomacy. Escaping the middle-income trap will demand more than just control over raw materials.

Moreover, the erosion of multilateral trade rules may heighten protectionist tendencies among major economies. As the U.S., EU, and China prioritize domestic industry and strategic autonomy, late-industrializing nations may struggle to access high-value global markets. The very same fragmentation that offers the Global South temporary leverage may also limit its long-term ascent.

Indeed, leverage is not destiny. Converting strategic resources and diplomatic flexibility into sustained prosperity and industrial strength will require cohesion, vision, and deft statecraft.

1. Latin America

Latin America, a vast and diverse region extending from Mexico in North America to Argentina and Chile in South America, embodies the Global South's identity as a collective shaped by shared economic struggles and a long history of resisting external domination. The roots of Latin American nationalism run deep, originating in anti-colonial movements against European powers—primarily Spain and Portugal. Iconic leaders such as Simón Bolívar and José de San Martín spearheaded independence efforts in the early 19th century, liberating much of the continent from Spanish rule and forging enduring ideals of sovereignty and self-determination.

The commitment to national autonomy persisted into the 20th century. Notably, Mexico's 1938 nationalization of its oil industry reclaimed control from American and British companies, becoming a lasting symbol of economic self-assertion and defiance. During the Cold War, many Latin American countries, including Brazil and Mexico, pursued non-alignment, seeking to avoid entanglement in the U.S.-Soviet rivalry. While exceptions like Cuba's alignment with the Soviet bloc stand out, the broader regional tendency has been to maintain a degree of strategic independence.

Latin America's strategic importance is amplified by its abundant natural resources, particularly its dominance in lithium—a mineral critical for electric vehicle batteries and renewable energy storage. Nearly half of the world's known lithium reserves are concentrated in the "Lithium Triangle" of Bolivia, Chile, and Argentina. Beyond mineral wealth, the region is home to over 600 million people, with a median age of 28, offering a large and youthful labor force that increasingly attracts foreign direct investment as companies seek alternatives to rising costs in China. Geopolitically, Latin America's relatively neutral stance amid intensifying U.S.-China competition is an asset: countries like Brazil secure technology investments from U.S. firms while also participating in Chinese-led initiatives such as the Belt and Road.

Driven by a nationalist desire to break the historical cycle of exporting raw materials and importing finished goods, Latin American countries are embracing resource nationalism and adopting assertive policies to control their resources and foster local industries. This trend is evident in recent moves to nationalize lithium sectors and restrict foreign corporate access, as well as efforts to form resource cartels and develop domestic value chains.

However, the region faces persistent challenges. Political instability and violence, as seen in Guatemala and Honduras, hinder industrial development, while economic overreliance on external powers—illustrated by Venezuela's substantial debt to China—can undermine autonomy. The waning influence of the United States, which once provided a measure of stability through military and economic support, has contributed to greater regional fragmentation. Issues such as narco-conflicts and political unrest threaten to derail nationalist ambitions, highlighting the tension between ideological aspirations and the practical difficulties of navigating an increasingly multipolar world.

2. Southeast Asia

Southeast Asia—spanning Indonesia, Malaysia, Vietnam, the Philippines, and beyond—stands as a linchpin of the Global South, defined by its economic dynamism and a deep-seated tradition of resisting foreign domination. Centuries of European colonization forged resilient nationalist movements, with leaders like Indonesia's Sukarno not only leading the struggle for independence but also shaping the region's postcolonial identity. Sukarno's pivotal role in the 1955 Bandung Conference helped launch the Non-Aligned Movement, setting a precedent for Southeast Asia's enduring commitment to regional autonomy and a careful balancing of global power interests.

This legacy of strategic autonomy remains central today. Malaysia skillfully navigates security ties with the United States while expanding trade with China. Vietnam, once a Soviet ally, now pursues an independent foreign policy, wary of overdependence on any single power. Such flexibility enables Southeast Asian countries to adapt to a multipolar world, leveraging their growing economic and geopolitical significance while mitigating the risks of great power rivalry.

The region's importance is amplified by its vast natural resources and youthful population. Resource nationalism is now a hallmark of Southeast Asian economic policy. Indonesia's bans on raw nickel and bauxite exports force foreign companies to invest locally, while Vietnam restricts rare earth exports to nurture domestic industries. Malaysia's tighter palm oil regulations further reflect the region's determination to capture more value from its resources. Ambitions for a 'Nickel OPEC' signal a desire to influence global markets, echoing the strategies of oil-exporting nations. Meanwhile, Southeast Asia's population—over 650 million strong, with a median age under 30—offers a dynamic labor force that attracts foreign investment, particularly as companies seek alternatives to China's rising costs.

Geopolitically, Southeast Asia is at the epicenter of U.S.-China competition, especially in the contested South China Sea. The Philippines hosts U.S. military bases, while Cambodia grants China privileged naval access—demonstrating the region's adeptness at engaging both superpowers. China's Belt and Road Initiative has funneled billions into Southeast Asian infrastructure, vying with U.S. efforts to strengthen regional ties. Russia's arms deals with Vietnam add another layer of strategic complexity.

Yet, significant challenges remain. Myanmar's ongoing civil conflict, aggravated by foreign intervention, threatens ASEAN unity. Stark disparities in development—such as Singapore's advanced economy versus Laos's underdeveloped infrastructure—hamper regional integration and stability.

At this crossroads, Southeast Asia's nationalist aspirations face both unprecedented opportunities and daunting obstacles. The region's future influence will depend on its ability to balance external pressures, foster internal cohesion, and translate resource wealth into sustainable development. If successful, Southeast Asia could emerge as a key architect of the Global South's evolving role in the international order.

3. Middle East

The Middle East, stretching from the oil-rich Persian Gulf states such as Saudi Arabia to resource-diverse nations like Jordan and Turkey, is a region where immense wealth coexists with persistent developmental challenges.

Its modern political landscape has been profoundly shaped by nationalism, which emerged in the early 20th century as a secular, anti-imperialist force in opposition to Ottoman and later Western domination. Figures like Egypt's Gamal Abdel Nasser epitomized this movement: his nationalization of the Suez Canal in the 1950s and leadership in rallying Arab states against British and French influence fostered a powerful sense of regional sovereignty.

While the ideal of Arab unity inspired movements across the Levant and North Africa, local ambitions and ideological rifts—between pan-Arabism, socialism, and later Marxism—often led to divergent national paths. Today, these historical legacies continue to shape the region's alignments. Saudi Arabia has long partnered with the United States, Iran has pursued an anti-Western trajectory since its 1979 revolution, and Qatar has maintained a carefully balanced neutrality—reflecting the broader Global South tendency to resist integration into any single bloc.

The Middle East's strategic significance remains anchored in its dominance of global energy markets. Saudi Arabia, Iraq, and other Gulf states collectively control a substantial share of the world's proven oil reserves—Saudi Arabia alone is the region's largest producer and a key player in OPEC, with its production decisions influencing global oil prices. Beyond oil, the region's resource profile is diversifying: Turkey holds 60% of the world's boron reserves, vital for high-tech manufacturing, and Jordan is a major producer of phosphates essential for global agriculture. These assets position the Middle East as a growing player in both traditional and emerging industries.

With a population nearing 400 million—60% under the age of 30—the Middle East offers a sizable labor pool, though skills development remains uneven compared to Asia. This demographic potential is both an opportunity and a challenge for attracting foreign direct investment and fostering sustainable growth.

Geopolitically, the region commands critical maritime chokepoints like the Strait of Hormuz, amplifying its leverage in the ongoing U.S.-China rivalry. The U.S. maintains a significant military presence in the Gulf, while China has invested heavily in regional infrastructure, including $400 million in port projects in Oman and the UAE by 2022, underscoring the Middle East's ability to balance competing superpower interests.

The Middle East also seeks to maintain and increase control over its resource wealth. Saudi Arabia's Vision 2030 initiative exemplifies this movement, having increased its domestic oil refining capacity to 3 million barrels per day by 2023, reducing reliance on raw exports. This strategy echoes the kingdom's founding ideology of controlling its oil destiny through OPEC, which was established in 1960. The UAE has similarly invested $15 billion in hydrogen projects by 2023, aiming to lead the clean energy market. Meanwhile, Jordan imposed restrictions on phosphate exports in 2022 to strengthen its fertilizer industry, reflecting a broader regional push to add value locally.

This resource nationalism intersects with the multipolar landscape—Russia's partnership with Saudi Arabia within OPEC+ led to coordinated oil production cuts in 2023, defying U.S. calls for increased output, while China's trade with Gulf states reached $20 billion in 2022. Iran, in turn, sold $1 billion worth of drones to Russia in 2023, further altering regional power dynamics.

However, the decline of U.S. influence in the region presents significant risks. Many conflicts in the Middle East could spiral out of control without American mediation,[30] as evidenced by the numerous past and ongoing instabilities in the region, with the greatest risk being between Israel and Iran (and its proxies). The lack of advanced technical skills across much of the region limits its ability to transition to high-value industries, leaving nationalist ambitions vulnerable to multipolar instability and internal divisions.

Persistent internal divisions, lagging technical skills, and the Arab League's ongoing struggle to unify disparate states complicate efforts to realize regional ambitions. In this fragmented landscape, the Middle East's future will depend on its ability to balance major-power relationships, invest in technological development, and overcome internal challenges to secure long-term stability and prosperity.

4. Africa

Africa, home to 54 nations and the world's youngest population (around 19 years of age!), epitomizes the paradox of the Global South: immense natural resource wealth alongside persistent developmental challenges. The continent holds a staggering share of global resources—30% of the world's mineral reserves, 12% of oil reserves, and vast deposits of cobalt, lithium, rare earths, and arable land. Yet, for much of its modern history, Africa's potential has been undermined by the legacy of colonial exploitation, which drained wealth and left behind fragmented societies and weak institutions.[31]

Nationalism in Africa gained momentum through visionary leaders such as Kwame Nkrumah, who led Ghana to independence in 1957 and championed pan-African unity and self-reliance, and Nelson Mandela, whose fight against apartheid became a global symbol of resistance to racial and economic oppression. This drive for sovereignty fueled Africa's non-alignment during the Cold War—a stance that endures today as countries like Nigeria and Kenya cautiously avoid entanglement with either U.S. or Chinese geopolitical blocs, prioritizing their own development agendas.

Strategically, Africa's location along critical trade routes, such as the Red Sea and Suez Canal, enhances its global leverage. Both the U.S. and China maintain military bases in Djibouti, underscoring the continent's ability to engage competing superpowers. Africa is navigating a complex multipolar world, attracting billions in Chinese loans and infrastructure projects while also receiving Western aid and investment.

Africa's economic importance is amplified by its mineral wealth. The Democratic Republic of Congo (DRC) controls about 70% of global cobalt reserves, underpinning its status as the world's largest cobalt producer. Zimbabwe's lithium and South Africa's rare earth elements are essential for the global transition to renewable energy and advanced technologies. Resource nationalism is increasingly shaping policy: Zimbabwe banned unprocessed (raw) lithium exports in 2022 to promote domestic processing, and the DRC is intensifying efforts to increase state revenue and local value addition from mining. Nigeria's $12 billion "Decade of Gas" initiative, launched in 2021, aims to boost domestic refining and transform the country into a gas-powered economy by 2023. These moves reflect a broader ideological rejection of colonial-era extraction and a push to retain more value from Africa's resources.[32]

However, the continent's resource wealth has too often fueled the "resource curse"—a cycle where weak institutions, corruption, and rent-seeking prevent resource revenues from translating into broad-based prosperity. Angola, for example, lost $42 billion in oil revenues to corruption since 2002, while conflicts in Somalia and elsewhere have displaced millions and undermined stability. Poor governance, lack of infrastructure, and limited technical skills further constrain Africa's ability to convert its natural capital into sustainable development. Meanwhile, the decline of UN peacekeeping operations, partly due to waning U.S. support, leaves a power vacuum.

Despite these challenges, there are examples of progress. Botswana, for instance, has managed its diamond wealth prudently through strong institutions and transparent policies, investing in infrastructure, education, and health. This highlights the critical role of good governance and economic diversification in overcoming the resource curse and achieving lasting prosperity.

Africa's future hinges on its ability to strengthen institutions, invest in human capital, and ensure that resource wealth is managed sustainably and equitably. Without these reforms, the continent's nationalist vision remains vulnerable to external dependency and internal fragmentation—risks that are heightened in today's competitive, multipolar landscape. Yet, if Africa can harness its vast resources effectively, it holds the potential not only to transform its own fortunes but also to play a decisive role in shaping the global economy of the 21st century.

5. India and Turkey

Even in the Global South, some countries are moving beyond the traditional strategy of balancing between great powers and are now seeking to carve out their own spheres of influence. India and Turkey stand out as prominent examples, each leveraging their geographic, economic, and political strengths to assert regional leadership and shape their neighborhoods according to their own interests.

While absolute national power is important for establishing a sphere of influence, relative power compared to neighboring states is often more decisive. In Latin America, for example, major players like Brazil, Argentina, and Mexico remain constrained by the proximity and dominance of the United States, limiting their ability to act as regional leaders. Similarly, Southeast Asian powers such as Indonesia and Vietnam must navigate China's overwhelming presence, while Central Asian states like Kazakhstan and Uzbekistan remain within Russia's orbit. In contrast, India's dominance in the Indian Ocean[33] and Turkey's strategic position at the crossroads of Europe and Asia[34] provide both countries with unique opportunities to shape regional dynamics.

India, with a population of 1.4 billion, is a pivotal actor in the Global South. Its modern identity was forged through anti-colonial struggle and the leadership of figures like Jawaharlal Nehru, who championed non-alignment and strategic autonomy during the Cold War—a tradition that continues today. India maintains robust ties with Russia through the BRICS grouping, while also engaging in security dialogues with the U.S.-led Quad. Economically, India is bolstered by abundant natural resources, including significant coal and rare earth reserves, and a skilled, youthful workforce (with a median age of 28) that underpins its globally competitive IT sector. India's strategic location along key Indian Ocean trade routes places it at the heart of U.S.-China competition, and its economic nationalism—exemplified by the 'Make in India' initiative—reflects a drive to reduce dependency on foreign powers and build domestic capacity.

Despite these advantages, India faces significant challenges. While rural literacy has improved to 77.5% (from 60%) as of 2023–24, gaps in education and skill development continue to limit the transition of its vast population into a fully skilled workforce. Persistent infrastructure deficits further hinder India's efforts to scale up its industrial capacity and fully realize its demographic dividend. Moreover, India remains at risk of falling into the middle-income trap, where economic growth could stagnate before achieving high-income status. These vulnerabilities could threaten India's long-term developmental goals and aspirations for regional leadership. Geopolitically, its ongoing border dispute with China remains a source of tension, with both countries continuing to strengthen their military presence along the Himalayan frontier. Meanwhile, Russia's increased oil exports to India—often in defiance of U.S. sanctions—highlight the delicate balancing act India faces on the global stage and add further complexity to its foreign policy.

Turkey, with a population of nearly 88 million, occupies a unique geostrategic position straddling Europe and Asia. Its control of the Bosphorus Strait and proximity to multiple conflict zones give it significant leverage over both Western and regional actors. Turkey's nationalist legacy, rooted in the vision of Mustafa Kemal Atatürk, continues to drive its pursuit of strategic autonomy. While a longstanding NATO member, Turkey under President Erdoğan has diversified its partnerships, engaging with Russia and China and refusing to fully align with any single bloc. Turkey's economic ambitions are supported by vast boron reserves and a diversified industrial base, with policies such as 'Vision 2023' aiming to boost domestic value-added industries and defense exports.

Nonetheless, Turkey's balancing act is fraught with risks. Its acquisition of Russian defense systems has strained NATO relations, while deepening economic ties with China introduce new dependencies. Should NATO cohesion weaken or Russian and Chinese influence expand, Turkey could find its strategic autonomy under threat.

Ultimately, both India and Turkey possess the potential to establish influential regional spheres, but their success will depend on their ability to navigate multipolar competition, balance external alliances, and address internal developmental challenges. As global power structures evolve, these countries are well-positioned to help reshape the regional order—provided they can convert their ambitions into sustainable influence without becoming marginalized in a rapidly shifting international landscape.

In Synthesis

Latin America's lithium boom, Southeast Asia's nickel drive, the Middle East's energy transformation, Africa's cobalt ambitions, India's tech ascent, and Turkey's push to capitalize on its boron reserves all share a common thread: a nationalist agenda that rejects the historical role of raw-material exporters. Armed with critical resources and growing labor forces, the Global South is no longer merely a passive supplier to global markets—it is actively reshaping the contours of multipolar globalization.

Geopolitically, the Global South occupies a pivotal position in balancing the interests of competing superpowers. Yet this neutrality—while strategically advantageous—is increasingly difficult to sustain as global powers intensify their scramble for influence. The more multipolar the world becomes, the more pressure is placed on nations to pick sides or risk marginalization.

At the same time, the forces propelling this new assertiveness are shadowed by deep structural challenges. Nationalist ambition alone cannot compensate for persistent internal gaps: limited technological capacity, insufficient education and infrastructure, political instability, and fragile institutions. The retreat of U.S. influence—once a stabilizing if controversial force—often gives way to regional power vacuums, while China's growing presence, especially through debt-financed infrastructure, raises fears of renewed dependency in a different guise.

Fragmentation further compounds these vulnerabilities. Latin America's ideological divides and the institutional weaknesses of the African Union hinder the emergence of a unified Global South voice. While regional cooperation exists in pockets, a coherent strategy for collective advancement remains elusive. Without it, the risk of falling into a renewed middle-income trap or becoming pawns in great power competition looms large.

The non-aligned movements of the Cold War once sought to carve an independent path between rival superpowers. Today, the Global South faces a similar test: whether it can translate its nationalist ambitions and economic leverage into enduring autonomy and influence—or whether it will fracture under the weight of a fractured world order. The outcome will help determine not only the fate of these nations, but the very structure of the global order to come.

Endnotes:

1 See among others, Richard Hass, "The Age of Nonpolarity: What Will Follow U.S. Dominance," Foreign Affairs (May 3, 2008); 곽노필, "2030년 세계는 '다극' 아닌 '다결절'을 향해 간다." 한겨레 (2019.9.16); "ESPAS Global Trends to 2030, the Future of Power in a 'Poly-nodal' World," uploaded in YouTube by the European Parliamentary Research Service (December 6, 2019); Randall Schweller, "Grand Strategy Under Nonpolarity," in Thierry Balzacq & Ronald Krebs (eds.), The Oxford Handbook of Grand Strategy (2021).

2 Some argue that broader nuclear deterrence could stabilize international relations. However, the risks associated with nuclear proliferation are substantial and multifaceted. To begin with, an increasing number of nuclear-armed states would multiply the potential scenarios for conflict, thereby heightening the overall risk of escalation or miscalculation. Furthermore, the likelihood that nuclear weapons could fall into the hands of rogue regimes or non-state actors—including terrorist organizations—would rise significantly. These dangers are further exacerbated by advances in artificial intelligence, cyber warfare, and digital espionage, all of which contribute to greater instability and increase the chances of catastrophic errors.

3 Whether China can serve as the anchor of a liberal trading order, however, remains an open question. Unlike the United States, which led the post-war trade regime, China has never fully opened its domestic market to foreign competition. While its reliance on exports has declined, the Chinese economy remains heavily dependent on external demand. Moreover, Chinese firms—bolstered by extensive state subsidies and chronic overcapacity—have severely undercut foreign industries through indiscriminate dumping. Beijing has also frequently used economic coercion to achieve political ends.

4 See Edwin Feulner, "What Are America's Vital Interests?", The Heritage Foundation (6 February 1996).

5 See America's National Interests report by the Commission on America's National Interests.

6 It should be noted that this approach partly reflected traditional realist concerns. Neoconservatives prioritized securing vital foreign resources (especially oil), countering revisionist regional powers, and expanding the liberal economic order. But they believed that the most effective long-term strategy was to proactively spread liberal values. By shaping global norms in advance, the United States could avoid having to respond to crises after they had erupted. In their view, ideological conversion was a more effective means of securing U.S. interests than mere containment or military deterrence.

7 Still, even conservative realists generally agreed, at least in principle, that promoting America's core values–market economics and liberal democracy–could ultimately serve U.S. security and economic interests. But they remained wary of an overly ex-

pansive approach. From their perspective, an excessive focus on spreading these ideals risked turning U.S. foreign policy into an "international social welfare program," draining resources and diverting attention from more pressing strategic priorities.

8   American exceptionalism, when stripped of its liberal foundations, becomes a precarious and ultimately unconvincing form of nationalism on which to base an expansionist agenda. Historically, expansionist ideologies have relied on some form of legitimizing narrative—whether to spread a superior political model, uplift neighboring regions, or impose order through a presumed rightful hierarchy. Liberal internationalism, Russia's Eurasianism, and China's Sinocentrism all provide such frameworks. Liberal internationalism casts expansion as the advancement of democracy and human rights; Eurasianism positions Russia as the natural guardian of a distinct civilizational space; Sinocentrism imagines China as the moral and cultural center of a hierarchically structured world. By contrast, a version of American exceptionalism divorced from its liberal ethos lacks a coherent ideological justification for either domestic imposition or global ambition. Bereft of moral or philosophical appeal, it invites internal backlash and external resistance, making any attempt at assertive projection costly and unsustainable.

9   The emergence of a regional hegemon undoubtedly challenges U.S. interests, but the concern is especially acute when that hegemon becomes a maritime power. Such a development could undermine the 'freedom of the seas'—a principle the United States has upheld since World War II. Freedom of navigation, taken for granted for decades, is in fact an anomaly in the broader arc of human history. Before the 1982 United Nations Convention on the Law of the Sea (UNCLOS) established a 12-nautical-mile territorial sea limit—formally enacted in 1994—internationally recognized territorial waters extended just three nautical miles from shore. This precedent was based on the 'cannon shot rule,' which dictated that territorial waters stretched only as far as a coastal state's cannons (viz. power) could reach. Historically, maritime boundaries were defined by military power rather than legal frameworks. If U.S.-enforced freedom of the seas were to collapse, the world's oceans could revert to a system where maritime zones are dictated by the naval strength of coastal states. In such a scenario, commercial shipping routes would no longer be determined solely by weather and distance but increasingly by the political and security dynamics between flag states and coastal nations. A more fragmented maritime order would heighten tensions, and contested waters would inevitably lead to clashes. Regional powers would seek to assert control over adjacent seas, undermining the long-standing principle of free navigation. Even if the U.S. were to adopt a more isolationist stance, it would be reluctant to allow such a scenario to unfold. However, how much longer it can guarantee the security of the world's oceans remains an open question. As military technology advances—particularly with the proliferation of hypersonic missiles and autonomous drone warfare—the absolute superiority of the U.S. Navy will inevitably erode, raising uncertainties about the future of global maritime stability.

10 States within the same region as a potential hegemon have inherent security incentives to resist its rise. In Europe, U.S. allies serve as a counterweight to Russia. In the

Indo-Pacific, Japan, Taiwan, and India play a similar role in balancing against China. In the Middle East, Israel and Saudi Arabia work to contain Iran. These states have strong strategic incentives to collaborate with Washington in maintaining regional power equilibrium.

11 Observing the accelerating shift in global power dynamics, with China's continued rise and Russia's limitations becoming clear, Dugin adjusted his earlier views, arguing for a concerted effort between China and Russia to strategically counter the influence of the United States.

12 유상철, "미-중 전쟁 나면 러시아는 어느 편 설까," 중앙일보 (2021.8.9). According to the English version of the Chinese diplomatic statement, prior to 2021, China designated only 14 countries as its so-called 'ironclad friends': Brazil, Egypt, Ethiopia, Kenya, Mali, Malta, Namibia, Pakistan, Romania, Serbia, Tanzania, Yemen, Zambia, and Zimbabwe. However, starting in 2022, China explicitly expanded this designation to include Russia as an 'ironclad friend.

13 Until the annexation of Crimea in 2014, political influence in Ukraine was nearly evenly split between pro-Western and pro-Russian factions. However, following two invasions, especially the war in 2022, it would not be an exaggeration to say that pro-Russian sentiment within Ukraine has been effectively eradicated. The shared sense of community that once bound Ukraine and Russia, rooted in their common Slavic heritage, has dissolved. Indeed, ethnicity is not an irreplaceable foundation for national identity. Yuval Noah Harari, in an article published shortly after the outbreak of the Ukraine war in The Guardian, noted that Ukraine has now cultivated an "anti-Russian" national identity. As the Ukrainian resistance against Russia continues to grow, each act of defiance contributes to Ukraine's evolving history, eventually shaping a national worldview that binds Ukrainians together in shared purpose. See Yubal Harari, "Why Vladimir Putin has already lost this war," *The Guardian* (28 February 2022). As Harari predicted, Ukraine's national identity will likely remain strongly defined by anti-Russian sentiment for the foreseeable future. In such a scenario, even if Russia were to achieve a decisive victory and fully occupy Ukraine, governing the country would be immensely difficult. Moreover, it would be virtually impossible to prevent Ukraine from re-emerging as an independent nation-state.

14 For Russia, which has long struggled with the lack of ice-free ports during winter, securing access to the Atlantic Ocean via the Black Sea (through the Mediterranean) and the Barents Sea (via the Baltic Sea and the Gulf of Finland) is of critical importance. To access the Barents Sea from Saint Petersburg, Russia must carefully manage its relations with Estonia, which forms the southern shore of the Gulf of Finland, and Finland, which forms the northern shore, as well as Sweden, which borders the Baltic Sea. But now that Finland and Sweden had joined NATO, the maritime route from the Gulf of Finland through the Baltic Sea to the Barents Sea fell entirely within NATO's sphere of influence. Although the ongoing melting of the Arctic due to global warming may reduce the strategic significance of the Gulf of Finland and the Baltic Sea for Russia, the NATO membership of Finland and Sweden has led to a situation where all Arctic

states, except Russia, are now NATO members. This shift in the region's security dynamics is likely to negatively impact Russia's position in the upcoming geopolitical competition in the Arctic.

15 Until just a month before the outbreak of the war, Russia's influence over Central Asia remained solid. In January 2022, when anti-government protests erupted in Kazakhstan, China expressed its willingness to offer support through the Shanghai Cooperation Organization (SCO). However, Kazakhstan chose to seek assistance from Russia rather than China. As a member of the Collective Security Treaty Organization (CSTO), which it leads, Russia sent peacekeeping troops to support the Kazakh government. This event underscored that, despite China's significant investments through its Belt and Road Initiative, Russia still held primacy in Central Asia and Eurasia as a whole. However, the situation shifted dramatically after the war broke out. In October 2022, at the CIS (Commonwealth of Independent States) summit in Kazakhstan, Tajikistan's President Emomali Rahmon made an unusually forceful statement in front of President Putin, declaring, "Respect us." Kazakh President Kassym-Jomart Tokayev even refused to hold a bilateral meeting with Putin. In the same month, Kyrgyzstan canceled joint military drills with Russia's CSTO just one day before they were set to take place. Meanwhile, in Southwest Asia, Azerbaijan launched an attack on Armenia, a Russian-backed nation, in September 2022. When Armenia sought military assistance from Russia through the CSTO, Russia, preoccupied with the war in Ukraine, was unable to respond. Armenia's Prime Minister Nikol Pashinyan criticized Putin, accusing the CSTO of failing to protect its members from external threats. By September 2023, Armenia hinted at a shift in its security alignment, holding joint military exercises with the United States. In October 2023, Armenia became a member of the International Criminal Court (ICC), which had issued an arrest warrant for President Putin. As Russia's influence waned in Central Asia and Southwest Asia, China swiftly stepped in. In September 2022, Chinese President Xi Jinping resumed his overseas visits, which had been paused due to the COVID-19 pandemic, with his first stop being Central Asia. Xi held consecutive meetings with Central Asian leaders, emphasizing "independence and sovereignty" and proposing increased involvement in the Belt and Road Initiative. The Central Asian leaders, who had previously been dismissive of Putin, greeted Xi with the highest honors, signaling a clear shift in allegiance. As Russia's de facto victory in Ukraine grew more evident, however, the political climate in Central Asia began to shift once more. At Moscow's 80th Victory Day parade in 2025, all five Central Asian leaders attended—a notable reversal from 2015, when Turkmenistan and Uzbekistan were absent. This time, Turkmenistan not only sent its president but also fielded a marching contingent, signaling the region's renewed, if pragmatic, alignment with Moscow.

16 During the COVID-19 pandemic, China dramatically tightened control over its population through the enforcement of a rigid 'Zero-COVID' policy, locking down entire cities and severely restricting movement. While much of the world pivoted toward a 'living with COVID' approach by late 2021 and early 2022, China maintained its strategy well into the following year, with prolonged lockdowns in major urban centers like Shanghai. Many speculated that the policy would remain in place until Xi

Jinping secured a third term as party leader, reinforcing a political climate in which criticism of the government could lead to detention. On October 13, 2022, just days before the 20th Communist Party Congress, two protest banners appeared on a Beijing overpass. One read: "We want food, not COVID tests; freedom, not lockdowns; truth, not lies; reform, not a Cultural Revolution; elections, not a leader; to be citizens, not slaves." The other called for Xi Jinping's removal. Though swiftly removed, the slogans soon reappeared in public spaces across China. In late November 2022, a deadly apartment fire in Urumqi, Xinjiang—widely attributed to COVID-related barriers that delayed rescue efforts—ignited nationwide protests. Initially aimed at the Zero-COVID policy, the demonstrations quickly escalated into political dissent, with chants such as "We don't want an emperor," "Xi Jinping step down," and even calls for the Communist Party's dissolution. Satirical comparisons between Xi and Adolf Hitler circulated widely. The government responded with force, yet the protests spread rapidly, signaling widespread discontent. Authorities eventually acknowledged that local governments had over-enforced COVID restrictions. After the death of former President Jiang Zemin on November 30, 2022, demonstrations briefly subsided. Following his funeral, the government quietly dismantled the Zero-COVID policy. By January 2023, Chinese authorities had begun discreetly arresting key figures in the so-called White Paper movement. In a conciliatory speech that same month, Xi Jinping emphasized the need for improved communication and responsiveness to the diverse needs of the Chinese people. The protests, especially the symbolic display of blank sheets of paper, revealed a segment of Chinese society with a clear yearning for greater freedoms. Still, while many appeared to favor a return to the more pragmatic governance style of Jiang Zemin or Hu Jintao, most protesters stopped short of demanding the Communist Party's complete overthrow.

17 Control over the South China Sea would give Beijing unchallenged authority over the waters within the Nine-Dash Line. This would allow China to dominate the Strait of Malacca, a vital chokepoint handling 20% of global maritime trade and ranking among the world's three most critical shipping lanes, alongside the Panama and Suez Canals. If China secures de facto control of the strait, it would command the primary maritime route connecting Northeast Asia to the Middle East, Africa, and Europe.

18 *Freedom in the World 2024*, Freedom House (February 2024). See also Larry Diamon, "How to End the Democratic Recession – The Fight Against Autocracy Needs a New Playbook," Foreign Affairs (22 October 2024).

19 During the 1950s, as the Cold War escalated, Western European nations, despite their conflicts a decade earlier, initiated cooperative efforts. The first significant step was the creation of the European Coal and Steel Community (ECSC) in 1951, formed by France, West Germany, Italy, Belgium, the Netherlands, and Luxembourg. Following World War II, coal and steel were vital for rebuilding. The ECSC sought to enhance efficiency in the production, distribution, and procurement of these resources while preventing any single member from dominating them—a key concern for France regarding a recovering Germany. For West Germany, participation in the ECSC facilitated reintegration into the international community. To achieve its objectives, the

ECSC assumed authority over national policies in specific areas, functioning similarly to a modern competition regulator. It had the power to set prices, control production, and supervise the coal and steel sectors across member states. Although some worried about the loss of national sovereignty, the ECSC succeeded. Encouraged by this achievement, the six ECSC members established the European Economic Community (EEC) in 1957. The EEC aimed to remove trade barriers, such as tariffs, and create a unified market for goods, services, capital, and labor. It also introduced joint policies in agriculture, transport, and energy, strengthening Europe's position in global trade negotiations. In 1967, these initiatives led to the formation of the European Community (EC), which combined the ECSC, the EEC, and the European Atomic Energy Community (EURATOM). The EC pursued political and social integration through economic unity. At a time when the United States and the Soviet Union dominated world affairs, European nations recognized the strategic benefits of collective action. Great Britain, historically cautious about such integration, joined the EC in 1973. The end of the Cold War in the early 1990s did not hinder this process; rather, it accelerated it. In 1993, the EC became the European Union (EU). Expansion continued, with Austria, Finland, and Sweden joining in 1995. In 1999, the EU launched the euro as a common currency, accompanied by a shared monetary policy and a cohesive trade framework.

20 The European Union (EU) is distinguished by its supranational structure, which grants it legal authority over its member states. This authority covers not only economic issues but also environmental regulations, consumer protection, human rights, and other areas. Powers not specifically assigned to the EU remain under national control. By 2023, the EU included 27 member states and functioned as a comprehensive supranational entity, supported by its own institutions: the European Commission (executive), the European Parliament (legislature), and the European Court of Justice (judiciary). These bodies enable member states to coordinate national interests into unified policies. The EU aligns closely with Immanuel Kant's concept of a "federation of free republics," as described in Perpetual Peace, emphasizing international law, free movement, and free trade. One measure of its achievement is the absence of armed conflict among member states, a significant departure from Europe's history of warfare. Led by Western European countries such as France and Germany, the EU prioritizes policies on climate change, poverty reduction, gender equality, and social justice. These topics, often divisive within individual nations, gain broader support through EU-level frameworks. As a result, the EU stands out as a leading international organization in addressing global challenges.

21 The Arab Spring uprisings in the early 2010s led to a significant flow of refugees from the Middle East and North Africa into Europe. This movement intensified in 2015 due to the Syrian Civil War, which prompted millions to seek asylum in the European Union (EU). At first, the EU adopted a humanitarian approach, prioritizing the acceptance of refugees. German Chancellor Angela Merkel supported this stance, acknowledging the difficulties of integrating culturally diverse populations but suggesting that sustained effort could strengthen Europe. As refugee numbers grew into the millions, however, challenges emerged. Member states accepting large inflows reported rises

in crime and security issues, prompting widespread opposition to immigration. This reaction challenged the EU's goal of unity and weakened its commitment to open policies. The rise in anti-immigration attitudes also bolstered nationalist movements, increasing the potential for far-right governments to gain influence in Europe.

22 Nationalists have historically viewed supranational organizations like the European Union (EU) with suspicion, arguing that they undermine national sovereignty. As far-right parties gain influence within EU member states, the risk of the EU weakening or fragmenting grows. A significant event occurred in 2016 when the Great Britain voted to leave the EU, a decision known as Brexit. This choice stemmed from concerns over high financial contributions, the arrival of EU migrant workers, and the belief that centralized EU policies limited national control. After Brexit, nationalist attitudes spread across Europe. In Austria, for instance, Norbert Hofer of the far-right Freedom Party proposed a referendum on EU membership, suggesting that the idea of EU dissolution was gaining traction. The increase in immigration and refugee arrivals has shifted political attitudes in Europe, challenging the dominance of liberalism and social democracy. Far-right parties, previously on the margins, have grown in prominence. In 2022, Italy elected Giorgia Meloni, a far-right nationalist, as prime minister. By 2023, even traditionally progressive nations like Finland and Sweden saw far-right parties achieve unprecedented electoral success. When combined with gains by center-right groups, the decline of left-leaning parties becomes more apparent. In Germany, the Alternative für Deutschland (AfD), an anti-EU far-right party, reached second place in polls by July 2023, indicating that the EU faces immediate challenges to its stability. This rise in nationalism threatens the EU's core structure. Nationalism strengthens unity within individual states but often opposes external cooperation, while liberalism prioritizes individual rights and supports cross-border integration. Thus, in effect, liberalism fosters collaboration between nations, whereas nationalism encourages separation.

23 The financial crisis triggered by Greece in 2009 quickly spread to Ireland and Portugal, compelling the EU to implement large-scale financial bailouts. However, the diagnosis of the crisis varied among member states. Less competitive economies blamed Germany, France, and the UK, arguing that these wealthier nations accumulated trade surpluses at the expense of weaker economies. For instance, Germany derived nearly 50% of its GDP from exports, with almost half of that coming from trade within the EU. On the other hand, wealthier EU members resented having to shoulder the debts of weaker economies, viewing the crisis as a result of poor fiscal management and excessive borrowing by those nations. This fundamental divide between creditor and debtor nations would go on to shape many of the EU's internal tensions.

24 In February 2025, French President Emmanuel Macron encapsulated Europe's transitional dilemma in a single remark: "This model, that is saying that you have the Chinese market as an outlet, you have the American security umbrella for our security, and you have cheap Russian gas to be able to produce, forget all three."

25 The term 'European Dream' was popularized by Jeremy Rifkin in his 2004 book, *The*

European Dream: How Europe's Vision of the Future is Quietly Eclipsing the American Dream. In this book, Rifkin contrasts the European approach to life with the American emphasis on individualism and materialism. According to Rifkin, the European lifestyle, unlike the American counterpart, places a strong emphasis on liberal values such as connectivity, inclusivity, respect for human rights, social welfare, and environmental responsibility.

26 After World War II, the United States, through General Douglas MacArthur's occupation administration, prohibited Japan from rearming and imposed a pacifist constitution. Article 9 of the 1947 Japanese Constitution renounced the right to engage in warfare, preventing Japan from maintaining a military. Instead of opposing this restriction, Japan shifted its resources from military spending to economic development. The Korean War, beginning in 1950, supported this shift by positioning Japan as a logistical hub for United Nations forces, generating capital for postwar rebuilding. Following the end of the U.S. occupation, the United States encouraged Japan to rearm to address military balance in Northeast Asia. Japan, citing Article 9, declined full rearmament and instead created the National Police Reserve, which evolved into the Japan Self-Defense Forces (JSDF) in 1954. Prime Minister Ichirō Hatoyama emphasized that the JSDF was limited to basic self-defense. Through its emphasis on economic growth, Japan overtook West Germany in 1968 to become the second-largest economy among non-communist countries. By 1985, Japan surpassed the Soviet Union, securing its rank as the world's second-largest economy, behind only the United States.

27 Following the Korean War, South Korea did not function as a liberal democracy for several decades. A liberal democratic system requires regular power transitions through elections, enabling competition and cooperation between ruling and opposition groups. However, the persistent threat from North Korea fostered an anti-communist stance that dominated politics, allowing leaders to silence opponents by accusing them of communist affiliations. Whether accurate or not, labeling rivals as communists proved an effective political strategy. Historical patterns indicate that politicians often seek to maintain power, with few exceptions. The Syngman Rhee government, particularly in its later terms, shifted toward an anti-communist authoritarian regime. Similarly, Park Chung-hee and Chun Doo-hwan established anti-communism as a core policy, using it to justify suppressing dissent. Despite this authoritarian control, a democratization movement persisted in South Korea. Leaders such as Kim Young-sam and Kim Dae-jung opposed military rule, contributing to the country's transition to liberal democracy by the late 1980s. South Korea stands out as one of the few nations to achieve both industrialization and democratization. Having faced colonial exploitation and a war that left it among the world's poorest countries, South Korea later attained economic growth and democratic governance. This outcome resulted from two main factors: Park Chung-hee's state-led economic policies, which supported industrial development and exports, and the sustained efforts of the pro-democracy movement led by figures like Kim Young-sam and Kim Dae-jung.

28 The Five Eyes alliance is one of the most powerful coalitions in the world today.

Comprising five countries, the alliance controls nearly 20% of the Earth's total land area and accounts for over 30% of world's nominal GDP. With the United States as a key member, the military power of the Five Eyes is unmatched. Additionally, the group holds one of the largest agricultural and livestock production capacity worldwide. In terms of natural resources, the Five Eyes nations possess vast reserves, including crucial minerals essential for the Fourth Industrial Revolution, such as lithium, nickel, cobalt, and copper. Despite their geographic distance—three of the members being continental-sized nations—the Five Eyes are connected by seas that they effectively dominate, granting them significant maritime power. In the context of the U.S.-China great power rivalry, the Five Eyes represent the United States' most formidable alliance asset.

29 For a critical analysis of the term 'Global South,' see Zachariah Mampilly's article, *What 'the Global South' Really Means – A Modern Gloss for Old Divisions*, published in *Foreign Affairs* on April 1, 2025. Mampilly contends that the term serves as a contemporary euphemism for the 'nonwhite world,' perpetuating colonial and racial hierarchies. He argues that while the phrase seeks to unify diverse nations under a shared identity, it oversimplifies nuanced realities, carries historical baggage, and is often exploited by dominant powers, such as China and Russia, for geopolitical advantage, highlighting the intricacies of global inequality.

30 At the conclusion of World War I, Britain and France, under the Sykes-Picot Agreement of 1916, decided to partition the Ottoman Empire, a defeated power, and divide the Middle East between them. This agreement laid the groundwork for the later partitioning of the Ottoman Empire and the creation several new states in the Levant and Mesopotamia, with borders established without consideration of existing cultural, religious, historical, or ethnic distinctions. These divisions contributed to ongoing disputes in the region. The interactions among the four major contemporary powers in the Middle East—Iran, Saudi Arabia, Israel, and Turkey—particularly over Mesopotamia, have remained complex. The presence of multiple influential states in a single region poses inherent geopolitical challenges, which were intensified by the Sykes-Picot Agreement's disruption of established patterns, compounded by ethnic and religious tensions. The United States has not fully resolved these regional conflicts, though no other power has emerged as a viable mediator. The significant military presence of the U.S. Fifth Fleet has, however, contributed to maintaining a degree of stability and order. Without this influence, the potential for increased instability in the region remains difficult to predict.

31 Africa, the second-largest continent after Asia, is the origin of modern humans. Excluding North Africa, often grouped geopolitically with the Middle East, sub-Saharan Africa alone has a population approaching one billion. The continent contains diverse ecosystems and significant natural resources. Despite this, many African countries face persistent economic challenges. In 2014, the United Nations identified 18 of the world's poorest nations, all located in Africa. Anthropologist Jared Diamond attributes this to the continent's arid environment, which complicates large-scale agriculture and livestock farming. These activities are necessary to generate surplus

resources and time for societal development, but their limited feasibility in Africa has constrained progress. Geopolitical analysts Peter Zeihan and Tim Marshall highlight additional barriers, such as the scarcity of navigable rivers and suitable coastlines, which have hindered trade and cultural exchange among African communities. Africa's underdevelopment also stems from historical actions by Western powers. The continent's borders, often drawn as straight lines, reflect colonial decisions rather than natural features or cultural boundaries. In the 19th and early 20th centuries, European nations—primarily Britain and France, alongside Germany, Spain, Portugal, Italy, and Belgium—competed for control of Africa. This rivalry risked escalating into broader conflict, prompting German Chancellor Otto von Bismarck to convene the Berlin Conference from November 1884 to February 1885. Building on his mediation of Balkan tensions in 1878, Bismarck sought to maintain European stability by dividing African territories among the powers based on their existing influence. The resulting borders disregarded local ethnic groups, cultures, and histories, contributing to ongoing conflicts. Post-World War II independence altered Africa's political map, but the Cold War introduced new challenges. The Soviet Union aimed to spread communism, while the United States countered these efforts. Many African nations pursued non-alignment, though avoiding superpower rivalry proved difficult. Political instability made Africa vulnerable to external interference, leading to proxy wars in countries like Angola and Mozambique. Regimes that emerged from this turmoil were often authoritarian, with successive leaders maintaining power through force, perpetuating cycles of instability. After the Cold War, Soviet engagement in Africa declined, and U.S. interest waned as the continent lost strategic priority. That being so, in the early 1990s, the United States supported United Nations peacekeeping efforts, including a limited intervention in Somalia's civil war. This operation, later depicted in the film *Black Hawk Down*, resulted in U.S. casualties and, facing domestic backlash, the Clinton administration withdrew in 1993, deeming Somalia strategically unimportant. Since then, U.S. involvement has largely been limited to economic aid. Africa continues to experience civil wars, coups, and authoritarian rule, with notable incidents in Sudan and Niger in 2023. Regional powers—South Africa, Nigeria, Egypt, and Ethiopia—lack the scope to address the continent's vast challenges. The African Union (AU), established in 2002 with leadership from South Africa and Libya, provides a framework for cooperation, but significant obstacles remain.

32 Globalization extended to Africa, introducing neoliberal policies and attracting private capital from around the world. Western multinational corporations, drawn by Africa's natural resources, established operations on the continent. However, the benefits of these investments often accrued to local dictators who negotiated directly with the corporations, leaving the broader population with limited gains. Without a developed industrial base, African countries relied heavily on exporting raw materials to earn foreign currency. Multinational corporations typically purchased these resources at low costs, processed them abroad, and sold the finished products elsewhere. The prices of these raw material exports were determined by international market rates, placing Africa in competition with other developing regions, such as Latin America and Southeast Asia. As a result, even within a free trade framework, African nations struggled to achieve substantial economic advantages.

33 India, having surpassed China in population in 2023, now stands as the world's most populous nation. Coupled with its status as the seventh-largest country by land area and the fifth-largest economy globally, India's rapid economic ascent strengthens its claim to future great-power status. This convergence of demographic heft, geographic scale, and economic momentum positions India as a potential superpower in the evolving multipolar order. Historically, the Indian subcontinent has been a major contributor to global economic output. Prior to the modern era dominated by the West, Chinese dynasties—such as the Han and Song—often led the world in GDP. Notably, during the mid-17th century, the Mughal Empire reached a level of economic output that, according to estimates by Angus Maddison (OECD, 2003), briefly surpassed that of the Ming and early Qing dynasties, marking the zenith of pre-modern Indian economic and political power. Over time, the Indian subcontinent's economic weight has varied relative to a more consistently unified Chinese state. Still, the region's historical economic prominence provides a foundation for its contemporary ambitions. Geopolitically, India enjoys a distinct advantage due to its central location in the Indian Ocean—a key artery of global trade. Situated at the nexus of maritime routes connecting Europe, Africa, the Middle East, and East Asia, India exerts de facto control over one of the most strategic chokepoints in the world. This includes influence over trade corridors such as the Suez Canal route, as well as emerging initiatives like the International North-South Transport Corridor. Crucially, the Indian Ocean remains relatively uncontested, with no regional power—aside from Pakistan, which relies heavily on Chinese support—capable of challenging India's maritime dominance in the near term. While China presents a long-term strategic challenge through its expanding naval footprint and the Belt and Road Initiative, India's geographic centrality and growing naval capabilities position it as a natural counterweight. In contrast to the United States, which faces direct military competition from China in the Western Pacific, India operates in a comparatively less crowded strategic environment. Its longstanding policy of non-alignment, rooted in Cold War geopolitics, continues to provide diplomatic flexibility—allowing India to engage major powers without being drawn into bloc-based confrontations. India's strategic trajectory hinges not on immediate confrontation but on the gradual consolidation of its economic, naval, and diplomatic influence. Its ability to shape the Indo-Pacific will depend on maintaining internal stability, sustaining economic growth, and navigating the geopolitical implications of China's infrastructure-driven expansionism. In the long term, India's rise will be determined by how effectively it leverages its unique combination of geography, demography, and economic potential within an increasingly competitive global order.

34 The Anatolian Peninsula, encompassing modern-day Turkey, occupies a strategically significant geographic location bridging Europe and Asia. Its position facilitates access to the Balkans, Eastern Europe (including the Black Sea region), the Caucasus, and the Middle East. This connectivity has historically fostered the rise of empires, most notably the Ottoman Empire, which exerted considerable influence over the Islamic world. Istanbul, situated across the Bosphorus Strait, exemplifies this strategic importance. Its location connecting the Black Sea and the Mediterranean has contributed to its enduring status as a major European city. Anatolia serves as a conduit for trade,

energy resources, and agricultural products, linking diverse regions. Turkey's geographic positioning aligns with the concept of a 'pivot state,' a role it has actively pursued. This strategic advantage has been amplified by geopolitical shifts in the region. During the Cold War, Turkey served as a frontline state for U.S. military operations against the Soviet Union. The dissolution of the Soviet Union and subsequent regional instability, including the emergence of independent states in the Caucasus and the weakening of neighboring Middle Eastern powers such as Syria, Iraq, and Iran, have created a power vacuum. The war in Ukraine has further weakened Russia's regional influence. This confluence of factors has positioned Turkey as a dominant regional power. Unlike Iran, which faces regional competition, or Israel, which contends with regional adversaries, Turkey possesses the capacity for regional intervention. Its Islamic identity and potential for Western support provide additional strategic advantages. Turkey maintains diplomatic relations with both Western and Eastern powers, enhancing its geopolitical flexibility. Turkey's political leadership, under President Recep Tayyip Erdoğan, has articulated ambitions for increased regional influence, drawing on the legacy of the Ottoman Empire. This ambition, coupled with Turkey's strategic advantages, suggests a potential for expanded regional hegemony. In summary, Turkey's geographic location, combined with regional geopolitical changes, has created a favorable environment for increased regional influence. The current leadership's ambitions, rooted in historical precedent, further reinforce this trajectory.

CHAPTER 14

MULTIPOLARITY VS. MULTILATERALISM
: WHY GLOBAL CHALLENGES DEMAND MULTILATERALISM

Si debbe considerare che non è cosa più difficile a trattare, né di successo più dubbio, né più pericolosa a maneggiare, che farsi capo nell'introdurre nuovi ordini.

It ought to be remembered that there is nothing more difficult to take in hand, more perilous to conduct, or more uncertain in its success, than to take the lead in the introduction of a new order of things.

Niccolò Machiavelli

Since the end of the Cold War in 1991, the liberal international order has aspired to build a world governed less by raw power and more by diplomacy, international norms, and multilateral cooperation. Anchored in a vision of economic liberalization and the global promotion of human rights, this system was sustained through multilateralism and international institutions that, for the first time in history, significantly constrained the unilateral impulses of great powers. The concurrent rise of the information technology revolution over the past three decades further accelerated globalization, driving exponential economic growth and empowering individuals on a scale never seen before. Yet beneath the surface of globalization lay entrenched structural inequalities. The implicit—and at times explicit—imposition of American-style liberalism sparked resistance from nations with deep-rooted civilizations and distinct cultural traditions.

Now, as U.S. hegemony recedes, the world is not transitioning into an era of peaceful equilibrium but returning to an age of classical geopolitics, marked by regional power rivalries and existential challenges to the liberal order. As a result, the contest over the future of global order has begun in earnest.

Competing Visions for the 21st Century

Major powers are now advancing competing models for the emerging international order, offering a glimpse into the worlds they each seek to shape. The United States and its Western allies had consistently reaffirmed their commitment to a 'rules-based international order'—a contemporary iteration of the liberal international order—as the foundational framework for 21st-century global governance.[1] Because U.S. hegemony was grounded in its ability to shape and enforce the 'rules' of international system, revisionist powers came to see such 'rules-based' order as inseparable from the U.S.-led order itself.

However, under the second Trump administration, the United States appears to have departed from this longstanding position. On February 4, 2025, President Trump suggested that the United States should "take over" the Gaza Strip, transform it into the "Riviera of the Middle East," and permanently relocate its 2.2 million Palestinian residents to other countries such as Egypt or Jordan. When a journalist challenged him by asking, "Take it under what authority?", Trump replied bluntly: "Under the U.S. authority."

Meanwhile, revisionist powers have long advocated for a multipolar world order in which multiple regional systems coexist. Within each of these regional orders, a dominant power holds sway as the central authority—directly challenging the core tenet of liberal internationalism: the diffusion of authority through universal rules and institutions.

Russia, for its part, champions an international system grounded in the primacy of state sovereignty and firmly rejects the ideological dominance of liberalism. Moscow has long contended that the liberal order's ideological hegemony has undermined the UN system, which was originally designed around the principle of sovereign equality among states.[2] The multipolarity Russia promotes is rooted in 'sovereign internationalism,' a vision that opposes the interventionist tendencies of liberalism and seeks to restore national sovereignty as the cornerstone of global governance.[3]

Yet Russia's proclaimed commitment to an 'international law-based order,' anchored in a rigid Westphalian interpretation of sovereignty, is shaped less by legal principle than by power politics.[4] Its behavior reveals a selective application of sovereignty, particularly with respect to states like Ukraine that fall within its perceived sphere of influence. In reality, a multipolar system does not inherently produce stability; it enables only great powers to assert greater autonomy while rendering smaller states more vulnerable to coercion.

China also envisions a multipolar world—one that challenges the U.S.-led liberal or "rules-based" international order.[5] In September 2023, China's Ministry of Foreign Affairs released the *Proposal on the Reform and Development of Global Governance*, stressing the inviolability of "sovereignty and territorial integrity of all countries." Like Russia, China professes support for "an international system with the United Nations at its core, an international order underpinned by international law, and fundamental norms governing international relations based on the purposes and principles of the UN Charter."[6]

Even these seemingly reassuring claims, however, must be interpreted through China's own ideological lens. When Chinese Foreign Minister Yang Jiechi rejected criticism over South China Sea disputes at the 17th ASEAN Regional Forum in July 2010, he unequivocally declared: "China is a big country, and other countries are small countries. And that's just a fact." This remark was not merely an assertion of power—it reflected a deeply rooted worldview. At its core, Confucian political philosophy emphasizes harmony through hierarchy and clearly defined roles. Internationally, China's vision draws from the ancient Tianxia (天下) concept: a hierarchical world order centered around Chinese leadership, in which global governance is based not on legal equality but on normative deference to the central authority of China. In this context, Yang's statement was an affirmation of normative authority—reinforcing the idea that 'big countries' exercise a natural and justified dominance over 'small countries' within China's hierarchical worldview.

For more than a decade, China's so-called 'wolf-warrior' diplomacy—marked by combative rhetoric and economic coercion[7]—largely failed to make its Tianxia-inspired model appealing to the global community. While this approach alienated many states, Beijing is now rebranding itself as a more benevolent and predictable alternative to an increasingly unilateralist America. Whether China can convincingly portray itself as a responsible hegemon remains to be seen. What is clear, however, is that the order China envisions institutionalizes a hierarchical global structure that prioritizes great power authority over equality. And like Russia's model, it offers no resolution to the instability inherent in multipolarity—unless or until China consolidates overwhelming power and reestablishes a form of unipolarity under its own leadership.

At the heart of these rival visions lies a resurgent nationalism intrinsic to the states that promote them. Trump and his "Make America Great Again" movement frame their worldview as essential to preserving 'Western civilization.' Putin positions Russia as the preeminent civilization-state of Eurasia, while Xi emphasizes China's status as the world's only continuously existing civilization-state. Leaders in India and Turkey likewise assert the uniqueness and historical grandeur of their respective civilizations. As universalism recedes, great powers increasingly lean into civilizational narratives, fostering nationalist pride that reinforces exclusionary and divisive politics.

In sum, each of the proposed alternatives to the liberal or rules-based international order ultimately constitutes a return to the traditional multipolar model. While some argue that multipolarity may bring greater fairness and stability, historical precedent offers little support for such optimism. Multipolarity is not novel—it defined most of human history prior to the Cold War's bipolar structure. In such a system, even great powers must navigate shifting alliances, while smaller states seek security through patronage—only to find themselves beholden to the interests of their more powerful protectors. The resulting world is rife with tension, where regional conflicts become arenas for great power rivalry.

The only mechanism known to mitigate oppression and war in such a system is the 'balance of power.' In a world bereft of compelling alternatives, even fleeting peace under a balance-of-power system or hegemonic stability may seem preferable to incessant conflict. But after centuries of geopolitical turmoil and bitter experience, is this truly the best humanity can hope for? If history is any guide, balance of power alone is neither sustainable nor reliable as a foundation for peace. It may serve as a temporary deterrent to catastrophe, but it has never produced enduring stability.

The collapse of the liberal international order without a viable replacement could usher in an era of instability unprecedented in modern times. Moreover, a return to unconstrained great power competition would mean discarding the hard-won lessons of the twentieth century—lessons etched in the devastation of two world wars and the brinkmanship of the Cold War—only to repeat them. The challenge we face is not merely the preservation of a particular order, but the fundamental question of whether the world can transcend the cyclical logic of power politics—or whether we are condemned to relive it once more.

The Limits of Multipolarity in Addressing 21st Century Global Challenges

Beyond its failure to provide a foundation for lasting peace, the most critical weakness of a multipolar system lies in its inherent inability to address global challenges that demand coordinated international cooperation.

Multipolarity often produces policy gridlock, fragmented responses, and geopolitical maneuvering that prioritizes national interests over collective well-being. Yet certain global threats can only be effectively mitigated through genuine multilateral cooperation. One such issue is the prevention of WMD proliferation. The non-proliferation regime functions like a net: the more countries participate, the stronger and more resilient it becomes. Conversely, any state excluded from multilateral cooperation creates a weak link, heightening the risk of proliferation.[8]

In the coming years, the nuclear non-proliferation regime under the Nuclear Non-Proliferation Treaty (NPT) will operate under conditions vastly different from those of the Cold War and post–Cold War periods, when it maintained relative effectiveness. Even under bipolar or unipolar systems, some states succeeded in developing nuclear weapons outside the NPT framework. In a truly multipolar world, however, intensifying security dilemmas across multiple regions could drive several states to pursue nuclear capabilities simultaneously, seeking 'self-help' strategic assurances for survival. With technological advancements significantly lowering the barriers to nuclear development, proliferation could unfold like a chain reaction—triggering a global domino effect. North Korea's successful nuclear program has already demonstrated that such developments are no longer insurmountable. A multipolar order, characterized by strategic uncertainty and shifting alliances, would only accelerate this trend.

Artificial intelligence (AI) represents another urgent challenge that demands global coordination. No longer merely a tool for human use, AI is increasingly replacing human roles across a wide range of sectors. What makes AI particularly concerning is the pace and scale of its development. With unlimited access to data and no need for rest, AI evolves continuously, rapidly outpacing both regulatory frameworks and societal adaptation.

While AI may generate new forms of employment, it is equally evident that exponentially more jobs will be displaced. The rise of deepfake technologies—capable of generating indistinguishable images, voices, and videos—raises serious concerns about misinformation, social unrest, and cybercrime. AI-powered terrorism and autonomous cyberattacks could pose unprecedented security risks, while the integration of AI with the Internet of Things (IoT) will embed it ever more deeply into essential infrastructure and our daily lives. The possibility of AI gaining control over critical societal functions—and even human decision-making—can no longer be dismissed as speculative fiction. The question is not whether AI will surpass human intelligence, but when—and whether it will remain under human control. In May 2023, the Center for AI Safety (CAIS) issued a warning signed by 350 leading scientists in the United States, urging that AI's existential risks be treated with the same urgency as nuclear war.

Recognizing these dangers, leading AI nations have rushed to establish regulatory frameworks, producing early-stage ethical guidelines aimed at risk mitigation. Yet these efforts are entangled in geopolitical rivalries. Premature regulation may place a country at a competitive disadvantage in the ongoing technological arms race, leading to reluctance in imposing effective restraints. Consequently, AI governance has become a zero-sum game in which unilateral efforts are insufficient. Without global coordination, fragmented approaches will fail to contain AI's unintended consequences—leaving the world vulnerable to a technological environment evolving beyond human control.

The prevention of WMD proliferation and the governance of AI are only two examples of global challenges that demand collective solutions. Climate change, too, will increasingly impact access to critical resources such as water and food, all while the free trade system erodes—spawning new sources of international conflict.[9] Meanwhile, global pandemics, cybersecurity threats, and emerging disruptive technologies—all complex, transnational in nature—underscore the impracticality of isolationism and great-power rivalry. These shared threats reinforce the need for robust international institutions and cooperative frameworks.

As the 21st century accelerates into an era of profound technological and geopolitical transformation, humanity faces challenges that no single nation—or group of nations—can resolve alone. Multilateralism is no longer merely a desirable framework for cooperation. It is an existential necessity.

Yet in a world where power is fragmented among rival states, achieving effective collective action becomes ever more difficult. Multipolar systems, by their very nature, foster great-power rivalry, zero-sum balancing, and a reluctance to compromise national interests for global stability. The return of multipolarity risks reviving patterns of unchecked military competition and shifting the international landscape away from cooperative stability toward geopolitical confrontation.

The erosion of multilateralism in favor of multipolar rivalry will not bring greater stability—it will deepen global disorder and make coordinated responses to shared crises virtually impossible. The choice before us is stark: embrace genuine multilateralism or resign ourselves to a future defined by unrestrained geopolitical competition.

The Future of Multilateralism in a Fragmented World

As unity among member states becomes increasingly difficult to achieve, the enforcement of international norms and agreements will weaken. Although existing international organizations and frameworks will continue to serve as platforms for dialogue and cooperation, their independence, authority, and influence will inevitably decline from the heights they reached during the era of the liberal international order.[10] In a fragmented global system, coordinated responses to crises will become more elusive—especially as the erosion of the free trade system deepens. As economic blocs seek to exert near-exclusive control over resources, the risk of economic fragmentation escalating into geopolitical conflict will rise.

For most states, the ideal outcome of the current transition would be the preservation of multilateralism within the international system.[11] Yet without a unipolar hegemon capable of enforcing cooperative norms, the global order is likely to drift back toward great power politics—albeit in more diffuse and regionalized forms.[12] In such an environment, states will increasingly seek partnerships with like-minded or strategically aligned peers, forming regional blocs and flexible coalitions.

As broad-based multilateral consensus becomes harder to achieve, many will turn to *minilateralism*—smaller, interest-driven groupings formed to address specific challenges. In a multipolar world, this fragmented and pragmatic approach to cooperation is likely to dominate.[13]

1. A Multilateralism Adapted to Multipolarity

Even if multipolarity becomes the defining feature of international politics, it remains essential to uphold the foundational principles of international law and multilateral cooperation. The rise of a fully *à la carte* world—where states engage selectively with international institutions, alliances, or norms based solely on narrow national preferences—would have deeply destabilizing consequences.

As diplomacy becomes more transactional and foreign policy increasingly shaped by short-term interests, a more individualized and pragmatic global dynamic appears inevitable. Nevertheless, establishing 'anchor' frameworks that unite diverse states under a shared umbrella remains crucial. The international community must continue to foster inclusive frameworks under common rules. The key challenge will be to ensure that minilateral arrangements—while flexible and interest-based—can coexist harmoniously within broader multilateral structures. Such a system would enable mediation between competing interests and facilitate unified responses to shared global challenges.

This will require enhancing the adaptability and resilience of core multilateral institutions such as the UN, the WTO, and the IMF—potentially through substantive reforms that reflect the shifting geopolitical and economic realities. These institutions, designed to bridge national interests and enable global cooperation, remain the most effective platforms for addressing complex transnational issues—even in the absence of a hegemonic power to enforce order. The enduring legacy of the liberal international order underscores the growing necessity of multilateralism as the world moves deeper into the 21st century.

2. The Evolving Role of International Law

In this rapidly transforming global order, the role and legitimacy of international law will also evolve. While the binding enforcement power of international law may weaken, its normative authority—grounded in voluntary compliance and broad recognition—will become increasingly important.[14] States may choose to adhere to legal norms not because they are compelled to do so, but because such adherence serves the common interest in maintaining stability, predictability, and institutional continuity amid uncertainty.

The current international system—shaped by the catastrophic lessons of two world wars and further reinforced by globalization in the post–Cold War era—stands as a testament to the necessity of multilateralism. Its imperfections, while real, call for refinement and strengthening—not for abandonment in favor of a return to the geopolitical rivalries of the 19th or early 20th centuries. If post–Cold War multilateralism was nurtured under the artificial stability of American hegemony, the multilateralism of the future must emerge as an essential mechanism for addressing the very crises humanity has brought upon itself.

The Crisis of Liberal Democracy and the Future of Multilateralism

As the pace of change accelerates in the 21st century, humanity will face an unprecedented array of challenges—many of which will prove insurmountable without genuine multilateral cooperation. Yet for such cooperation to transcend diplomatic formalities and take meaningful shape, a foundational liberal consensus remains indispensable.

The core principles of the liberal international order—respect for territorial sovereignty irrespective of power, adherence to international law, and the promotion of free trade—form the structural basis for broad-based international cooperation. Without at least a modicum of liberal internationalism, multilateralism risks becoming a purely realist framework, reminiscent of the Concert of Europe or the narrow, issue-specific alignments of the Cold War era. Both models, though historically significant, ultimately failed to address the systemic global challenges of their time—and are even less suited to the far more complex and interdependent crises of the 21st century.

At this critical juncture, it is worth recalling Immanuel Kant's insight: true cosmopolitanism—and by extension, meaningful multilateralism—can only emerge on the foundation of liberal-democratic values. For such a system to endure, liberal democracy must be not only politically viable but also widely recognized as a normative force in international society. This recognition, however, depends on the internal vitality of liberal democracy within individual states.

In a world marked by cultural and political pluralism, sustaining a liberal-led, rules-based international order requires a coherent and resilient coalition of liberal-democratic nations at its core. Today, however, that foundation is under strain. Liberal democracies around the world are confronting deep-seated ideological and political vulnerabilities—from democratic backsliding and rising populism to the appeal of authoritarian alternatives. Concurrently, the fragmentation of the international order is accelerating, weakening the normative coherence necessary for multilateralism to function effectively. Without a renewed and principled commitment to liberal-democratic ideals, multilateralism risks becoming a hollow construct—incapable of mobilizing the collective will required to address the defining transnational crises of our time.

Endnotes:

1. The term 'liberal international order' inherently implies liberalism as its foundational value, evoking associations with neoliberalism, a concept that has fueled resentment in many countries. Having witnessed firsthand the backlash of ideological imposition, the United States and its Western allies may have found it necessary to adopt a less overtly ideological term—the 'rules-based international order,' which carries broader appeal and resonance. However, the rules-based international order, as championed by the U.S. under the Biden administration, is not synonymous with the traditional liberal international order. A critical distinction lies in the absence of free trade as a core pillar. Unlike the classic liberal order, which was fundamentally built on free trade principles, Biden's vision of a rules-based order notably excluded free trade as a guiding principle. Without free trade, the rules-based order diverges from the traditional liberal international order in its truest sense. Under the second Trump administration, the United States even abandoned the rhetoric of a rules-based international order, signaling an even greater departure from past commitments to international governance frameworks.

2. See among others, 강봉구, 「자유주의 국제질서의 균열과 러시아의 주권적 국제주의」, 『슬라브研究』 제35권 4호. (2019) pp. 1-33.

3. Russia perceives the 'rules' in the West-promoted rules-based international order as extending beyond international law, which is established strictly through sovereign agreements and legally grounded practices among states. Instead, Moscow argues that these rules also include norms unilaterally imposed by the United States and its Western allies—rules that lack broad international consensus and are formulated privately by specific nations or blocs. From Russia's perspective, the rules-based order is merely a rebranded version of the liberal international order—a 'Liberal International Order 2.0' designed to impose liberal ideological principles on other states under a new label.

4. While Moscow insists that its vision of sovereign internationalism—anchored in a rigid Westphalian interpretation of sovereignty—constitutes an 'international law-based order,' the effectiveness of any legal system is inevitably shaped by the political structures and power dynamics that sustain it.

5. Notably, while China has expressed an interest in reforming various aspects of the existing international order, it does not appear intent on dismantling or overthrowing it entirely. As a primary beneficiary of the U.S.-led system, China recognizes the advantages it has reaped. Nonetheless, guided by its Sinocentric vision and far-reaching ambitions, China may ultimately aim to replace the United States as the dominant hegemonic power within the global system that it seeks to shape.

6. See Paul Gewirtz, "China, the United States, and the future of a rules-based international order," Brookings (22 July 2024), citing Article 19 of China's *Foreign Relations Law* (2023).

7 This is particularly ironic, as the Confucian ideal of governance emphasizes virtue (德, dé) and moral leadership, both of which are intended to foster an inclusive system rooted in the principle of harmony (和, hé).

8 This was precisely the logic behind the Proliferation Security Initiative (PSI), which was launched in response to the rise of extremist terrorism following the 9/11 attacks. The initiative, which brought together 105 countries, aimed to prevent terrorist organizations from acquiring WMDs by closing off global proliferation loopholes.

9 For more information, see among others, Michael Albertus, "The Coming Age of Territorial Expansion – Climate Change will Fuel Contests – and Maybe Wars – for Land and Resources," Foreign Affairs (4 March 2025).

10 The effectiveness of international organizations ultimately depends on the collective will of their member states.

11 Multilateralism, as it is understood today, is a progressive achievement of the liberal international order and the Pax Americana. The international community has long sought to realize what Immanuel Kant once envisioned as a "federation of free states" capable of securing perpetual peace. This aspiration first materialized in the League of Nations after World War I and was later revived through the United Nations following World War II—both attempts to embed democratic ideals within an international system historically dominated by great powers. Yet idealism alone proved insufficient. The League of Nations, despite its initial promise in the immediate aftermath of World War I, collapsed under the weight of resurgent great power politics within a decade. During the Cold War, the United Nations struggled to implement meaningful multilateralism, often reduced to serving as a diplomatic intermediary between the United States and the Soviet Union. It was only under Pax Americana—when the United States emerged as the unchallenged global hegemon—that true multilateralism became feasible. In the decade following the Cold War, multilateralism experienced its golden age. Rather than unilaterally dictating global terms, the U.S. opted—at least outwardly—to lead through multilateral institutions. Under the stabilizing framework of unipolar hegemony, multilateralism flourished. However, this liberal order encountered its first major rupture in 2003, when the U.S., in launching the Iraq War, bypassed the UN Security Council and set a precedent for sidelining multilateral consensus. Even then, Washington sought to maintain the appearance of restraint, favoring 'minilateralism'—coalitions of willing partners—over broad-based international endorsement. A revealing moment of this mindset appears in an episode of the American political drama The West Wing, where White House officials, struggling to secure wide international backing for a controversial initiative, reframe their coalition by emphasizing the participation of all NATO members, presenting it as though it enjoyed broad global legitimacy. The scene illustrates a deeper truth: even the world's lone superpower once felt compelled to justify its actions through the language of multilateralism, attesting to the strength and normative pull of the liberal international system. In such a world, even weaker states could leverage multilateralism to exert pressure on great powers—a striking departure from historical precedent.

12 Securing the future of multilateralism will become increasingly difficult if regional hegemons emerge in the wake of U.S. unipolarity. A regional hegemon—particularly an authoritarian one—would likely seek to subordinate its sphere of influence through a system of client states, thereby eroding the sovereignty of its neighbors and hollowing out the foundations of multilateral cooperation. If such a power were to manipulate international institutions by demanding a one-state, one-vote system while simultaneously controlling a bloc of dependent states, other great powers would almost certainly reject multilateralism as illegitimate. This would hasten its collapse, plunging the world into a new era of rivalry and confrontation. Moreover, the emergence of one regional hegemon would incentivize others to pursue similar dominance within their own regions, accelerating the fragmentation of the international order. In contrast, if the rise of regional hegemons can be averted, multilateralism may yet endure.

13 If multilateralism is about securing broad international cooperation to advance globally shared objectives, then minilateralism represents a more limited, pragmatic form of that ambition—focused on specific issues among a select group of states. In some cases, minilateralism is deliberately chosen to address localized or regional concerns, as exemplified by organizations like the European Union or the African Union. More often, however, minilateral initiatives arise as a fallback when global consensus proves elusive. The underlying logic is that incremental, issue-specific agreements—however narrow or fragmented—can help bridge wider divides among states. If widely accepted and normalized, such minilateral arrangements are hoped to evolve into broader multilateral consensus. Yet this optimistic assumption does not always hold. A striking example is the failure of WTO reform. Despite repeated efforts to modernize and strengthen the global trade regime, the Doha Round collapsed after years of impasse. In response, states increasingly turned to bilateral and regional Free Trade Agreements (FTAs)—a form of minilateralism in international trade. The expectation was that a critical mass of FTAs could cumulatively support global trade liberalization and eventually catalyze a multilateral breakthrough at the WTO. However, despite the proliferation of FTAs since the mid-2000s, this trend never translated into meaningful reform of the multilateral trading system. The WTO case illustrates a broader truth: minilateralism does not necessarily serve as a stepping stone to multilateral progress. In some cases, it may even entrench fragmentation. Minilateral arrangements can harden into exclusive coalitions aimed at countering rival blocs, rather than facilitating global cooperation. When multiple groups pursue separate, overlapping minilateral initiatives—each aligned with competing strategic or ideological interests—the risk of conflict increases. In a world where multilateralism remains the dominant framework, such tensions can be managed through institutional coordination. But in an era marked by great-power competition and balance-of-power politics, even minor frictions can escalate into broader geopolitical confrontations. Under such conditions, minilateral groups may quickly evolve into rigid alliance blocs, deepening polarization and undermining any remaining prospects for global integration. Despite these risks, minilateralism is likely to play an increasingly prominent role in the remainder of the 21st century. The urgency of interstate cooperation has never been greater, yet the weakening of multilateral institutions makes achieving broad global consensus more difficult than ever. Within these con-

straints, carefully navigating the limitations of minilateralism—while maximizing its potential—appears to be the only viable path forward. As such, multilateralism in the 21st century will likely be more fragmented, adaptive, and issue-specific, with minilateralism emerging as the dominant operational mode of international cooperation among states that share strategic or normative affinities.

14 정하늘, 『21세기 국제질서 맥락으로 이해하기 - 패권 전환기 속 대한민국의 미래』 국제법질서연구소 (2023), p. 541.

CHAPTER 15

LIBERAL DEMOCRACY'S EXISTENTIAL CRISIS

Remember, democracy never lasts long.
It soon wastes, exhausts, and murders itself.
There never was a democracy yet that did not commit suicide.
It is in vain to say that democracy is less vain, less proud, less selfish, less ambitious, or less avaricious than aristocracy or monarchy.
It is not true, in fact, and nowhere appears in history.
Those passions are the same in all men, under all forms of simple government, and when unchecked, produce the same effects of fraud, violence, and cruelty. When clear prospects are opened before vanity, pride, avarice, or ambition, for their easy gratification, it is hard for the most considerate philosophers and the most conscientious moralists to resist the temptation.
Individuals have conquered themselves.
Nations and large bodies of men, never.

John Adams

1. The Expansion and Fragmentation of Liberal Ideologies

The political crisis engulfing liberal democracies today is deep, complex, and multifaceted. Each nation faces its own particular challenges—from the algorithmic amplification of political polarization through social media to escalating disputes over immigration, identity, and governance. Yet beneath these varied symptoms lies a common and more profound reality: liberal democracy itself is in crisis.

As with the liberal international order, liberal democracy is rooted in the tradition of liberalism. But while contemporary liberalism traces its intellectual lineage to the classical liberalism of the Enlightenment, it has evolved into something markedly different—broader in scope, more fragmented in structure, and, in many ways, internally incoherent.

At its core, liberalism is a philosophy of individual freedom. If its essence were to be distilled into a single moral principle, it would be Immanuel Kant's categorical imperative: never treat human beings merely as means to an end, but always as ends in themselves.[1] No matter how noble a cause, ideology, or movement may be, individuals must never be reduced to instruments in its service. Each person is to be respected as an autonomous subject, endowed with inherent dignity, agency, and the right to self-determination. From this principle flowed the liberal commitment to individual rights, constitutional limits on power, and institutions designed to safeguard liberty.

Yet over time, liberal thought has expanded into a sprawling and often contradictory constellation of ideas. Today, "liberalism" encompasses such a broad and diverse array of positions—ranging from libertarianism to progressive egalitarianism—that it resists coherent definition.[2] Like many concepts in the social sciences, liberalism has undergone recursive cycles of interpretation, critique, and reinvention, resulting in a tradition that is as internally diverse as it is ideologically unstable. In the 21st century, this unchecked proliferation of liberal paradigms—rather than fortifying democracy—has begun to erode its normative and institutional foundations.

Importantly, this crisis is not confined to the West. Non-Western societies that have adopted Western-style liberal democracy are experiencing similar strains, suggesting that the problem lies not in localized historical or cultural variables, but in a more profound transformation of liberalism's conceptual core. To fully understand the fragility of liberal democracy today, it is necessary to retrace the intellectual arc of liberalism itself—from the rationalist foundations of the Enlightenment to the philosophical pluralism and identity-based politics that characterize the modern era.

The Rationalist Foundations of Liberalism

The Enlightenment—often regarded as the philosophical foundation of classical liberalism—was also, more fundamentally, an age of rationalism. If modern philosophy begins with Descartes, its defining methodology is inductive reasoning, as articulated by Francis Bacon in *Novum Organum* (1620). Prior to Bacon, philosophical inquiry was dominated by deductive logic in the Aristotelian tradition, which derived particular conclusions from general premises. Bacon's inductive method reversed this process: it sought to derive general principles from empirical observation and methodical experimentation, thereby laying the groundwork for the boundless expansion of human knowledge.[3]

Liberalism, shaped within this rationalist milieu, emerged as a product of logic and systematic reasoning. Enlightenment thinkers, most notably Immanuel Kant, applied the principles of pure reason to moral and political life, constructing the intellectual architecture of classical liberalism around the dignity of the individual, the autonomy of the will, and the necessity of legal and institutional constraints on power.

Yet the Enlightenment's rationalist legacy did not remain unchallenged. In the 19th century, philosophers such as Georg Wilhelm Friedrich Hegel, Karl Marx, and Friedrich Nietzsche radically expanded the horizons of philosophical inquiry—probing dimensions of human experience that reason alone could not fully capture. Nietzsche, in particular, foresaw the dissolution of traditional religious and moral worldviews as civilization progressed. In *Thus Spoke Zarathustra* (1885), Nietzsche famously proclaimed the "death of God"—a metaphorical expression of the decline of traditional religious and moral foundations in an increasingly secular and rationalist world. Every society, he observed, is sustained by foundational dogmas—transcendent values that provide coherence, direction, and meaning. With the erosion of these inherited absolutes, Nietzsche warned, modern humanity would confront a void of meaning, a condition he termed 'nihilism.'

To resist this descent into meaninglessness, Nietzsche proposed the doctrine of 'eternal recurrence': the idea that one should live each moment in such a way that one would will its eternal repetition, exactly as it is. In doing so, existence would acquire intrinsic value—not by appeal to divine or objective standards, but through the full embrace of one's own life, freely and consciously lived.

Eternal recurrence, however, places immense responsibility on the individual. A life that holds value under this doctrine must be not only freely chosen but actively affirmed. Nietzsche thus rejected the absorption of the self into collective identities—whether religious, national, or ideological—and called instead for the creation of the autonomous self: a self that transcends societal conventions and asserts its own will to power.

The 20th-Century Turn: From Rationalism to Subjectivity

Nietzsche's ideas exerted a profound influence on 20th-century existentialist thought, which further deepened the rejection of preordained meaning. Thinkers such as Jean-Paul Sartre and Martin Heidegger argued that human beings are not born with intrinsic purpose but must define themselves through their own choices and actions. Nietzsche's emphasis on autonomy, freedom, and personal responsibility found fuller articulation in existentialism's call for radical self-definition.

As industrialization and geopolitical upheavals accelerated, traditional worldviews and moral frameworks eroded with unprecedented speed. The result, as Nietzsche had foreseen, was a deepening individualism. The collapse of inherited values coincided with the secularization of political institutions and the progressive detachment of societal norms from religious foundations.

Simultaneously, as societies came to prize personal experience and uniqueness, the rigid architecture of Enlightenment rationalism began to give way. The modern era witnessed a shift from the primacy of objectivity to a growing emphasis on subjectivity, profoundly reshaping the philosophical landscape. Abstract and conceptual inquiry, increasingly liberated from empirical constraints, began to dominate intellectual discourse.

As with all dominant intellectual movements, these philosophical developments reverberated far beyond the academy. They left a powerful imprint on cultural domains such as literature, art, and music. This sweeping intellectual and aesthetic transformation—rooted in the radical questioning of tradition, authority, and inherited meaning—came to be known as *Modernism*.

Despite its revolutionary spirit, Modernism—like Nietzsche's doctrine of eternal recurrence—remained tethered to the search for universal meaning. It sought to discover new truths and values that could replace the disintegration of the old. Yet by the mid-20th century, even this pursuit began to falter. Western societies were becoming increasingly diverse—ethnically, culturally, and ideologically—rendering the ideal of a singular, cohesive worldview ever more elusive. At the same time, the devastation wrought by two world wars shattered the Enlightenment's faith in reason and scientific progress. The atrocities committed under totalitarian regimes—Nazism, Fascism, Stalinism—discredited the grand ideologies that had once claimed to offer ultimate meaning. Meanwhile, decolonization and civil rights movements in the 1950s and 1960s further upended prevailing moral and political dogmas, accelerating a broader cultural shift toward relativism and pluralism.

It was in this context that a new intellectual movement emerged: *Postmodernism*. Rejecting grand narratives and absolute truths, postmodernism emphasized the relativity of knowledge and the multiplicity of cultural and ideological perspectives.[4] It placed renewed focus on individual experience and subjective perception as the primary lenses through which reality is interpreted.

With its rejection of universals and embrace of relativism, postmodernism encouraged critical examinations of how societies construct and convey meaning—through language, culture, and institutional power. This intellectual orientation gave rise to 'deconstructionism,' a powerful analytical method that seeks to expose the internal contradictions, hidden assumptions, and ideological underpinnings embedded within seemingly stable concepts.

The influence of postmodernism soon extended far beyond philosophy. It became a defining force across the humanities and social sciences, reshaping the study of politics, economics, culture, and identity. Like the Enlightenment and Modernism before it, postmodernism transformed not only how knowledge was produced, but also how power, discourse, and meaning were understood.

Collaborative Solidarity of Postmodernism and Socialism

During this period, postmodernism intersected with the socialist tradition, which had long provided critical insights into power, class, and hierarchy. At first glance, the two may appear philosophically incompatible—postmodernism rejects universality and absolute truths, while socialism is rooted in a universalist vision of class struggle and collective emancipation. Yet beneath these surface tensions lay a shared critique: both traditions insisted that social structures are neither natural nor immutable, but are instead historically, culturally, and politically constructed.

Moreover, postmodernism's emphasis on cultural diversity and the rights of marginalized groups resonated with socialism's long-standing commitment to defending the oppressed. This intellectual and ethical alignment laid the groundwork for a growing ideological and activist convergence under the banner of 'social justice.' Over time, postmodernist and socialist thought began to coalesce within progressive movements, profoundly shaping the trajectory of left-wing politics and academic discourse.

A pivotal intellectual influence during this convergence was Antonio Gramsci's theory of cultural hegemony. While deconstructionism became a widely adopted methodological tool for social critique, Gramsci's work offered a strategic vision for transformative politics. Gramsci argued that ruling elites maintain dominance not merely through coercion, but by shaping cultural norms, values, and institutions in ways that legitimize and naturalize their authority. Through education, media, religion, art, and even familial structures, the dominant class embeds its worldview into the fabric of everyday life, rendering its ideology synonymous with 'common sense.' This form of cultural hegemony ensures that subordination is often internalized and consented to unconsciously. To resist this subtle form of domination, Gramsci called for the construction of alternative value systems and narratives—what he termed 'counter-hegemony.' Such a project required both critical deconstruction of prevailing ideologies and the proactive articulation of new frameworks that could empower subordinate groups and challenge the status quo.

The growing alliance between postmodernism and socialism gave rise to a broad-based left-wing coalition encompassing progressive intellectuals, socialists, feminists, LGBTQ+ activists, racial minorities, and their allies. United by a shared commitment to social justice and emancipation, this coalition launched a comprehensive challenge to existing cultural and institutional hierarchies. Their goal was to dismantle the entrenched systems of power that structured social life, while advancing alternative visions of equality, inclusion, and collective dignity.

The Quest for Progress Continues

By the late 20th century, the struggle for social justice had achieved significant gains across multiple domains of Western society. Diversity and minority rights became central to political discourse, institutional discrimination was largely dismantled, and cultural narratives that had long marginalized minority groups were critically reexamined and revised. Even language became a site of contestation, as efforts to reform terminology and promote new expressions in line with progressive ideals gained traction.

Yet even as leftist discourse came to dominate academia and much of mainstream culture, the drive for transformation did not abate. In the perpetual evolution of political thought, yesterday's progressivism often becomes today's conservatism. To retain its identity as the vanguard of change, leftist discourse grew ever more "progressive," continuously shifting its focus and refining its objectives.

With institutional discrimination largely addressed, the movement turned its attention to structural discrimination—forms of inequality embedded not in overt laws or policies, but in the implicit norms, expectations, and cultures of society. This conceptual expansion was strongly influenced by the work of the philosopher John Rawls, who argued in *A Theory of Justice* (1971) that inequalities based on morally arbitrary factors—race, gender, intelligence, or social background—should be considered unjust.[5] In Rawls's ideal society, only those advantages earned through individual effort or merit would be legitimate.[6]

In pursuit of this vision, persuasion increasingly gave way to activism, and process yielded to outcomes. The objective was not merely to present compelling arguments but to secure cultural hegemony—to reshape the ideological terrain itself. A central rationale for this approach was moral urgency. Despite the ascendancy of progressive values in public discourse, many minority groups remained vulnerable to private discrimination and exclusion. If opposing narratives were freely tolerated, it was feared that harmful ideologies could resurface, threatening hard-won gains. However, the methods used to identify and address structural discrimination often proved difficult to defend through empirical scrutiny. Definitions of structural bias were frequently contested—even among progressives—and efforts to measure or eliminate it lacked consistent standards. Nevertheless, such concerns were often dismissed as secondary. If empirical validation became a prerequisite for social justice, progress would be delayed.

Rawls's egalitarian ideal was nearly unassailable in principle, yet the pathways to realizing it were deeply divisive. Disagreements over means, strategy, and acceptable trade-offs were inevitable. Without a degree of flexibility and pragmatic compromise, rigid adherence to idealistic methods risked unintended consequences. And indeed, this is precisely what unfolded.

A number of influential thinkers—both sympathetic and critical—sounded alarms about the trajectory of progressive liberalism. Political philosopher John Gray, for example, coined the term "hyper-liberalism" well before the more polemical label "woke" entered popular discourse. According to Gray, modern progressivism had veered away from its pragmatic roots—anchored in tolerance, individual liberty, and pluralism—toward a form of moral authoritarianism. He argued that by elevating radical individual autonomy to the highest good, where identity is seen as entirely self-defined and socially constructed, the movement undermines shared values, erodes social cohesion, and fragments collective identity. Moreover, Gray warned that this shift promotes a kind of moral relativism that ultimately destabilizes the very idea of objective truth.[7]

A more moderate critique came from the eminent historian Timothy Snyder, who, while committed to liberal democracy, expressed concern about the excesses of individualism. In his reflections on freedom and totalitarianism,[8] Snyder argued that true freedom is not simply the absence of constraint or the assertion of personal autonomy. Rather, it is sustained through social bonds, mutual responsibility, and a collective commitment to truth. He emphasized that a functioning free society depends on citizens who actively seek reliable information, engage in critical reflection, and resist the allure of propaganda and falsehood.[9] For Snyder, freedom is inseparable from truth—and truth, in turn, is a shared civic duty.

The Quest for Progress Hits a Dead End

Over time, certain factions within the left began to elevate not only their goals but also their methods to the level of orthodoxy. This growing rigidity fostered increasing hostility toward dissent. As the struggle for cultural hegemony intensified, a proliferation of new terms, norms, and symbolic gestures emerged—often carrying implicit or explicit social mandates. Individuals who resisted these shifts or failed to adopt the latest terminology risked being labeled bigots or reactionaries.[10]

Criticism of leftist ideas was increasingly framed as 'backlash'—a term that, while neutral in definition, took on a pejorative tone, suggesting that opposition was inherently regressive or unjust. Rather than engaging critics through open debate, dissenting voices were frequently marginalized through social pressure, personal attacks, and what became known as 'cancel culture.' In this climate, political correctness became not merely a courtesy, but a prerequisite for full participation in public life. While not all left-wing activists endorsed these aggressive tactics, many tacitly accepted or enabled them. Ironically, the movement that had long championed classical liberal principles—especially freedom of conscience and expression—began to drift away from those very ideals.[11]

During this period of ideological ascendancy, minority rights expanded considerably, and liberal democracies grew more pluralistic. In some respects, deeper social integration was achieved. Yet after successfully deconstructing mainstream discourses, the postmodernist left turned its critical gaze to some of the very foundations of society itself. The movement sought to supplant these foundational principles with experimental, often underdeveloped alternatives—frequently pursued with aggressive zeal. This bold agenda exposed internal contradictions and strategic limitations. A societal backlash was inevitable. Many individuals and communities—some of whom had previously supported or tolerated the left's aims—grew disillusioned.

Rather than reflecting on this shift, however, the left largely reverted to familiar defensive strategies, branding critics as reactionaries, much as it had done when it operated from the margins. This was a profound miscalculation. When a movement operates on the fringes, its critical posture alone can justify its place in public discourse. But when it becomes mainstream—or seeks institutional dominance—it faces a new burden: it must prove capable of offering a coherent, stable, and sustainable vision of social order. Because progressive discourse had never before functioned as the dominant societal framework, it faced an even steeper challenge. Yet despite its expanding influence—and despite its increasing proximity to power—the left often remained trapped in the combative mindset of a dissident movement. Even as it blurred the lines of whether cultural hegemony now lay with the left or the right, it continued to behave as if it were the outsider.

The progressive left could have pursued cultural hegemony by welcoming rigorous criticism, cultivating institutional maturity, and practicing internal correction and self-restraint. Instead, the left clung to outdated tactics—invoking backlash theories and dismissing critique instead of engaging with it substantively. But in the context of institutional dominance, such tactics were no longer tenable. Without genuine mechanisms for self-correction, the left became vulnerable to a level of scrutiny and backlash it was unprepared to confront.

That vulnerability was swiftly recognized. Right-wing forces—long alienated by the trajectory of the progressive movement—intensified their opposition. But this time, they were joined by center-right voices who had quietly observed the contradictions of the new cultural order. The backlash was broader and more potent than any before. As the left pursued increasingly radical reforms, the right responded with an equally transformative counter-narrative—one that framed its agenda not simply as opposition, but as a "restoration" of a world they believed had been upended. Yet the left, still viewing itself through the lens of resistance, failed to recognize that many now saw it as the dominant force imposing its will. The right, in turn, rallied against what it perceived as a new tyranny: a progressive orthodoxy that held sway over both cultural and institutional domains.

The result is an unprecedented political landscape in which both ends of the spectrum now advocate for their own versions of cultural revolution. The ideological conflicts engulfing contemporary Western democracies have reached levels unseen in recent memory.

Internationally, the consequences have been striking. Authoritarian states, once cautious in their engagement with liberal democratic narratives, now openly mock the dogmatic excesses of Western progressivism. Where they once felt compelled to respond to liberal ideals, they now use its contradictions as evidence of Western decline.

Given that nearly half the population in many liberal democracies opposes these progressive agendas, it is unsurprising that the rest of the world views the West's ideological fragmentation with indifference—or even skepticism. In his 1977 inaugural address, President Jimmy Carter declared, "The best way to enhance freedom in other lands is to demonstrate here that our democratic system is worthy of emulation." But today, the internal discord that once symbolized democratic vitality increasingly risks undermining the very credibility of the Western model itself.

2. The Perils of Polarization
: How Extremism Threatens Liberal Democracy

What is particularly alarming is not just the scale of these conflicts, but their accelerating trajectory. In many liberal democracies, the left and right are now locked in an unrelenting struggle for cultural and political hegemony. Though both sides claim to engage in democratic debate, the true objective often seems to be the political neutralization—or outright marginalization—of the opposition. This confrontational approach has become increasingly normalized across the ideological spectrum.

Political ideologies, whether left or right, are ultimately rooted in distinct value systems and worldviews. They cannot be eradicated through argument, coercion, or force. Yet today's political discourse increasingly frames ideological disagreement as a moral confrontation—a zero-sum battle between truth and falsehood, justice and injustice, good and evil. This moral absolutism calcifies political positions into dogma, transforming democratic pluralism into a fight for supremacy.

As ideologies harden into dogmas, the space for compromise narrows. Dialogue gives way to domination, and political opponents are recast as enemies to be vanquished, not participants in a shared democratic endeavor. The result is a deepening cultural and social conflict that erodes the mutual respect and coexistence essential to a functioning democracy.

The Erosion of the 'Rule of Law' and the Path to Radicalization

Most alarmingly, political polarization is exerting profound pressure on the rule of law and the legitimacy of judicial institutions. Across many liberal democracies, public confidence in the judiciary is in decline, as court rulings that run counter to prevailing ideological expectations are increasingly dismissed as politically motivated or illegitimate.

Historically, judicial decisions were viewed not only as mechanisms for dispute resolution but also as society's most credible source of authoritative truth. When courts found political figures guilty of unlawful conduct, the consequences extended far beyond legal penalties—striking at the heart of their political legitimacy. In most liberal democracies, a court verdict still retains formal legal force. Yet the judiciary's broader authority—its capacity to shape public understanding of justice and truth—is increasingly under question. In high-profile, politically charged cases, losing parties often denounce rulings as biased. More troublingly, the general public has become more inclined to disregard judicial outcomes when evaluating the moral or political fitness of convicted leaders. As a result, the judiciary's role as a check on political power is steadily eroding—a symptom of the wider unraveling of the rule of law.

To be sure, the judiciary is not without blame. When court decisions appear ideologically slanted or detached from social realities, public trust erodes. A judiciary perceived as insular, elitist, or unaccountable risks further alienation, deepening the crisis of institutional legitimacy. This erosion of trust has been compounded by the growing politicization of the courts, which undermines the perception of impartiality that judicial authority depends upon.

Nevertheless, an independent, well-functioning judiciary is indispensable to safeguarding the rule of law and preserving the republican principles of checks and balances. Without these institutional guardrails, individual liberty and democratic governance are placed in grave jeopardy.[12] In *Politics*, Aristotle warned that when the rule of law is weakened in a democratic society, demagogues rise to fill the void—paving the way for tyranny.[13] His warning remains timely. Like the canary in the coal mine, the judiciary's weakening authority signals something deeper: an early warning of democratic decay and societal radicalization. As judicial institutions lose their ability to command legitimacy across ideological lines, the very foundations of liberal democracy come under threat.

Ideological Divide

History offers sobering lessons. Whenever radical ideological movements—whether from the left or the right—have succeeded in capturing the state, their lofty promises have more often produced repression, purges, and tyranny.[14] By contrast, examples of ideological restraint and moderation in power are exceedingly rare.[15] If current trends persist, the defining virtue of liberal democracy—the peaceful coexistence of competing worldviews—may become untenable.

The trajectory of these conflicts is especially troubling. While political struggles in liberal democracies might once have followed a dialectical logic of thesis, antithesis, and synthesis,[16] the current escalation risks pushing these conflicts beyond reconciliation. Polarization is no longer simply a matter of policy disagreement; it is becoming existential.

Across much of the democratic world, the left and right are drifting toward their respective extremes. Although liberal democracies have institutional safeguards against the seizure of power by radicals, a more insidious dynamic is unfolding: as one side radicalizes and gains momentum, the other, rather than moderating in response, radicalizes as well. As Nietzsche warned, "If you stare into the abyss long enough, the abyss will stare back at you." Each cycle of backlash intensifies the next, as opposing camps adopt mirror-image strategies—escalating polarization, entrenching ideological conformity, and widening social divides. Political victory—or even defeat—can produce a kind of euphoria that deepens ideological commitment and accelerates radicalization. If this spiral continues, liberal democracies may veer away from Hegel's vision of historical progress through synthesis and instead descend into systemic fragmentation or collapse.[17] At the heart of this crisis is a deepening ideological rupture.

Modern progressive liberal thought—once championed primarily by the left—has undergone profound evolutions. Yet since the mid-2010s, a new intellectual current—*post-liberalism*—has emerged to challenge the very foundations of progressivism and, indeed, the liberalism itself.

Post-liberalism now serves as the philosophical bedrock for many contemporary right-wing movements. Though diverse in expression, its core tenets reject liberalism's emphasis on individual autonomy and instead prioritize communitarian values. Post-liberal thinkers also call for a shift away from market-oriented neoliberalism towards state-centered approaches to economic and social life.

One of the most prominent figures in this movement, Patrick Deneen, argues in *Why Liberalism Failed* (2018) that liberalism contains the seeds of its own undoing. He contends that liberalism's relentless pursuit of individual freedom and expanded personal choice gradually dissolves the very social structures—family, tradition, and community—that sustain a stable society. In the era of progressive liberalism, this dismantling has only accelerated, fragmenting society into increasingly atomized identity groups. Liberalism, which once relied on structured order to liberate individuals from a pre-modern 'state of nature,' now undermines the foundations that make such liberation possible. As Deneen sees it, liberalism is not evolving—it is imploding.

Post-liberalism is also heavily influenced by religious moral frameworks, particularly Catholic social thought. Many of its proponents argue that liberalism's secular trajectory has precipitated moral decay and cultural disintegration, thereby eroding the normative legitimacy of the liberal order itself.

This confrontation between progressive liberalism and post-liberalism is not a mere contest over policy—it is a fundamental clash of values and worldviews. As such, the political divide of our time is arguably deeper than at any point in recent history.

For those disillusioned by the sweeping cultural and political transformations of recent decades, post-liberalism's call for a return to tradition can appear not as regression but as a necessary course correction. Yet the danger lies in the velocity and direction of the backlash. How far back would the movement rewind the clock? Figures like Steve Bannon, who proudly describes himself as "anti-modernity," envision a wholesale rejection of Enlightenment ideals. In this worldview, the United States is no longer the product of liberal modernity but a vessel for the ancient Western traditions of Athens, Jerusalem, and Rome.[18] Even classical liberalism, once the foundation of American political thought, is now viewed as suspect.

Domestically, post-liberalism's political influence is still bounded by electoral realities. But its implications in international relations are more alarming. Globally, post-liberalism rejects the cosmopolitan ethos of liberal internationalism. It views globalism as a threat to cultural and national sovereignty and as a tool that empowers capital at the expense of local identity. Instead, it embraces nationalism—arguing that each nation must prioritize its own interests above all else.[19] Unfortunately, a global order rooted in competing nationalisms is likely to revert to multipolarity—a system that history has proven dangerously unstable. On this critical issue, post-liberalism offers no viable solution for ensuring global stability.

Identity Politics and the Rise of Tribalism

Another significant factor exacerbating political divisions in modern liberal democracies is the rise of tribalism and identity politics. To be sure, identity politics has played a constructive role in amplifying the voices of historically marginalized groups and fostering solidarity for necessary social change. At the same time, however, it has absorbed elements of the socialist tradition of class struggle, often identifying and targeting perceived enemies in increasingly aggressive terms.

Human relationships are almost always shaped by power dynamics, making the formation of social hierarchies virtually inevitable. A critical awareness of these dynamics is essential for diagnosing social injustices and proposing effective remedies from a progressive perspective. However, while power undeniably influences social hierarchies, it does not necessarily constitute a fixed or uniform class structure. Power is fluid, contingent, and highly context-dependent. A hierarchical relationship within the workplace, for example, may carry little meaning outside that specific domain. Unlike rigid class systems, modern power dynamics are situational and role-specific. An individual who wields authority in one arena cannot be permanently classified as belonging to a dominant class.

In contemporary societies, therefore, these power relations emerge from complex, multifaceted interactions rather than neatly defined class boundaries. Reducing these intricate dynamics to simplistic class narratives risks obscuring the true nature of social relations and misrepresenting the lived realities of individuals. Such reductionism often leads to frameworks that define entire groups by a single dimension of identity, distorting the fluid and overlapping nature of human interaction.

More troubling, however, is that political movements built around narrow and exclusionary identities frequently fail to account for the interconnected and multilayered relationships among diverse social groups. This tunnel vision fosters an instinctive tribalism—an "us versus them" mentality—giving rise to political forces that are inherently adversarial. When identity politics frames certain groups as enemies to be dismantled rather than as participants in a shared political community, it ceases to function as a tool for inclusion and progress. Instead, it becomes an instrument of division, exclusivity, and conflict.

Indeed, identity-based political struggle almost inevitably involves the identification of an adversary. However, when a particular group is persistently targeted in political discourse, it is only natural for that group to organize in response. While a certain level of criticism is not only inevitable but necessary in democratic politics, when it crosses a critical threshold—perceived as existential or fundamentally unjust—it often prompts a counter-movement. This backlash is also animated by a basic political instinct: the drawing of a line between friend and enemy.[20] This reactive dynamic almost always follows the same pattern: the counter-force turns its energy against the original aggressor, fueling a self-reinforcing cycle of hostility and polarization.

From this cycle, two possible trajectories emerge. In a more hopeful scenario, the existence of rival political forces can serve as a check on extremism, producing a rough equilibrium in which moderation and compromise are incentivized. Such a balance may prevent any single faction from consolidating excessive power and help preserve democratic norms. However, the more pessimistic—and perhaps more likely—outcome is a descent into zero-sum tribal warfare, where each side views total victory over the other as the only acceptable resolution. In such a world, politics ceases to be a space for deliberation and becomes a battlefield for domination. The breakdown of cooperation and shared civic values in this scenario could unravel the very fabric of democratic society. At this stage, public discourse no longer functions as a forum for reasoned debate but instead becomes a theater of ideological warfare, where the goal is not understanding but the silencing or destruction of opponents. Political dialogue degenerates into a contest of willpower, where logical persuasion and factual reasoning are abandoned in favor of emotional appeals, propaganda, and rhetorical warfare.

The rise of postmodern relativism has already weakened the status of objective truth, and in today's environment, truth itself is increasingly supplanted by personal belief and subjective emotion. The public sphere has thus been transformed into a post-truth battlefield, in which feelings routinely overpower facts, and narratives displace evidence. This post-truth culture, when combined with extreme political polarization, leads individuals to reject any form of authority or information that challenges their preexisting beliefs. In its most extreme form, this cognitive closure renders meaningful political engagement impossible. Once this threshold is crossed, no amount of evidence or logic can alter the convictions of committed partisans. History suggests that societies in such a state of epistemic and ideological fragmentation often teeter on the brink of collapse or fall into civil strife.

This is the fundamental crisis confronting contemporary liberal democracies. The erosion of trust in shared norms, coupled with the descent into tribalized politics, poses an existential threat to the liberal democratic order. If this cycle remains unbroken, the very survival of liberal democracy may be imperiled.

3. Potential Remedy
: Rise of the Political Center

Today, most liberal democracies have already stepped into the coliseum of post-truth politics. Are we truly powerless to halt this decline? Must we simply accept the inevitable collapse of liberal democracy?

It has become clear that neither the left nor the right offers a viable solution to this crisis. Both seem to operate under the illusion that securing political and cultural hegemony will somehow restore stability. Beyond this pursuit of dominance, genuine answers are in short supply. Yet the truth remains: neither side can permanently erase the other from the political arena, nor can it impose lasting cultural supremacy over its opponents. Any attempt to do so—whether through coercion, suppression, or ideological warfare—will only deepen the existing polarization. Such a trajectory leads inevitably toward a political landscape so fractured that the liberal democratic system itself becomes unsustainable.

If we are to avert this looming catastrophe, we must chart an alternative course. Fortunately, one path remains: the consolidation and rise of the political center.

Political Center as Anti-Extremist Force

In an era of extreme polarization, only the political center can serve as a counterweight to the forces of radicalization. Both left- and rightwing movements, in seeking to consolidate power, are often drawn toward their most extreme elements. Within ideologically homogeneous groups, these extremists tend to wield disproportionate influence, gradually pulling the broader faction toward their views. As a result, political movements that succumb to extremism frequently reject not only the policies but also the fundamental values associated with their opponents.

As political discourse shifts from deliberation and compromise to a battlefield defined by absolute confrontation, even extreme measures are increasingly justified as necessary weapons in the fight against a perceived enemy. Governance and problem-solving are no longer the primary objectives; instead, the overriding goal becomes the demonization and defeat of the other side. This dynamic perpetuates a vicious cycle of polarization, in which each side's radicalism feeds the other's, escalating conflict with no clear path to resolution. To break free from this cycle and achieve meaningful reconciliation, extremism must be decisively rejected. Yet the growing influence of radical voices has deeply entrenched both the left and the right, making internal course correction increasingly unlikely. Polarization has become a self-reinforcing system—each side's radicalism legitimizes and strengthens the other's, leaving neither with the capacity or incentive to reverse course. In such an environment, the prospects for a grand project of national integration or healing remain bleak.

This paralysis is not confined to internal party dynamics—it extends to the broader public discourse. Once a political faction embraces extremism, meaningful engagement with outsiders becomes nearly impossible. Even when one side effectively exposes the contradictions or flaws in the other's position, it remains equally open to scrutiny and criticism in return. Debates devolve into defensive performances and rhetorical point-scoring, entrenching divisions rather than bridging them. These exchanges do little to foster mutual understanding; they serve instead to consolidate in-group loyalty, reinforcing polarization without contributing to any constructive resolution.

Within this landscape, the political center holds a critical structural advantage. By definition, centrists resist the gravitational pull of ideological extremes. At most, they may lean moderately to the left or right—but they do not operate within rigid ideological frameworks. As a result, they are far less susceptible to the tribalist impulses that dominate polarized factions. Centrists are not emotionally bound to defending a fixed worldview, which enables them to prioritize pragmatism over dogma, and cooperation over confrontation. Unburdened by ideological rigidity, centrists are better positioned to engage with diverse perspectives, navigate complex political challenges, and promote the stability and cohesion necessary for democratic governance.

In a polarized age, the center may be the only force capable of restoring balance and preserving the democratic promise of pluralism.

Centrists' Inherent Limitations

That being said, the reality is far more complex. Carl Schmitt, the controversial German political philosopher and jurist, was among the most incisive critics of liberal democracy. He argued that democracy—dependent on the accommodation of diverse opinions and interests—is inherently ill-equipped to deal with moments of crisis that demand decisive state action. In exceptional circumstances, he claimed, the democratic principle of deliberation loses its relevance; what is needed instead is sovereign authority capable of immediate decision.

Schmitt's core assertion was that politics does not begin with consensus or balance, but with the fundamental distinction between friend and foe. From his perspective, there was no rationale for treating the political center as an independent force. In a polarized environment, he believed, centrism would inevitably be engulfed by the ideological forces to its left and right.[21] In today's deeply divided political landscape, his prediction seems increasingly prescient: the center faces unprecedented challenges in asserting itself as a distinct political actor.

Indeed, Schmitt's diagnosis has largely borne out in practice. In most liberal democracies, the center has rarely emerged as an autonomous force. It has functioned primarily as a moderating influence, nudging left-wing parties rightward and right-wing parties leftward—particularly in the lead-up to elections. Beyond this role, however, the center has struggled to establish itself as a significant or enduring political movement.

One of the central weaknesses of centrism is its lack of a clear and compelling political vision. Unlike the left and right, which often mobilize support through ideological conviction and a strong sense of mission, centrism frequently fails to inspire similar levels of political enthusiasm or commitment. Centrists often find themselves trapped in a posture of 'both-sides criticism,' motivated more by a desire to maintain balance than by any deep-seated convictions. This instinctive caution, while valuable for fostering dialogue, makes them hesitant to engage in ideological confrontation—a stance that limits their ability to galvanize mass support.

Moreover, centrism often lacks a distinct political identity beyond its opposition to extremism. As ideological tides shift, the center is frequently absorbed into the dominant agendas of the left or the right. In today's political climate—defined by identity politics, tribal affiliations, and intensifying polarization—centrism finds itself at a structural disadvantage. The space for pragmatic, non-ideological discourse has been dramatically reduced, making it increasingly difficult for the center to gain traction as a viable and influential force.

A Centrist Activism

Yet despite its often-overlooked role, centrism has always been indispensable in preserving liberal democracy. It is often said that the left and right are the two wings of a bird—both necessary for flight. Without a body to anchor them, however, the wings would simply fall apart. In much the same way, centrists have served as the unifying force that holds democratic societies together, ensuring their coherence and stability.

It is worth recalling that many of history's great thinkers did not regard democracy as the ideal political system. Both Plato and Kant, for instance, expressed deep skepticism about its foundations. In *The Republic*, Plato warned that the masses, more susceptible to emotion than reason, could easily fall prey to charismatic demagogues. Such figures, he argued, would ultimately lead democracies into tyranny. He also feared that excessive freedom would encourage citizens to prioritize personal indulgence over virtue and morality, unleashing societal chaos. Kant, too, was wary of democracy's pitfalls—particularly the "tyranny of the majority," in which the whims of the many could trample the rights of the few. He believed democratic leaders were often tempted to pander to the volatile desires of the public, rather than uphold enduring moral principles.

The vulnerabilities of democracy identified by Plato and Kant remain relevant today, as both the left and the right struggle with their own forms of ideological excess. Yet the force that has historically mitigated these vulnerabilities—directly or indirectly—has always been centrism. Societies lacking a robust centrist presence are especially prone to radicalization and polarization. By prioritizing balance, pragmatism, and restraint, centrism has served as a stabilizing force, checking populist surges, defending constitutional norms, and preserving the rule of law.

But today, as both the left and the right increasingly resort to revolutionary rhetoric and treat one another as existential threats, centrism can no longer afford to remain a passive force. It must evolve from a quiet stabilizer into an active political entity—one capable not only of tempering excesses, but of leading in its own right.

The first step in empowering centrism is to cultivate an environment in which it can thrive. No matter how capable individual centrist leaders may be, they cannot succeed in a system rigged against moderation. The effort must begin with individuals who currently identify as center-left or center-right. Rather than subordinating themselves to broader partisan identities, they must embrace 'centrist' as a political identity in its own right. The formation of a critical mass of centrists is essential. While traditional identity politics has revealed its polarizing and often toxic effects, a centrist identity—by its very nature—is less likely to devolve into extremism. Done right, it can serve as a unifying framework for those alienated by ideological tribalism.

Second, centrists must foster a culture in which their views can be expressed without fear of reprisal. Today, centrist voices are often attacked from both flanks—dismissed by the left as veiled conservatives, and by the right as closet progressives. With no organized coalition to support them, many centrists choose silence. This culture must change. The goal should not be for centrists to retreat from public discourse, but to make the extremes fear centrist critique. Only when extreme rhetoric is challenged by measured, principled arguments will it begin to lose its grip on political debate.

Third, centrism must reclaim the practice of constructive 'both-sides criticism.' The left and right are locked in cycles of mutual delegitimization, in which attacks on one's opponent serve primarily to distract from internal contradictions. Centrists, by contrast, are uniquely positioned to offer structural critiques of both extremes. Such critiques must not be opportunistic or cynical, but principled—aimed at illuminating blind spots and fostering common ground.

Fourth, structural reform is essential for strengthening the centrist perspective over time—across politics, education, society, and academia. In the political arena, winner-takes-all electoral systems should be replaced with alternatives such as ranked-choice voting, runoff elections, proportional representation, etc., to give centrists a fighting chance.

In education, students should be taught to engage with contrasting historical interpretations and ideological frameworks in a fair and balanced manner. Indoctrination—whether left or right—must be replaced by intellectual pluralism. In academia, more research should be devoted to balanced critiques of both sides, especially in contentious fields where polarization has narrowed acceptable discourse.

Culturally, public debate must be revived as a civic norm. Polarizing rhetoric often collapses under scrutiny when subjected to transparent, reasoned debate. To that end, centrist voices should be integrated as a third position in televised debates and panel discussions. The default structure should shift from two-sided confrontation to three-sided deliberation.

Finally, if centrism is to become a lasting force in real-world politics, it must establish a viable party infrastructure capable of sustaining itself within existing democratic systems.[22] The value of centrist politics lies not in neutrality, but in the ability to pursue the most reasonable solution to each issue[23]—sometimes aligning with the left, other times with the right. But without an independent political vehicle, the center will continue to be absorbed by one side or the other. A functional centrist party must be rooted in institutions, constituencies, and leadership capable of resisting this gravitational pull.

The core mission of centrist politics is not to revolutionize society, but to prevent its collapse. Grand visions are welcome, but not necessary. What is essential is that centrism act as a counterweight to extremism, a defender of liberal democracy's procedural and ethical foundations. It does not need overwhelming power to play this role. A decisive minority—holding the casting vote—can be enough. Centrism's strength lies in guiding governing coalitions toward pragmatism, compromise, and good governance.

In an era where polarization threatens to unravel liberal democracy, centrism's role as a philosophical and political anchor has never been more vital. Drawing on traditions as old as Aristotle's *Golden Mean* and Confucius's *Ethic of Harmony*, it can offer a path forward based not on domination, but on balance. By defending pluralism, upholding reasoned discourse, and resisting ideological excess, centrism can serve as democracy's last line of defense.

In truth, it has played this role all along—quietly, persistently, and often without recognition. The time has come for it to claim its place in the political arena, openly and on its own terms.

4. The Future of Liberal Democracy and the Fate of the Multipolar World

In this chapter, we have explored the domestic political implications of the crisis confronting liberal democracy. Yet its impact extends far beyond national borders, reverberating throughout international relations. Foreign policy, after all, is an outward projection of domestic priorities and values, shaping the international order as their global expression.

Even from a strictly realist perspective—one that brackets liberalism's intrinsic normative appeal—the political stability of liberal democracies is indispensable. Should democracy falter, the already complex dynamics of multipolarity would grow exponentially more volatile, further destabilizing the international system.

Stephen Walt, a prominent realist scholar, advanced the 'Balance of Threat Theory' in his 1987 work *The Origins of Alliances*. Walt argued that alliances form not simply in response to power imbalances but in reaction to perceived threats. A state's threat level is assessed based on several factors: its aggregate capabilities (population, economic capacity, and military strength), geographical proximity, offensive potential, and—most importantly—its perceived intentions. Hostile intent magnifies a state's threat perception.

In general, liberal democracies—where citizens directly impacted by war possess electoral power—are less likely to engage in military conquest against other nations. This framework helps explain why, after World War II, European powers—despite centuries of conflict—ceased viewing one another as security threats. It also sheds light on why enduring tensions between East Asian countries, such as South Korea and Japan, have not led to diplomatic collapse. In both cases, the stabilizing presence of liberal democracy has tempered historical grievances and fostered mutual trust.

Democratic Peace Theory[24] reinforces this analysis. It posits that institutional features of liberal democracies—checks and balances, separation of powers, and the tempering force of public opinion—systematically reduce the likelihood of war between them. Shared values, sustained diplomatic engagement, and economic interdependence further strengthen these relationships, lowering the risk of miscalculation or escalation. Empirical evidence supports this: while liberal democracies often come into conflict with non-democratic states, armed conflict between liberal democracies remains exceptionally rare, if not absent.

In other words, the erosion of liberal democracy threatens to dismantle these stabilizing mechanisms. As checks and balances weaken and institutional integrity declines, states become more susceptible to erratic, populist, or extremist decision-making—thereby increasing the risk of confrontation. Political extremism, often accompanied by resurgent nationalism, fractures the shared norms that underpin democratic alliances and undermines both diplomacy and economic cooperation.

A global decline in liberal democracy would not only leave democratic states more vulnerable to external threats but could also drive them into zero-sum competition with each other—reproducing the dynamics of classical realist geopolitics. This fragmentation would deepen global divisions, encourage the formation of rival power blocs, and render the international system more unstable and prone to crisis.

Today, liberal democracy faces an existential test. In some countries, cultural tensions over immigration have reached a boiling point. In others, deepening political polarization threatens the very foundations of democratic governance. Addressing this crisis requires bold and decisive action. The stakes could not be higher: unless liberal democracy proves resilient enough to withstand these mounting pressures, it risks fading into the annals of history.

Endnotes:

1 One of the most famous articulations of this principle can be found in Immanuel Kant's *Groundwork of the Metaphysics of Morals:* "Act so as to treat humanity, whether in your own person or in that of another, always as an end, and never merely as a means." Even before Kant, thinkers like John Locke and Jean-Jacques Rousseau advanced similar ideas, arguing that individuals possess inherent value and should be respected for their freedom and dignity in their own right. Locke's natural rights theory emphasized life, liberty, and property as fundamental human entitlements, while Rousseau's social contract theory underscored the importance of individual autonomy within a collective political order. These philosophical traditions laid the groundwork for modern conceptions of human rights, shaping the ethical and political frameworks that continue to influence contemporary discourse on justice and governance.

2 Liberalism, in domestic politics, generally manifests as a movement that opposes political and social structures or customs that suppress individual freedom. Beyond political science, liberalism also plays a significant role in economics and sociology. Within these disciplines, liberalism has developed into various factions, particularly in economic and international political thought, with neoliberalism emerging as a notable sub-branch. Over time, the expansion and reinterpretation of liberal ideas within these sub-factions have led to increasingly complex and sometimes contested definitions of liberalism. Contemporary liberalism cannot be neatly categorized as either progressive or conservative. Some forms of liberalism align more closely with progressive ideals, while others resonate with conservative principles. In economic matters, conservatives typically favor classical liberalism, advocating for minimal government intervention in the market and maximizing the freedom of economic agents. However, in cultural and social spheres, conservatives often prioritize community customs and traditional norms over individual freedoms. Progressives, by contrast, tend to reject neoliberal free-market policies, emphasizing wealth redistribution through government intervention, while placing a higher priority on individual freedoms in cultural and social issues, often challenging traditional norms and customs. Even among those who embrace the core tenets of liberalism, significant ideological differences can arise. These differences frequently result in internal conflicts within liberal thought. For example, the protection of minority rights is a fundamental liberal value. In recent years, debates in Western societies have intensified over the extent to which this principle should be enforced. Many on the cultural left advocate not only for banning hate speech against gender minorities but also for compelling the use of specific language when referring to them. This stance has sparked opposition from conservatives, who argue that compelled speech contradicts the foundational liberal principle of freedom of expression. Such tensions illustrate the evolving and often contradictory nature of liberalism in contemporary political discourse.

3 Inductive and deductive reasoning are two foundational methods of drawing conclusions. Inductive reasoning moves from specific observations to broader generalizations and serves as the engine of scientific discovery. For example, after observing that a certain medication consistently reduces symptoms across multiple clinical trials, re-

searchers may inductively conclude that the drug is effective. While such conclusions are open to revision, they provide the essential groundwork for forming hypotheses, constructing theories, and generating new lines of inquiry. Deductive reasoning, by contrast, begins with a general principle and applies it to a specific case. If all birds lay eggs and a pigeon is a bird, it logically follows that pigeons lay eggs. Deductive reasoning offers certainty—so long as its premises are valid—but it cannot generate new knowledge beyond what is already contained in those premises. In this way, deductive reasoning ensures internal coherence, while inductive reasoning opens the door to discovery, creativity, and scientific advancement.

4 In his 1979 seminal work *The Postmodern Condition*, Jean-François Lyotard, one of the leading thinkers of postmodernism, succinctly defined the postmodern as an "incredulity toward metanarratives"—the grand, overarching narratives that overshadow all other historical narratives by determining the legitimacy of such subsidiary narratives. According to Lyotard, these metanarratives impose a totalizing structure on knowledge and history, thereby marginalizing alternative perspectives. Postmodernism, in rejecting these dominant narratives, emphasizes the plurality of viewpoints and the contingent, fragmented nature of truth.

5 John Rawls' concept of the 'veil of ignorance' is a central element of his *Theory of Justice*. This thought experiment asks individuals to design the fundamental principles of justice for society without knowing their own social status, race, gender, or other personal characteristics. The purpose of this hypothetical scenario is to ensure impartiality—since individuals behind the veil of ignorance could end up in any position within society, they would rationally choose principles that guarantee fairness and equality for all. By doing so, Rawls argues, they would prioritize justice as fairness, favoring rules that protect the most disadvantaged rather than policies that benefit only specific groups.

6 Later thinkers such as Daniel Markovits and Michael Sandel have critiqued even meritocracy, arguing that social advantages often attributed to personal effort or merit are largely shaped by structural inequalities. Sandel, in particular, builds on his longstanding critique of Rawls' theory—which he sees as overly detached from lived experience and too focused on individual rights over the communal realities that define us—to challenge the meritocratic ideal. He questions the elevation of personal effort and merit as a fair basis for distributing social goods, exposing how it masks systemic disparities. See among others, Michael Sandel, *Liberalism and the Limits of Justice*, Cambridge University Press (1982); David Markovits, *The Meritocracy Trap: How America's Foundational Myth Feeds Inequality, Dismantles the Middle Class, and Devours the Elite*, Penguin Press (2019); Michael Sandel, *The Tyranny of Merits: What's become of the Common Good?* Farrar, Straus and Giroux (2020).

7 See John Gray, *Straw dogs: Thoughts on humans and other animals*, Granta Books (2002); *Black Mass: Apocalyptic religion and the death of utopia*, Allen Lane (2007); *The silence of animals: On progress and other modern myths*, Allen Lane (2013).

8   See Timothy Snyder, *Bloodlands: Europe Between Hitler and Stalin*, Basic Books (2010).

9   See generally, Timothy Snyder, *On Tyranny: Twenty Lessons from the Twentieth Century*, Crown (2017); Timothy Snyder, *On Freedom*, Crown (2024).

10 In a thought-provoking private conversation I had with a left-wing social scientist, he tried to defend the movement by invoking the theories of Richard Dawkins. Dawkins, a vocal proponent of secular humanism, champions an ethics grounded in 'empathy'—arguing that social norms should be based on concern for human well-being. My interlocutor claimed that this perspective provides a theoretical foundation for restricting expressions or discourse deemed offensive or uncomfortable to marginalized individuals or vulnerable groups. It is worth noting, however, that Dawkins himself has consistently defended free speech and expressed skepticism toward efforts to curtail discourse—even when such discourse is perceived as offensive or uncomfortable by some. Furthermore, Dawkins is a staunch supporter of scientific (and empirical) rationalism. To put this discussion in perspective, in The God Delusion (2006), Dawkins rejects traditional religion as a moral foundation, claiming that its irrationality ultimately makes it harmful to society. He argues that religious doctrines often incite conflict and suffering rather than offering a reliable ethical framework. In place of religion, Dawkins advocates for a humanistic ethics rooted in scientific rationalism—one based on empirical evidence and logical reasoning. To counter the claim that morality depends on religion, Dawkins points to the evolutionary origins of empathy. He argues that empathy evolved to foster cooperation and social cohesion, enabling humans to behave ethically without relying on divine commandments. By grounding morality in human nature and evolution, Dawkins challenges the idea that religious belief is necessary for ethical decision-making.

11 In *A Letter Concerning Toleration* (1689), John Locke presents a compelling case for freedom of thought and expression, arguing that they are essential to a just society. First, he asserts that neither individuals nor governments possess absolute knowledge or truth. Since no one can claim infallibility, suppressing dissent risks silencing what may, in fact, be the truth. Even when ideas are flawed, Locke maintains that open debate helps refine existing beliefs and uncover deeper truths. Thus, all ideas—correct or mistaken—must remain subject to public discussion. Locke also emphasizes that exposure to diverse perspectives strengthens logic and reasoning, fostering intellectual and societal progress. He argues that freedom of conscience, particularly in religious matters, is a fundamental right that must be safeguarded from government interference. Truth, he insists, is not established through coercion but through reason. Suppressing thought and expression leads only to hypocrisy and resentment, not genuine conviction. Moreover, Locke warns that enforced intellectual uniformity breeds social unrest, while a peaceful society must accommodate differing views. Finally, he underscores that protecting free expression is vital to preventing tyranny. Silencing dissent lays the groundwork for despotism, whereas open dialogue keeps power in check and sustains a healthy democratic order. Through this argument, Locke highlights the indispensable role of tolerance in maintaining a just and stable society.

12 The authority of judicial decisions, despite their shortcomings, rests on a social consensus that legitimizes institutionalized procedures for dispute resolution. This consensus is essential to the maintenance of a liberal social order. When courts yield to external political, ideological, or populist pressures, their legitimacy begins to erode. Without public confidence in judicial decisions, the judiciary can no longer fulfill its role as a provider of peaceful dispute resolution. In the absence of such mechanisms, social discord inevitably deepens, the legal order weakens, and disputes degenerate into power struggles or self-help. A society governed in this way ceases to function not only as a true republic, but also as a liberal democracy.

13 Aristotle's analysis in Politics establishes a strong connection between the rule of law and the rise of demagogues. He argued that in lawful democracies, where constitutional principles and legal frameworks prevail, the 'best citizens' naturally lead, preventing demagogues—who manipulate public opinion through emotional appeals—from gaining power. However, when the rule of law weakens, democracies devolve into systems where the collective will of the majority (demos) overrides legal constraints. In such conditions, demagogues consolidate authority through populist decrees, replacing legal governance with arbitrary rule. Aristotle likened this lawless democracy to tyranny, as both centralize power and enable despotic rule. The majority, acting as a singular entity rather than as individuals, becomes tyrannical, while sycophants (flatterers) reinforce the demagogue's dominance, further undermining institutional checks. For Aristotle, a constitution ceases to exist when laws lose their supremacy, highlighting that democratic stability depends on legal authority prevailing over populist whims. See Aristotle, Politics, Book 4, section 1292a, translated by H. Rackham (retrieved from Perseus Digital Library).

14 On the left, historical examples include Robespierre and the Jacobins' purges during the French Revolution (1793), the Bolshevik Great Purge following the Russian Revolution (1917), the Cultural Revolution's purges in China (1960s), and the Khmer Rouge purges in Cambodia (1970s). On the right, they include Mussolini's Fascist regime in Italy (1920s), Nazi Germany's brutal oppression (1930s), and Franco's authoritarian military dictatorship in Spain (1930s–1970s).

15 The 1974 Carnation Revolution in Portugal and the peaceful transfer of power following the dismantling of apartheid in South Africa during the 1990s stand out as rare exceptions to the historical pattern of political upheaval. Unlike most revolutions or regime changes, these transitions avoided the violent purges and brutal repression that often accompany such shifts.

16 The German philosopher Georg Wilhelm Friedrich Hegel developed this dialectical framework to explain how contradictions drive historical progress. According to Hegel, history unfolds through a process of thesis, antithesis, and synthesis, in which an initial idea (thesis) is challenged by a counter-idea (antithesis), and the conflict between the two is eventually reconciled into a higher-order synthesis that resolves their contradictions.

17 Hegel viewed history as a structured progression toward greater freedom and reason, culminating in what he called the realization of Absolute Spirit.

18 See Freddie Hayward, "The godfather of the Maga right: Steve Bannon on a US-Russia alliance, kinship with Blue Labour, and his war on modernity," *The New Statesman* (26 February 2025).

19 Neoliberalism, which flourished under the liberal international order, is often seen as the ideological counterpart to leftist liberalism. While the two differ on key issues such as government intervention and market freedom, they both share a commitment to cosmopolitanism. In contrast, post-liberalism—advocating for the revival of traditional values and communitarianism—explicitly rejects globalism and cosmopolitanism. This rejection stands in direct opposition to the ideals of perpetual peace through global cooperation, as espoused by thinkers like Immanuel Kant and political leaders such as Woodrow Wilson.

20 Conversely, if a group is persistently targeted yet fails to mount an adequate response, the legitimacy of the attacks against it should be questioned.

21 See Carl Schmitt, *Political Theology: Four Chapters on the Concept of Sovereignty* (originally in 1922), University of Chicago Press (2005); Carl Schmitt, *The Concept of the Political* (originally in 1932), University of Chicago Press (2007); Carl Schmitt, *The Crisis of Parliamentary Democracy* (originally in 1923), MIT Press (1988).

22 The specific requirements for establishing such a political party will vary depending on the country, society, and political environment.

23 Many often mistake the political concept of 'centrism,' which fundamentally strives for 'golden mean (mesotes)' between two extremes, for 'neutrality.' In addition, centrism does not always settle for the so-called "middle ground." Rather, it prioritizes the most balanced and effective outcome. When circumstances demand bold action to achieve this balance, centrists are willing to embrace and pursue such measures.

24 For a comprehensive analysis on the Democratic Peace Theory, see Michael Doyle, "Why They Don't Fight – The Surprising Endurance of the Democratic Peace," Foreign Affairs (June 18, 2024).

CHAPTER 16

NAVIGATING THE UNCERTAINTIES
: CONCLUDING REFLECTIONS ON A CHANGING WORLD

> The important thing is not to stop questioning.
> Albert Einstein

We are living through an era of profound transformation.

Not only is the liberal international order—which has structured global relations for decades—undergoing fundamental change, but so too is the liberal democratic foundation upon which it was built. Assumptions once taken for granted no longer hold; scenarios once deemed unthinkable are now within reach.

The forces driving this transformation are manifold and complex. Most immediately visible is the shifting global balance of power, which has altered the structural landscape of international relations. But this is only part of the story. The behavior of states and societies is also deeply shaped by the values and worldviews of their people—worldviews that evolve alongside changing realities and prevailing ideologies.

Today, we are once again witnessing a clash between liberal and nationalist-realist worldviews, each offering contrasting visions of international order and governance. Liberals have long maintained that deeper international cooperation and economic interdependence would guide humanity toward a more peaceful and stable future. Realists, by contrast, have rejected this vision as utopian, insisting that the international system remains, at its core, a self-help arena defined by competition for power and security. The global resurgence of nationalism only reinforces this realist conviction.

Yet this iteration of the clash is unlike any before. In the past, liberals sought to build a cooperative order atop a realist world—a system that, while imperfect and unequal, proved beneficial to many. Never before, however, have we seen the liberal international order itself unravel.

As we enter this uncertain era of hegemonic transition, one thing is clear: no one can say with certainty what comes next.

The United States, having come to terms with the inevitability of a multipolar world, now grapples with the challenge of redefining its role—not as the singular global hegemon, but as the preeminent great power among many. Meanwhile, revisionist states that once sought to dismantle unipolarity must now formulate grand strategies suited to a rapidly emerging multipolar era. The vast majority of nations, caught off guard by the suddenness of this transition, are anxiously preparing to navigate the uncertainties of the 21st century.

A world once steadily integrating under the banner of international liberalism now faces mounting challenges on every front. The fate of a world without a singular hegemon remains uncertain. While some nations may find opportunity in the new order, from a broader global perspective, the return of multipolarity is an ominous development. This multipolarity will differ in kind—not just in degree—from that of previous eras. Most critically, the defining challenges of the coming decades—climate change, unregulated AI, WMD proliferation, and more—cannot be resolved through the limited and often fragile cooperation typical of past multipolar or bipolar systems.

Tragically, the intensification of geopolitical rivalries and the erosion of liberal values are likely to weaken multilateralism. In a fractured and distrustful international community, the capacity to address existential risks may be diminished. The deterioration of free trade and global cooperation could further destabilize societies, compounding economic hardship and fueling new sources of international conflict. Any one of these trends could trigger a crisis of catastrophic proportions. That is why collective security frameworks, international cooperation, and multilateral trade mechanisms are not optional—they are indispensable in the 21st century.

If humanity fails to mount a collective response to the unprecedented crises of this century, the worst-case scenario is not mere instability—it is extinction. Indeed, our species may not survive to see the end of the century. This is not an exaggeration.

For this reason, we must not abandon multilateralism. Even if the form of multilateralism pursued under the liberal international order was viable only in the context of U.S. unipolarity, we cannot afford to discard it altogether. Rather, we must seek a new, updated form of multilateralism—one that can function effectively in the emerging world order.

The illusions of liberalism, however, have come to an end. That is the undeniable reality of our time. The grand experiment that began with classical liberalism, evolved through Woodrow Wilson's vision of international liberalism, and culminated in the post–Cold War liberal international order has reached its limits. The once-prevalent belief that all nations would inevitably embrace liberal democracy has lost its hold. The narrative of the "End of History" no longer commands belief.

Yet some core values of liberalism must be preserved. At the very least, human civilization must not regress to the point of forsaking the foundational legacies of classical liberalism. The principles it espoused—freedom, human rights, the rule of law, and rationalism—are intellectual assets that transcend civilizations, ethnicities, regions, and cultures. Unlike neoliberalism or 21st-century progressivism, these timeless tenets, first championed centuries ago, remain values even the most traditionalist states can recognize as universal. Anchored by these principles, we must engage in sincere, open dialogue across nations, cultures, and individuals to rediscover the truly universal values of humanity. The enduring project of achieving lasting global peace must begin again from this foundational starting point.

Reimagining the international order will require a careful reassessment of global governance structures. This may involve reforming existing institutions or even creating an entirely new system. Such an undertaking demands deep technical deliberation and sustained effort, and can proceed at a measured pace. After all, every system is ultimately built upon political dynamics that allocate responsibilities among stakeholders based on necessity, legitimacy, and rationality. But before we embark on that long-term endeavor, one urgent task must take precedence: securing immediate peace in the face of mounting conflicts.

At the time of this writing, the international community is confronting a grave and unpredictable security crisis. No one can foresee how far the instability sparked by shifting power dynamics will spread. Ukraine, the Taiwan Strait, the Korean Peninsula—any miscalculation in these flashpoints could trigger a chain reaction with devastating consequences. In this volatile period of transition, escalation could quickly spiral out of control. No nation is immune to the catastrophe such a scenario could bring.

The international community must urgently prioritize collective action to address immediate crises amid the ongoing reconfiguration of global power. At the same time, we must lay the groundwork for a resilient and sustainable international order—a long-term endeavor whose success ultimately depends on the restoration of a stable equilibrium.

The road ahead is long and uncertain, marked by risk and volatility. To pretend otherwise would be naïve. And yet, a silver lining remains: for the first time in history, humanity possesses the collective knowledge, historical insight, and analytical tools that might—just might—enable us to navigate this transition without catastrophe. Equipped with these assets, we have a rare opportunity to rise above the failures of the past and chart a new course toward a more hopeful future.

If we can face each challenge with clarity, endure the turbulence with resolve, and remain steady amid upheaval, the situation will eventually improve. History teaches us that all great dilemmas are either resolved with time or lose their urgency in its wake. The crises of our time are no exception. When the solutions are beyond our immediate reach, endurance itself becomes a form of resistance. And if we endure—if we outlast the crises—we will, in the end, overcome it.

I close this book with a line from Christopher Nolan's 2014 cinematic masterpiece, *Interstellar*: "We will find a way. We always have."

BIBLIOGRAPHY

English materials

_____, *Decade Forecast: 2000-2010*, Stratfor Global Intelligence (1 January 2000)

_____, *Decade Forecast: 2005-2015*, Stratfor Global Intelligence (7 February 2005)

_____, *Decade Forecast: 2010-2020*, Stratfor Global Intelligence (21 January 2010)

_____, *Decade Forecast: 2015-2025*, Stratfor Global Intelligence (23 February 2015)

_____, *Decade Forecast: 2020-2030*, Stratfor Global Intelligence (12 February 2020)

_____, *Freedom in the World 2022*, Freedom House (February 2022)

_____, *Freedom in the World 2024*, Freedom House (February 2024)

_____, *Pacific Historical Review*, Volume 55, Number 1 (February 1986)

_____, *World Trade Report of 2023*, World Trade Organization (2023)

Adam Smith, *An Inquiry into the Nature and Causes of the Wealth of Nations* (ed. C.J. Bullock), Collier (1937)

Adam Tooze, *Crashed: How a Decade of Financial Crisis Changed the World* (Penguin Books, 2019)

Alexander Downes, "Regime Change Doesn't Work," Boston Review (September/October 2011)

Aleksandr Dugin, *The Foundations of Geopolitics: The Geopolitical Future of Russia*, Arktogeja (1997)(English Translation 2020)

Alexander Wendt, "Anarchy Is What States Make of It: The Social Construction of Power Politics," International Organizations, Volume 46, Number 2 (Spring 1992), pp. 391-425.

Aloysius Uche Ordu & Danielle Resnick, "After the US-Africa Leaders Summit, the US must ensure accountability and strengthen coordination," Brookings (23 December 2022)

Amitav Acharya, *The End of American World Order*, Polity Press (2015)

Anique Ginneken, *Historical Dictionary of the League of Nations*, Scarecroww Press (2006)

Angus Maddison, *Development Centre Studies – The World Economy: Historical Statistics*, OECD (2003)

Anne-Marie Brady, "Magic Weapons: China's political influence activities under Xi Jinping," Conference paper presented at the conference on "The corrosion of democracy under China's global influence, supported by the Taiwan Foundation for Democracy," hosted in Arlington, Virginia, USA, 16-17 September 2017

Anshu Siripurapu and Noah Berman, "Is Industrial Policy Making a Comeback?" Renewing America (18 November 2022)

Antonios Tzanakopoulos, *Disobeying The Security Council*, Oxford University Press (2013)

Arthur Nussbaum, *A Concise History of the Law of Nations*, Macmillan Company (1954)

Arvind Subramanian, "The Inevitable Superpower: Why China's Dominance Is a Sure Thing," Foreign Affairs, Volume 90, Number 5 (September/October 2011)

Ben Bland, "Trump's tariffs will push Southeast Asia uncomfortably close to China," Chatham House (8 April 2025)

Benjamin Valentino, "The True Costs of Humanitarian Intervention," Foreign Affairs, Volume 90, Issue 6, (November/December 2011)

Bernard Hoekman and Petros C. Mavroidis, "WTO Reform: Back to the Past to Build for the Future," Global Policy Volume 12, Supplement 3 (April 2021)

Bill Emmott, *The fate of the West: the battle to save the world's most successful political idea*, Public Affairs (2017)

Brian Katulis & Peter Juul, "The Lessons Learned for U.S. National Security Policy in the 20 Years Since 9/11," CAP Article (10 September 2021)

Bruce Hoffman, *Inside Terrorism*, Columbia University Press (2006)

Bruce Jones & Susana Malcorra, "Competing for Order – Confronting the Long Crisis of Multilateralism," Brookings (October 2020)

Carl Schmitt, *Political Theology: Four Chapters on the Concept of Sovereignty*, University of Chicago Press (2005)

Carl Schmitt, *The Concept of the Political*, University of Chicago Press (2007)

Carl Schmitt, *The Crisis of Parliamentary Democracy*, MIT Press (1988)

Caroline de Gruyter, "Putin's War is Europe's 9/11," FP (28 February 2022)

Carter Malkasian, "The Korea Model: Why an Armistice Offers the Best Hope for Peace in Ukraine," Foreign Affairs (July/August 2023)

Chad P. Bown and Soumaya Keynes, "Why Trump Shot the Sheriffs: The End of WTO Dispute Settlement 1.0", Peterson Institute for International Economics (March 2020)

Charles Lois Montesquieu, *The Spirit of Laws* (originally in 1748), Prometheus (2002)

Christian Goeschel, *Mussolini and Hitler: The Foreging of the Fascist Alliance*, Yale University Press (2018)

Christopher Layne, "Kant or Cant: The Myth of the Democratic Peace," International Security, Volume 19, Number 2 (Fall 1994)

Chris Miller, *Chip War: The Fight for the World's Most Critical Technology*, Scribner (2022)

Clyde Prestowitz, "CHIPS as usual: A defense of US industrial policy," hinrich foundation (30 August 2022)

Colin Gray, *The Second Nuclear Age*, Lynne Reinner Publishers (1999)

Craig Calhoun, "Cosmopolitanism and Nationalism," Nations and Nationalism, Volume 14 (2008), pp. 427-448

Dale Copeland, *The Origins of Major War*, Cornell University Press (2000)

Dani Rodrik, *The Globalization Paradox: Democracy and the Future of the World Economy*, Norton (2011)

Daniel Drezner, *The System Worked: How the World Stopped Another Great Depression*, Oxford University Press (2014)

David Easton, *A Systems Analysis of Political Life*, John Wiley & Sons (1965)

David Kang, *East Asia Before the West: Five Centuries of Trade and Tribute*, Columbia University Press (2010)

David Markovits, *The Meritocracy Trap: How America's Foundational Myth Feeds Inequality, Dismantles the Middle Class, and Devours the Elite*, Penguin Press (2019)

David Steigerwald, "The Synthetic Politics of Woodrow Wilson," Journal of the History of Ideas, Volume 50, Number 3 (July-September 1989), pp. 465-484

Dexter Tiff Roberts, "China is ready to 'eat bitterness' in the trade war. What about the US?" New Atlanticist (10 April 2025)

Donald Trump, *Crippled America: How to Make America Great Again*, Simon & Schuster (2015)

Doni Rodrik, *The Globalization Paradox, Why Global Markets, States, and Democracy Can't Coexist*, Oxford University Press (2012)

Doo-Sik Kim & Haneul Jung, "Special Report: The Legal Status of the Northern Limit Line", Korean Yearbook of International Law, Volume 2 (2015), pp. 191-203

Douglas Irwin, "Globalization enabled nearly all countries to grow richer in recent decades," Peterson Institute for International Economics (16 June 2022)

Douglas Irwin and Oliver Ward, "What is the Washington Consensus?", *Peterson Institute for International Economics* (2021)

Dukgeun Ahn, "Why Reform is Needed: WTO 'Public Body' Jurisprudence", Global Policy Volume 12, Supplement 3 (April 2021)

Edgar Feuchtwanger, Bismarck, Routledge Historical Biographies (2002)

Edward Carr, *The Twenty Years' Crisis, 1919-1939*, Macmillan (1951)

Edward Carr, *What is History?*, Vintage (1967)

Edward Luce, *The retreat of western liberalism*. Atlantic Monthly Press (2017)

Edwin Feulner, "What Are America's Vital Interests?", REPORT Political Porcess, The Heritage Foundation (6 February 1996)

Eleanor Lattimore, "Pacific Ocean or American Lake?" Far Eastern Survey, Volume 14, Number 22 (7 November 1945), pp. 313-316

Eric Schmidt, "Innovation Power – Why Technology Will Define the Future of Geopolitics," Foreign Affairs (28 February 2023)

Francis Fukuyama, "The End of History?", The National Interest, Number 16 (1989), pp. 3-18

Francis Fukuyama, "The End of History and the Last Man", Free Press (2006)

Francis Fukuyama "Against Identity Politics: The New Tribalism and the Crisis of Democracy", Foreign Affairs, Volume 97, Number 5 (2018) pp. 90-114

Francis Fukuyama, Barak Richman, and Ashish Goel, "How to Save Democracy from Technology Ending Big Tech's Information Monopoly", Foreign Affairs (January/February 2021)

Gail Braybon, *Evidence History, and the Great War: Historians and the Impact of 1914-18*, Berghahn Books (2004)

George Friedman, *The Next 100 Years: A Forecast for the 21st Century*, Knopf Doubleday Publishing Group (2010)

George Modelski and William Thompson, *Leading Sectors and World Powers: The Coevolution of Global Economics and Politics*, University of South Carolina Press (1996)

Gerhard Weinberg, *A World at Arms: A Global History of World War II* (2nd ed.), Cambridge University Press (2005)

Gideon Rose, "Get Ready for the Next Nuclear Age – How Trump might drive proliferation," Foreign Affairs (8 March 2025)

Graham Allison, *Destined for War: Can America and China Escape Thucydides's Trap?*, Houghton Mifflin Harcourt (2017)

Graham Allison, "The Myth of the Liberal Order: From Historical Accident to Conventional Wisdom", Foreign Affairs, Volume 97, Number 4 (2018), pp. 124-133

Graham Allison, Kevin Klyman, Karina Barbesino, Hugo Yen, "The Great Tech Rivalry: China vs the U.S.", Avoiding Great Power War Project, Harvard Kennedy School Belfer Center for Science and International Affairs (December 2021)

Graham Allison and Robert Blackwill, *America's National Interests*, The Commission on America's National Interests (1998)

Hal Brands and Michael Beckley, "China is a Declining Power – and That's the Problem," Foreign Policy (24 September 2021)

Hal Brands, "The Age of Amorality – Can America Save the Liberal Order Through Illiberal Means?" Foreign Affairs (20 February 2024)

Hal Brands, "The Renegade Order – How Trump Wields American Power," Foreign Affairs (25 February 2025)

Halford Mackinder, "The Geographical Pivot of History", The Geographical Journal, Volume 23, Number 4 (1904), pp. 421-437

Haneul Jung, "Decoding Global Politics: The Complex Workings of International Relations", SiLO Perspectives No. 3 (September 26, 2024)

Haneul Jung & Nu Ri Jung, "Enforcing 'Purely' Environmental Obligations Through International Trade Law: A Case of the CPTPP's fisheries Subsidies", Journal of World Trade, Volume 53, Issue 6 (2019), pp. 1001-1020

Haneul Jung, "Kant's Perpetual Peace: The Foundation of the Liberal Worldview", SiLO Perspectives No. 6 (2025)

Haneul Jung & Nu Ri Jung, "Longstanding Riddle about the Doctrine of Legitimate Expectation Under International Investment Law – Ascertaining Legal Tests for the Customary International Law's Minimum Standard of Treatment", Northwestern Journal of International Law and Business, Volume 42, Issue 2 (2022)

Haneul Jung & Jeongmeen Suh, "Preventing Systematic Circumvention of the SCM Agreement: Beyond the Mandatory / Discretionary Distinction", World Trade Review, Volume 15, Issue 3 (2016), pp. 475-493

Haneul Jung, et al., "Responding to Foreign Anti-Dumping Investigations: Exclusion of Korean PVC Shrink Film Products from Colombian Anti-Dumping Duties", Lexology (29 November 2013)

Haneul Jung, "Tackling Currency Manipulation with International Law: Why and How Currency Manipulation should be Adjudicated?", Manchester Journal of International Economic Law, Volume 9, Issue 2 (2012)

Haneul Jung, "The Age of Reason: How the European Enlightenment Shaped Modern Civilization", SiLO Perspectives No. 5 (December 2, 2024)

Haneul Jung, "The Ends Justify the Means? Realpolitik's Clash with Legitimacy Through History", SiLO Perspectives No. 4 (14November 2024)

Haneul Jung, "The European Balance of Power: The 19th Century Geopolitics Behind the World War II", SiLO Perspectives No. 7 (2025)

Haneul Jung, "Welcome to Our Changing World: Why the World Order is Shifting and Why It Matters", SiLO Perspectives No. 2 (7 June 2024)

Hans Kelsen, *Pure Theory of Law*, The Lawbook Exchange (2009)

Hans Kundnani, "What is the Liberal International Order?", German Marshall Fund (3 May 2017)

Hans Morgenthau, *Politics Among Nations* (7th ed), McGraw-Hill Education (2005)

Henry Farrel and Abraham Newman, "Weaponized Interdependence: How Global Economic Network Shape State Coercion", International Security, Vol. 44, No. 1 (2019)

Henry Kissinger, *Diplomacy*, Simon & Schuster (1994)

Henry Kissinger, *World Order*, Penguin Books (2015)

Henry Sokolski, "Getting Ready for a Nuclear-Ready Iran: Report of the NPEC Working Group," in *Getting Ready for a Nuclear-Ready Iran*, ed. Henry Sokolski and Patrick Clawson, Strategic Studies Institute (2005), pp. 1-10

Hippolyte Forack, "US-Africa Leaders Summit could make history – if leaders recalibrate trade relations," Atlantic Council (12 December 2022)

Holger Herwig, *The Influence of A.T. Mahan upon German Sea Power*, U.S. Naval War Collge (1990).

Hope Seck, "The Navy Wants to Decommision 24 Ships. Are Plans for A Mega-Fleet Dead?" SANDBOXX (3 April 2022)

Hope Seck, "Hypersonic Weapons Could Rescue The Navy's Stealth Destroyer" SANDBOXX (3 April 2022)

H.L.A. Hart, *The Concept of Law*, Oxford University Press (1997)

H. P. Willmott, *First World War*, Dorling Kindersley H/B (2003)

Ian Hurd, *International Organizations: Politics, Law, Practice*, Cambridge University Press (2011)

Ian Hurd, "Legitimacy and Authority in International Politics," International Organization (1999), pp. 379-403

Immanuel Kant, *Perpetual Peace – A Philosophical Essay*, CreateSpace Independent Publishing Platform (2016)

International Bank for Reconstruction and Development (The World Bank): "The 2011 World Development Report"

Isaac Chotiner, "Why John Mearsheimer Blames the U.S. for the Crisis in Ukraine," The New Yorker (1 March 2022)

Jack Donnelly, "The Ethics of Realism", in Christian Reus-Smit & Duncan Snidal (eds.), The Oxford Handbook of International Relations, Oxford University Press (2008)

Jaemin Lee, "IHR 2005 in the Coronavirus Pandemic: A Need for a New Instrument to Overcome Fragmentation?," ASIL Insights, Volume 24, Issue 16 (2020)

Jaemin Jeon & Haneul Jung, "Korea" Chapter, Brian Facey (ed.), Foreign Investment Regulation Review, Law Business Research (2016)

James Fearon, "Rationalist Explanations for War," *International Organization*, Volume 49, Number 3 (Summer 1995), pp. 379-414

Jamie Gaida, Jennifer Wong Leung, Stephan Robin & Danielle Cave, "ASPI's Critical Technology Tracker – The global race for future power," Australian Strategic Policy Institute (2 March 2023)

Jared Diamond, Guns, Germs, and Steel, W. W. Norton (2005)

Jean Jacques Rousseau, *The Social Contract* (originally 1762), Ozymandias Press (2018)

Jeannette Money, "Globalization, international mobility and the liberal international order," International Affairs, Volume 97, Issue 5 (2021), pp. 1559-1577

Jeff Colgan and Robert Keohane, "The Liberal Order is Rigged: Fix it Now or Watch it Wither," Foreign Affairs, Volume 96, Number 3 (2017) pp. 36-44

Jeremy Baum & John Villasenor, "How close are we to AI that surpasses human intelligence?" Brookings (18 July 2023)

Jeremy Rifkin, *The European Dream: How Europe's Vision of the Future is Quietly Eclipsing the American Dream*, Jeremy P. Tarcher Inc. (2004)

John Culver, "How to Read Xi Jinping – Is China Really Preparing for War?", Foreign Affairs (6 June 2023)

John Delaney, et. al, "2022 Emerging Technology Trends, Perkins Coie LLP (January 2022)

John Gray, *Straw dogs: Thoughts on humans and other animals*, Granta Books (2002)

John Gray, *Black Mass: Apocalyptic religion and the death of utopia*, Allen Lane (2007)

John Gray, *The silence of animals: On progress and other modern myths*, Allen Lane (2013)

John Ikenberry, *After Victory: Institutions, Strategic Restraint, and the Rebuilding of Order after Major Wars*. Princeton University Press (2001)

John Ikenberry, *A World Safe for Democracy: Liberal Internationalism and the Crises of Global Order*. Yale University Press (2020)

John Ikenberry, "Is American Multilateralism in Decline?", Perspectives on Politics, Volume 1, Number 3 (2003), pp. 533-550

John Ikenberry, *Liberal Leviathan: the origins, crisis, and transformation of the American world order*. Princeton University Press (2011)

John Ikenberry, *Liberal Order and Imperial Ambition: Essays on American Power and International Order*. Princeton University Press (2011)

John Ikenberry, *Power, Order, and Change in World Politics*. Cambridge University Press (2014)

John Ikenberry, "Salvaging the G-7", Foreign Affairs, Vol. 72, No. 2 (1993), pp. 132-139

John Ikenberry, "The End of liberal international order?", International Affairs, Issue 94, Volume 1 (2018), pp. 7-23

John Ikenberry, "The Future of the Liberal World Order", Foreign Affairs, May/June (2011), pp. 56-68

John Ikenberry, "The Illusion of Geopolitics: The Enduring Power of the Liberal Order", Foreign Affairs, Volume 93, No. 3 (2014) pp. 80-90

John Ikenberry, "The Plot Against American Foreign Policy: Can the Liberal Order Survive?", Foreign Affairs, Volume 93, No. 3 (2017) pp. 2-9

John Kane, "Democracy and world peace: the Kantian dilemma of United States foreign policy," Australian Journal of International Affairs (2012), Volume 66, pp. 292-312.

John Lewis Gaddis, The Cold War: A New History, Penguin Books (2006)

John Lewis Gaddis, "Why Would Anyone Want to Run the World? – The Warnings in Cold War History," Foreign Affairs (7 June 2024)

John Locke, *Two Treatises of Government* (originally in 1689), CreateSpace Independent Publishing Platform (2014)

John Mearsheimer, "Bound to Fail: The Rise and Fall of the Liberal International Order", International Security, Vol. 43, No. 4 (Spring 2019), pp. 7-50

John Mueller, "PAX AMERICA is a Myth: Aversion to War Drives Peace and Order," The Washington Quarterly (Fall 2020), pp. 115-136

John Pomfret & Matt Pottinger, "Xi Jinping Says He is Preparing China for War – The World Should Take Him Seriously," Foreign Affairs (29 March 2023)

John Rawls, *A Theory of Justice*, Belknap Press (1999)

John Ruggie, "International Regimes, Transactions, and Change: Embedded Liberalism in the Postwar Economic Order", International Organization, Vol. 36, No. 2 (1982), pp. 379-415

John Ruggie, "Multilateralism: The anatomy of an institution", in John Ruggie (ed.), Multilateralism Matters: The Theory and Praxis of an Institutional Form, Columbia University Press (1993), pp. 3-47

J.V. Stalin, Questions & Answers to American Trade Unionists: Stalin's Interview with the First American Trade Union Delegation to Soviet Russia (September 15, 1927), Marxists Internet Archive

John Stuart Mill, *On Liberty* (originally in 1859), Dover Publications (2002)

John Weitz, *Hitler's Banker: Hjalmar Horace Greeley Schacht*, Warner Futura (2002)

Jon Western & Joshua Goldstein, "Humanitarian Intervention Comes of Age, Lessons From Somalia to Libya," Foreign Affairs, FRNA, 48, Volume 90 (2011)

Jonathan Kirshner, "Bring Them All Back Home? Dollar Diminution and U.S. Power," The Washington Quarterly, Volume 36, Issue 3 (Summer 2013), pp. 27-45

Jonathan Kirshner, "Trump's 'America First' is Not Realism," Foreign Affairs (22 January 205)

Joseph Ebeghulem, "The Failure of Collective Security in the Post World Wars I and II International System", International Journal of Peace and Conflict Studies. Volume 1, Number 1 (2012)

Joseph Nye and David Welch, *Understanding Global Conflict & Cooperation: Intro to Theory & History* (9th Ed.), Pearson Education (2014)

Karen Mingst, Heather Mckibben, Ivan Arreguín-Toft, *Essentials of International Relations* (8th Ed.), W.W. Norton (2019)

Karl Marx & Frederick Engels, *Manifesto of Communist Party*, Foreign Language Press (1972)

Keith Rockwell, "The drums echoing: Africa's rising clout in global trade and geopolitics," hinrich foundation (8 August 2023)

Kenneth Oye, "Explaining Cooperation under Anarchy: Hyopthesis and Strategies," World Politics Volume 38, Issue 1 (1985), pp. 1-24

Kenneth Waltz, "Globalization and Governance," Political Science and Politics, Volume 32, Number 4 (December 1999), pp. 693-700

Kenneth Waltz, *Theory of International Politics*, Waveland Press (2010)

Kenneth Waltz, "Why Iran Should Get the Bomb: Nuclear Balancing Would Mean Stability," Foreign Affairs, Volume 91, Issue 4 (2012)

Kenton Thibaut, *Chinese Discourse Power: Capabilities and Impact*, Atlantic Council (August 2023)

Kevin Grier and Robin Grier, "The Washington Consensus Works: Causal Effects of Reform, 1970-2015", Journal of Comparative Economics, Vol. 49 (8 September 2020), pp. 59-72

Kofi Annan, "Reflections on Intervention," The Question of Intervention: Statements by the Secretary-General (United Nations, 1999)

Larry Diamon, "How to End the Democratic Recession – The Fight Against Autocracy Needs a New Playbook," Foreign Affairs (22 October 2024)

Lisa Martin, "Interests, Power, and Multilateralism", International Organization, Volume 46, Number 4, (1992), pp. 765-792

Lori Damrosch, et al., *International Law – Cases and Materials* (4th ed), West Group (2002)

Louis Henkin, *How Nations Behave – Law and Foreign Policy* (2nd ed), Council on Foreign Relations (1979)

Luke Amadi, "Globalization and the changing liberal international order: A review of the literature", Research in Globalization 2 (2020)

Malcolm Jorgensen, "The German National Security Strategy and International Legal Order's Contested Political Framing," European Journal of International Law Blog (5 July 2023)

Mario Coccia, "Why do nations produce science advances and new technology?", Technology in Society 59 (2019)

Mark Esper, *A Sacred Oath: Memoirs of a Secretary of Defense During Extraordinary Times*, William Morrow (2022)

Mark Gunzinger & Bryan Clark, "Winning The Salvo Competition: Rebalancing America's Air and Missile Defenses," Center for Strategic and Budgetary Assessments (20 May 2016)

Mark Copelovitch, Sara Hobolt & Stefanie Walter, "Challenges to the contemporary global order. Cause for pessimism or optimisim?", Journal of European Public Policy, Volume 27, Issue 7 (2020), pp. 1114-1125

Markus Kornprobst and T. V. Paul, "Globalization, deglobalization and the liberal international order," International Affairs, Volume 97, Issue 5, (2021) pp. 1305-1316

Martin Gilbert, *First World War*, Stoddart Publishing (1994)

Matt Gobush, "Resurrecting Woodrow Wilson: A Christian Critique of Liberal Internationalism," Providence (29 June 2018)

M. E. Sarotte, "Why They Fight – What's at Stake in the Blame Game Over Ukraine," Foreign Affairs (9 April 2025)

Mette Eilstrup-Sangiovannia and Stephanie C. Hofmann, "Of the contemporary global order, crisis, and change," Journal of European Publis Policy, Volume 27, Issue 7 (2020) pp. 1077-1089

Michael Albertus, "The Coming Age of Territorial Expansion – Climate Change will Fuel Contests – and Maybe Wars – for Land and Resources," Foreign Affairs (4 March 2025)

Michael Cox, "Power Shifts, Economic Change and the Decline of the West," International Relations, Volume 26, Issue 4 (2012)

Michael Desch, "Benevolent Cant? Kant's Liberal Imperialism," The Review of Politics, Volume 73, Number. 4 (2011) pp. 649-656

Michael Doyle, "Why They Don't Fight – The Surprising Endurance of the Democratic Peace," Foreign Affairs (June 18, 2024)

Michael Doyle, "Kant, Liberal Legacies, and Foreign Affairs," Philosophy & Public Affairs, Volume 12, Issue 3 (1983), pp. 205-235

Michael Kimmage, "The World Trump Wants – American Power in the New Age of Nationalism," Foreign Affairs (25 February 2025)

Michael Kofman and Rob Lee, "Beyond Ukraine's Offensive – The West Needs to Prepare the Country's Military for a Long War," Foreign Affairs (March 10, 2023)

Michael Mandelbaum, *The Case for Goliath: How America Acts as the World's Govern-*

ment in the 21st Century, Perseus Books (2005)

Michael Mandelbaum, *The ideas that conquered the world: peace, democracy and free markets in the twenty-first century*. Public Affairs (2004)

Michael Sandel, *Liberalism and the Limits of Justice*, Cambridge University Press (1982)

Michael Sandel, *The Tyranny of Merits: What's become of the Common Good?*, Farrar, Straus and Giroux (2022)

Mike Pence, *So Help Me God*, Simon & Schuster (2022)

Miles Kahler, "Multilateralism with Small and Large Numbers," International Organization, Volume 46, Number 3, (1992), p. 681

Mitch McConnell, "The Price of American Retreat – Why Washington Must Reject Isolationism and Embrace Primacy," Foreign Affairs (16 December 2024)

Moisés Naím, "Globalization," Foreign Policy (March/April 2009), pp. 28-34

Monica Toft, "The Return of Spheres of Influence – Will Negotiations Over Ukraine Be a New Yalta Conference that Carves Up the World?" Foreign Affairs (13 March 2025)

Nicola-Ann Hardwick, "The UN During the Cold War: 'A tool of superpower influence stymied by superpower conflict?'", E-International Relations (2011)

Nicholas Lardy, "Issues in China's WTO Accession," Brookings Testimony (9 May 2001)

Nicholas Lardy, "How serious is China's economic slowdown?" Peterson Institute for International Economics (17 August 2023)

Niccolo Machiavelli, *The Prince*, Penguin Classics (2015)

Noam Chomsky, *World Orders Old and New*, Pluto Press (1994)

Norrin Ripsman, "Globalization, deglobalization and Great Power Politics," International Affairs, Volume 97, Issue 5, (2021), pp. 1317-1334

Odd Arne Westad, *The Cold War: A World History*, Basic Books (2019)

Oona Hathaway & Scott Shapiro, *The Internationalist: How a Radical Plan to Outlaw War Remade the World*, Simon & Schuster (2017)

Pankaj Ghemawat, "Why the World Isn't Flat," Foreign Policy, Number 159 (March/April 2007), pp. 54-60

Pascal Lamy, "The slow American protectionist turn," VOX (27 March 2023)

Paul Bracken, The Second Nuclear Age: Strategy, Danger, and the New Power Politics, Times Books (2012)

Paul Gewirtz, "China, the United States, and the future of a rules-based international order," Brookings (22 July 2024)

Paul Kennedy, *The Rise and Fall of the Great Powers: Economic Change and Military Conflict from 1500 to 2000*, Random House (1989)

Paul Krugman, "China's Future Isn't What It Used to Be," The New York Times (22 December 2022)

Peter Drysdale & Charlie Barnes, "How India can realize its ambitions to become a great power," hinrich foundation (23 August 2022)

Peter Gries, *China's New Nationalism: Pride, Politics, and Diplomacy*, University of California Press (2004)

Peter Hays Harris, "Losing the International Order: Westphalia, Liberalism and Current World Crises," The National Interest (10 November 2015)

Peter Zeihan, *Disunited Nations: The Scramble for Power in an Ungoverned World*, HarperCollins (2020)

Peter Van den Bosshe, *The Law and Policy of the World Trade Organization* (2nd Ed.), Cambridge University Press (2008)

Petros C. Mavroidis and André Sapir, "All the Tea in China: Solving the 'China Problem' at the WTO," Global Policy Volume 12, Supplement 3 (April 2021)

Philip Setler-Jones, "Welcome to the New Deal-based Order," World Economic Forum (2017)

Pierre Lemieux, "Dispelling Supply Chain Myths," CATO Institute (Summer 2022)

Pratap Bhanu Mehta, "Indispensable Nations – The Fall and Rise of Nationalism," Foreign Affairs (25 February 2025)

Rakesh Kochhar, Richard Fry, and Molly Rohal, "The American Middle Class is Losing Ground," Pew Research Center (9 December 2015)

Rakesh Kochhar & Stella Sechopoulos, "How the American middle class has changed in the past five decades," Pew Research Center (20 April 2022).

Randall Schweller, "Grand Strategy Under Nonpolarity," in Thierry Balzacq & Ronald Krebs (eds.), The Oxford Handbook of Grand Strategy (2021)

Richard Hass, "The Age of Nonpolarity: What Will Follow U.S. Dominance," Foreign Affairs (3 May 2008)

Richard Haas, "World Order 2.0," Foreign Affairs, (January/February 2017)

Richard Helms, "Memorandum for the Director of Central Intelligence: Meeting with the Attorney General of the United States Concerning Cuba" (19 January 1962)

Richard Kohn, "An Essay on Civilian Control of the Military," Diplomacy, March (1997)

Robert Art, "American Foreign Policy and the Fungibility of Force," Security Studies, Volume 5, Number 4 (Summer 1996), pp. 7-42

Robert Art, "To What Ends Military Power?" International Security, Volume 4, Number 4 (Spring 1980), pp. 3-35

Robert Art & Robert Jervis (eds.), *International Politics: Enduring Concepts and Contemporary Issues* (12th ed), Pearson (2015)

Robert Gilpin, *U.S. Power and the Multinational Corporation*, Basic Books (1975)

Robert Jervis, "Cooperation Under the Security Dilemma," World Politics, Volume 30, Number 2 (January 1978), pp. 18-214

Robert Jervis, "Theories of War in an Era of Leading-Power Peace: Presidential Address, American Political Science Association, 2011," American Political Science Review, Volume 96, Number 1 (March 2022), pp. 1-14

Robert Kagan, "The Ambivalent Superpower: America and the world aren't getting a divorce. But they are thinking about it," Politico Magazine (March/April 2014).

Robert Kagan, *The World America Made*. Vintage Books (2012)

Robert Kagan, "The twilight of the liberal world order," Brookings Report (24 January 2017)

Robert Keohane, "International Institutions: Can Interdependence Work?" Foreign Policy, Issue 110 (Spring 1998), pp. 82-94

Robert Powell. 1991. "Absolute and Relative Gains in International Relations Theory," The American Political Science Review, Volume. 85, Number 4:1303-1320

Robert Ross and Zhu Feng (eds.), *China's Ascent: Power, Security, and the Future of International Politics*, (Cornell University, 2008)

Ronald Dworkin, *Law's Empire*, Harvard University Press (1986)

Samuel Barkin and Bruce Cronin, "The state and the nation: changing norms and the rules of sovereignty in international relations," International Organization, Volume 48, Issue 1 (1994), pp. 107-130

Samuel Huntington, *The Clash of Civilization and the Remaking of World Order*, Simon & Schuster (2011)

Samuel Huntington, *The Third Wave: Democratization in the Late Twentieth Century*, Volume 4, University of Oklahoma Press (1993)

Sherzod Shadikhodjaev, "Steel Overcapacity and the Global Trading System," Asian Journal of WTO & International Health Law and Policy, Volume. 16, Number 2 (Sep 2021), pp. 179-218

Sid Simpson, "Making liberal use of Kant? Democratic peace theory and Perpetual Peace," International Relations, Volume. 33, Issue 1 (2019) p. 109-128

Simon Newman, "The Hegelian Roots of Woodrow Wilson's Progressivism," American Presbyterians, Volme 64, Number 3 (Fall 1986), PP. 191-201.

Sonali Das, "China's Evolving Exchange Rate Regime," IMF Working Paper (March 2019)

Stephen Brooks, John Ikenberry and William Wohlforth, "Lean Forward: In Defense of American Engagement," *Foreign Affairs*, Volume 92, Number 1 (2013), pp. 130-142

Stephen Brooks, "The Trade Truce? – When Economic Interdependence Does – and Doesn't – Promote Peace," Foreign Affairs (18 June 2024)

Stephen McGlinchey, "Nuclear Weapons and International Relations," *E-International Relations* (2022)

Stephen Walt, "China Wants a 'Rules-Based International Order,' Too," *FP* (31 March 2021)

Stephen Walt, *The Origins of Alliances* (Cornell University Press, 1990)

Stephanie Hofmann, "Global Ordering and Organizational Alternative for Europe: NATO vs. the European Union?", Texas National Security Review (2019), pp. 13-20

Steve Chan, "Challenging the liberal order: the US hegemon as a revisionist power," International Affairs, Volume 97, Issue 5 (2021), pp. 1335-1352

Steven Croley & John Jackson, "WTO Dispute Procedures, Standard of Review, and Deference to National Government," American Journal of International Law Volume 90, Number 2 (April 1996), pp. 193-213

Steven Ratner, "International Law: The Trials of Global Norms," Foreign Policy, Issue 110 (Spring 1998), pp. 65-75

Suisheng Zhao, *A Nation-State by Construction: Dynamics of Modern Chinese Nationalism*, Stanford University Press (2004)

Tanisha Fazal, "The Power of Principles – What Norms are Still Good For," Foreign Affairs (18 June 2024)

Ted Galen Garpenter, "The Imperial Lure: National Building as a US Response to Terrorism" Mediterranean Quarterly (Winter 2006), pp. 34-47

The White House, *Indo-Pacific Strategy of the United States* (February 2022)

Thomas Friedman, *The Lexus and the Olive Tree*, Farrar, Straus, Giroux (1999)

The White House, "United States Strategic Approach to the People's Republic of China," (May 20th, 2020)

Thomas Hobbes, *Leviathan* (originally in 1651), Hackett Publishing Company (1994)

Thomas Paine, *Rights of Man* (originally in 1791), Dover Publications (1999)

Thomas Schelling, *Arms and Influences*, Yale University (1966)

Thucydides, *History of the Peloponnesian War*, Rex Warner (1954)

Tim Marshall, *Prisoners of Geography: Ten Maps that Explain Everything About the World*, Scribner (2015)

Tim Chapman, *The Congress of Vienna 1814-1815*, Routledge (1998)

Timothy Snyder, *Bloodlands: Europe Between Hitler and Stalin*, Basic Books (2010)

Timothy Snyder, *On Tyranny: Twenty Lessons from the Twentieth Century* (Crown, 2017)

Timothy Snyder, *On Freedom* (Crown, 2024)

Tong Zhao, "Will China Escalate? – Despite Short-Term Stability, the Risk of Military Crisis is Rising," Foreign Affairs (2 May 2025)

Tom Buchanan, *Europe's Troubled Peace, 1945-2000*, Blackwell Publishing (2006)

Tom Wright, *All Measures Short of War: The Contest for the 21st Century and the Future of American Power*, Yale University Press (2012)

Tomuschaat Christian, *The United Nations at Age Fifty: A Legal Perspective*, Martinus Nijhoff Publishers (1995)

United States Trade Representative, 2018 Trade Policy Agenda and 2017 Annual Report of the President of the United States on the Trade Agreements Program (2018)

United States Trade Representative, 2021 Report to Congress on China's WTO Compliance (February 2022)

Umut Aydin, "Emerging middle powers and the liberal international order", International Affairs, Volume 97, Issue 5 (2021), pp. 1377-1394

Walden Bello, *Deglobalization: Ideas for a New World Economy*, Zed Books (2004)

Ward Wilson, *Five Myths about Nuclear Weapons*, Houghton Mifflin Harcourt (2013)

William Thompson, *Power Concentration in World Politics: The Political Economy of Systemic Leadership, Growth and Conflict*, Springer (2020)

Yubal Harari, "Why Vladimir Putin has already lost this war," The Guardian (28 February 2022)

Zachariah Mampilly, "What 'the Global South' Really Means – A Modern Gloss for Old Divisions," Foreign Affairs (1 April 2025)

Zbigniew Brzezinski, *The Grand Chessboard: American Primacy and Its Geostrategic Imperatives*, Basic Books (1998)

Korean materials

_____, 『2021 국제정세전망』, 국립외교원 외교안보연구소 (2020.12)

_____, 『2022 국제정세전망』, 국립외교원 외교안보연구소 (2021.12)

_____, 『2023 국제정세전망』, 국립외교원 외교안보연구소 (2022.12)

_____, 『2022 국방백서』, 대한민국 국방부 (2023.2)

_____, 『미-중 기술패권 경쟁에 대응한 주요국 산업정책 방향』, 한국산업기술진흥원 (2021.7)

_____, 『중국의 디지털 실크로드: 중화 디지털블록(China-centered Digital Bloc)과 디지털 위계질서(digital hierarchy)의 부상』, 현대중국연구 21(4)(2020)

강봉구, 「자유주의 국제질서의 균열과 러시아의 주권적 국제주의」, 『슬라브研究』 제35권 4호. (2019) pp. 1-33

강정인, 이상익 「유교적 국제질서의 이념과 그 현대적 함의」, 『한국철학논집』 제47집 (2015), pp. 171-206

강선주, 『미국의 자유주의 패권질서의 지속가능성: 국내정치 필요조건과 포스트-코로나 국제질서에 함의』, 국립외교원 외교안보연구소 (2020)

강선주, 「미국 주도의 자유주의 국제질서: 과거, 현재, 그리고 미래」, 『국제정치논총』 제60집 제2호. (2020) pp. 301-330

김경숙, 「아시아·태평양에서 인도·태평양으로 무게중심 이동」, 『월간〈통상〉』 (2022.3) pp. 2-3

김동기, 『지정학의 힘: 시파워와 랜드파워의 세계사』 아카넷 (2020)

김두식, 정하늘, 김종우, 「해외건설 분쟁 해결 - 'ISD 중재'가 대안이다」, 『K-Build』 2016년 6월호, pp. 34-43

김상배 엮음, 『4차 산업혁명과 미중패권경쟁』, 서울대학교 국제문제연구소 총서 34

(2020)

김수민, 「중국 사법체계는 우리와 어떻게 다를까? - 법률해석과 사법해석을 중심으로」, 법률신문 (2022.4.11.)

김양희, 「미국 주도 '신뢰가치사슬'의 구축 전망과 함의」 IFANS FOCUS (2021.11.8.)

김양희 「21세기 보호주의의 변용, '진영화'와 '신뢰가치사슬(TVC)'」, 국립외교원 외교안보연구소 (2022)

김일기, 채재병, 「북한의 개정 당규약과 대남혁명전략 변화 전망」, 『INSS 전략보고』 (2021. 12.)

김재천, 「인도·태평양으로 보폭을 넓혀가는 세계의 중추 국가들」, 『월간 〈통상〉』. (2022.3), pp. 4-7

김정호, 『법과 경제학』, 한국경제연구원 (1997)

김종현, 『경제사』, 경문사 (2010)

김진아, 「한반도 위기의 핵벼랑끝 구조와 심리·인지적 변수에 대한 고찰」, 『국방정책연구』 제32권 제1호 (2016)

남궁곤, 「오바마 시대 '자유 국제주의 이념 3.0 버전'의 운영체계와 구성요소」, 『동향과 전망』, 92호 (2014), pp. 212-251

남동우·김덕기, 「러시아·우크라이나 갈등의 역사적 근원과 러시아의 우크라이나 침공이 한반도 안보에 주는 전략적 함의」, 『인문사회21』 제13권 제2호 (2022)

남윤선·이정·허성무, 『4차 산업혁명 시대 중국의 역습:반도체 전쟁』 한국경제신문 (2017)

니컬러스 웝숏, 『새뮤엘슨 vs 프리드먼』, (이가영 옮김) 부키(주) (2022)

도널드 부드로, 『하이에크는 어떻게 세상을 움직였나』, (최지희 옮김) 지식발전소·프레이저연구소 (2021)

론 처노, 『금융 권력의 이동』, (노혜숙 옮김) 플래닛 (2008)

마이클 샌델, 『정의란 무엇인가』, (이창신 옮김) 김영사 (2010)

박건영, 「핵무기와 국제정치: 역사, 이론, 정책, 그리고 미래」, 『한국과 국제정치』 제27권 제1호 (2011), pp. 1-45

박재적, 「인태 지역을 둘러싼 아세안과 인도의 관점」, 『더 특별한 통상, 월간 〈통상〉』. (2022.3), pp. 8-11.

박지영, 「미중 기술패권경쟁의 의미」 아산정책연구원 (2020.5.28.)

박원곤·설인효, 「트럼프 행정부 안보국방전략 분석/전망과 한미동맹 발전 방향」, 『국방연구』, 60권 4호 (2017), pp. 1-27

제임스 뷰캐넌·존 버튼·리차드 와그너, 『케인스는 어떻게 재정을 파탄냈는가』, (옥동석 옮김) 자유기업원 (2021).

신각수, 「유엔 가입 30년과 새로운 30년: 국제평화와 정의를 위한 한국의 역할」, 『서

울국제법연구』, 29권 1호 (2022), pp. 1-11.

연원호 · 나수엽 · 박민숙 · 김영선, 『미 · 중간 기술패권 경쟁과 시사점』. 대외경제연구원 (2020.8.31.)

오종혁, 「미중 기술패권 경쟁의 최근 동향」 소프트웨어정책연구소 (2021.5.24)

유영신, 「4차 산업혁명을 대비하는 중국의 ICT 산업 및 정책 동향」, 『ICT Spot Issue』 정보통신기술진행센터(2017)

유지영, 「국가 안보 위협 논란에 따른 미국의 1962년 무역확장법 232조 수입조치에 대한 통상법적 쟁점」, 『통상법률』 138호 (2017)

유희복, 「국제질서의 다면성과 '자유주의 국제질서'의 미래: 중국의 시각을 예로」, 『아태연구』 제4호. (2018) pp. 129-169

윤성원, 「윈스턴 처칠과 유럽통합」 『통합유럽연구』 통권 제17호 (2018), pp. 115-140

윤우진, 「중국 환율제도의 변화와 영향」 『e-kiet 산업경제정보』 (산업연구원) 제485호 (2010.7.15.)

윤혜령, 「4차 산업혁명시대 미중기술패권 경쟁과 시사점 - 화웨이, 틱톡, 텐허 분쟁 사례를 중심으로」, 『2020 STEPI Fellowship』

이근, 「국제적 공간에서의 시장의 진화와 공적영역의 형성: 자유주의 국제질서(Liberal International Order)의 재해석」, 『국제ː지역연구』 33권 4호 (2024) pp. 85-114

이재현, 「신남방정책과 인도 · 태평양 정책의 협력」, 『더 특별한 통상, 월간 〈통상〉』. (2022.3) pp. 12-15

이지용, 「21세기 세계질서와 미중 관계」, 『KINU 통일+』. (2015 여름호) pp. 99-109

이신화 · 박재적, 「미중 패권경쟁시대 인태 지역의 자유주의 국제질서: 도전과 전망」, 『국제지역연구』 제25권 제2호. (2021) pp. 2019-250

이승주, 「불확실성 시대의 국제정치경제: 자유주의 국제질서의 위기?」, 『국제정치논총』 제58집 4호 (2017) pp. 237-271

이혜정, 『냉전 이후 미국 패권: 자본주의와 민주주의, 전쟁의 변주』 한울아카데미 (2017)

이혜정 · 전혜주, 「미국 패권은 예외적인가?: 아이켄베리의 자유주의 국제질서 이론 비판」, 『한국과 국제정치』 제34권 제4호. (2018) pp. 1-31

임미원, 「칸트의 영구평화론」, 『법철학연구』 제14권 제1호. (2011) pp. 43-68

장세호, 「러시아-우크라이나 전쟁 이후 푸틴체제의 안정성 평가」, 『INSS 전략보고』 제193호 (2022년 11월)

장하준, 『나쁜 사마리아인들』, (이순희 옮김) 도서출판 부키 (2011)

장하준, 『사다리 걷어차기』, (형성백 옮김) 도서출판 부키 (2011).

정경록, 『중국일람 - 상하이 주재 상무영사의 비즈니스 에세이 64』 비아북 (2017)

정누리 & 정하늘, 「반덤핑조치 시 덤핑률편승(Rate Shopping) 방지를 위한 실무적 고려사항: 미국식 이해승계인 심사기준의 도입 필요성에 관한 검토를 중심으로」, 『통상법률』 제118호 (2014), pp. 16-48

정성철, 「일극체제와 상호의존을 통해 본 21세기 국제정치」, 『KINU 통일+』 통일연구원 (2015), pp. 45-55

정진영, 「중국의 부상과 국제통화·금융질서의 미래: 자유주의 국제질서가 붕괴될 것인가?」, 『한국과 국제정치』 33권 1호 (2017), pp. 131-168

정하늘, 『21세기 국제질서 맥락으로 이해하기 – 패권 전환기 속 대한민국의 미래』 국제법질서연구소 (2023)

정하늘, "국제재판에서 재심사되는 국내법원 판결들", 『법률신문』 (2022.8.11)

정하늘, "대한민국의 국제분쟁 대응역량 강화를 위한 해묵은 제언", 『법률신문』 (2022.12.8)

정하늘, "우크라이나 전쟁과 진퇴양난에 처한 국제사법재판소", 『법률신문』 (2022.8.29)

정하늘, 「문언외적 해석에 관한 법 해석규칙의 실증적 분석: WTO 판례에 대한 고찰을 중심으로」, 『통상법무정책』 제1호 (2021), pp. 1-27

정하늘, 『미국법 해설』 박영사 (2011)

정하늘, 「투자자-국가 분쟁해결제도(ISDS)에서의 국가책임 발생범위 확장 가능성에 대한 연구」, 『국제법학회논총』 제61권 제1호 (2016), pp. 221-245

정하늘, 「한반도 해역의 법적 지위와 해상작전법」, 『Strategy 21』 제26호 (2010), pp. 5-46

정홍상, 『국제기구 멘토링: 10년의 국제기구 경험담과 GCF 유치과정 스토리』 도서출판 하다 (2013)

존 미어샤이머, 『강대국 국제정치의 비극 – 미중 패권경쟁의 시대』, (이춘근 옮김) 김앤김북스 (2017)

차정미, 「미중기술패권경쟁과 중국의 강대국화 전략 – '기술혁신'과 '기술동맹' 경쟁을 중심으로」, 『국제전략 Foresight』 Vol. 03 (2021.8.12.)

차정미, 「중국의 4차산업혁명 담론과 전략, 추진체계」, 『동서연구』 30(1)(2018)

차태서, 「트럼프 현상과 자유주의세계질서의 위기」, 『JPI정책포럼』 제189권 (2017)

최우선, 「미국의 INF 조약 탈퇴와 미중 군사경쟁」, 『IFANS 2019-23』 국립외교원 외교안보연구소

최은미, 「동북아평화협력플랫폼 활성화를 위한 추진과제」 IFANS 주요국제문제분석 2018-54

한국금융연구원, 「제조강국을 목표로 한 '중국제조 2025'의 내용 및 평가」, 『China Inside 중국 내 주요 연구 동향』 제27권 17호

한승완, 「'정체성 정치'(Identity Politics)와 자유주의 국제질서」, 『국가안보전략연구원 Issue Brief』 18-52 (2018)

한인택 · 변영학 · 장지향 · 성일광 · 강충구 『민주주의 위기, 국제질서 혼란』 아산정책연구원 (2020년 12월)

허성무, 「반도체 패권을 둘러싼 한국중국미국 간 경쟁양상에 대한 연구」, 『통상정보연구』 제20권 4호 (2018)

Beyond the sources explicitly listed above, I have drawn from a vast array of materials—many of which I cannot specifically identify. Over the years, the news articles, books, magazines, reports, and videos I have encountered daily, stretching back to my childhood, have all played a role in shaping my thought process. While I may not be able to cite each source individually, their direct and indirect influence on this book is undeniable. Moreover, throughout my career, I have amassed a wealth of knowledge that has inevitably informed my perspective and reasoning. Although I am confident that this book contains no confidential information, I recognize that my professional experiences have contributed significantly to the development of the ideas presented in this book.

ABOUT THE AUTHOR

Haneul Jung is the founding principal of System for International Law and Order (SiLO) LLC, an independent research and publishing entity dedicated to exploring the complex interplay between international law and global governance.

Haneul's passion for international trade law was ignited back in 2005 during his law school years, when he became captivated by the multilateral trading system under the auspices of the World Trade Organization (WTO). To the young Haneul, the WTO seemed to have successfully brought the principle of the 'rule of law' to life in the anarchic international landscape. He believed that the concept of 'Triangulating Peace,' regarded as the cornerstone of achieving lasting global harmony, was embodied in the WTO's multilateral trading framework.

Upon graduating from law school, Haneul remained committed to his career aspirations. During his mandatory military service, he gained hands-on experience in public international law by serving as an international law specialist for the Republic of Korea (ROK) Joint Chiefs of Staff and as a staff judge advocate for a counter-piracy task force deployed to the Gulf of Aden. In private practice at SL Partners and Shin & Kim, he was not always able to focus exclusively on international trade or public international law. Nevertheless, he actively sought every opportunity to work on such matters, while also handling a wide range of international disputes and cross-border transactions. To deepen his theoretical knowledge, Haneul diligently authored scholarly articles on international trade law and public international law. Luckily, his efforts were recognized with numerous accolades, including constant professional recognition as a 'Leading Individual in International Trade' by Chambers & Partners (Asia-Pacific/Global) and the prestigious Shimdang Scholarly Award on International Trade, among other honors.

From 2018 to 2022, Haneul served as Director of the Trade Dispute Settlement Division at the Ministry of Trade, Industry and Energy of the Republic of Korea, where he led Korea's international trade disputes. In this capacity, Haneul handled nearly a quarter of Korea's total WTO dispute cases to date.

By the end of his tenure as a government director, however, the liberal international order was showing signs of significant erosion, and the multilateral trading system—Haneul's North Star for nearly two decades—faced a parallel decline. This unfortunate yet pivotal moment inspired Haneul to dedicate the rest of his career to studying the foundations of an international system capable of fostering a stable and enduring global order.

www.ingramcontent.com/pod-product-compliance
Lightning Source LLC
LaVergne TN
LVHW011943060526
838201LV00061B/4192